A FRAGILE INHERITANCE

SALONI MATHUR

A FRAGILE INHERITANCE

Radical Stakes in Contemporary Indian Art

DUKE UNIVERSITY PRESS · DURHAM AND LONDON · 2019

Printed in the United States of America on
acid-free paper ∞
Designed by Matthew Tauch
Typeset in Quadraat Pro by Tseng Information Systems, Inc.

Library of Congress Cataloging-in-Publication Data
Names: Mathur, Saloni, author.
Title: A fragile inheritance : radical stakes in contemporary
Indian art / Saloni Mathur.
Description: Durham : Duke University Press, 2019. |
Includes bibliographical references and index.
Identifiers: LCCN 2019006362 (print) |
LCCN 2019009378 (ebook)
ISBN 9781478003380 (ebook)
ISBN 9781478001867 (hardcover : alk. paper)
ISBN 9781478003014 (pbk. : alk. paper)
Subjects: LCSH: Art, Indic — 20th century. | Art, Indic — 21st
century. | Art — Political aspects — India. | Sundaram, Vivan —
Criticism and interpretation. | Kapur, Geeta, 1943 — Criticism
and interpretation.
Classification: LCC N7304 (ebook) |
LCC N7304 .M384 2019 (print) |
DDC 709.54/0904 — dc23
LC record available at https://lccn.loc.gov/2019006362

Cover art: Vivan Sundaram, *Soldier of Babylon I*, 1991, diptych made
with engine oil and charcoal on paper. Courtesy of the artist.

Duke University Press gratefully acknowledges the UCLA Academic
Senate, the UCLA Center for the Study of Women, and the UCLA
Dean of Humanities for providing funds toward the publication
of this book.

This title is freely available in an open access edition thanks to the
TOME initiative and the generous support of Arcadia, a charitable
fund of Lisbet Rausing and Peter Baldwin, and of the UCLA Library.

CONTENTS

PREFACE

I still recall my first encounter with the works of art and critical writing by Vivan Sundaram and Geeta Kapur that situate the central concerns of this study. I was a graduate student pursuing my MA in anthropology at the University of Western Ontario, Canada. It was around 1990, before the internet and other communication technologies had revolutionized the way that images and information are available to people around the world. My thesis supervisor had returned from a research trip to India with a sampling of contemporary art catalogues—pamphlets, really—that she had collected from galleries, museums, and bookshops in Delhi. They were a gift; I knew nothing, except that I found them riveting and befuddling. Included were some images of paintings by Vivan Sundaram, featuring fantastical tropes in soft pastels of boats, journeys, and elusive female subjects, with titles like *Arabesque* and *The Orientalist*, which seemed to prompt a visual dialogue, however obliquely, with the writings of Edward Said. Within a year or two, I moved to New York to continue my studies as a PhD student, where for the first time I read Geeta Kapur, whose intense and discriminating prose seemed somehow to *get under the skin* of a painting or a sculpture and break open its vertiginous realities in a way that recrystallized its exquisite complexity just beyond the reach of what could be grasped. I struggled with the destabilizing formulations of her texts and made photocopies from journals like *South Atlantic Quarterly* and *Third Text*, along with coveted issues of the *Journal of Arts and Ideas*, brought to me by friends from India. I also photographed Sundaram's images to add to my collection of 35 mm cardboard-frame slides, which I projected on the wall for class presentations or viewed on a light box, a major purchase at the time. What strikes me today is the *preciousness* that came with these modes of engagement at a distance; the novelty of an image or text that had traveled physically from New Delhi to the remote corners of Ontario or New York; the endless chain of questions that emerged from a thing that appeared out of its context in this way; and the slow gestation of ideas and responses that came from a sustained process of wondering over time. Somehow these conditions of reception and prolonged puzzlement and contemplation seem a far cry from the voracious appetites for consumption and modes of instantaneous access that characterize the new technologies and globalized circuits of contemporary art today.

The point is not to invoke nostalgia for an earlier, preglobalized set of networks for art but to clarify some of my own locations and investments in this study at the outset. This book does not represent an "insider" account of contemporary Indian art or the Delhi art world. Although it is my birthplace, I do not live in India or operate within the everyday conditions of art and activism that proliferate and thrive on the subcontinent today. I have nonetheless engaged with the creativity of these milieus intimately through travel, research, professional collaboration, friendships, and family ties over the course of a two-decade-long career in the North American academy. Thus, at the crucial core of this book is a heightened sensitivity toward the processes by which cultural knowledge is mediated and transmitted and the possibilities for connection in the realm of aesthetics across the dialectics of distance and proximity. My interest is in the critical procedures that *open out* a discourse about modernism or aesthetics emerging from a particular era and locale and *make it available* to outsiders across distance and time—that is, make its problems and questions available for others to inhabit in a way that transcends the parochial claims to "insider" or "outsider" status. These are the kinds of radical operations and effects that I see present in the work of Sundaram and Kapur and that lead not to a stable or settled point of arrival for the modern and contemporary art of the subcontinent but to a proliferation of difficulty, uncertainty, and untethered possibilities. Theirs is a model of cultural practice that has consistently sustained such effects over time and that has forged a project of critical reinvention in and through scrupulous attention to preexisting ideas and ways of seeing. To my mind, this is the opposite of the insatiable quest for that which is "new" in contemporary art, or the reductive search for the next big thing, which can sometimes dictate art's institutional agendas. Instead, their intense mode of working entirely in the present while simultaneously calling up a relation to the past in order to give creative shape to the future serves to challenge such progressivist approaches to the history of art with a more profound and dissonant temporal sensibility. At the same time, this book actively resists fixing a stable or unchanging intellectual contribution or constructing a hagiography that idealizes its subjects. It is rather an attempt to articulate some of the difficulty and fragility of such a critical inheritance, to follow its lines of flexibility and diversity and to amplify its points of intellectual vitality, in ways that continue Sundaram's and Kapur's ongoing projects of radicality and diversification. To this end, it seeks not to offer the final word on their different contributions but to expand and alter the terms through which their practices have been understood thus far.

It would be a number of years before I would meet Vivan Sundaram and Geeta Kapur or even realize that the artwork and texts to which I was repeatedly drawn represented the output of a married couple. While their careers are distinguished by many major individual projects, at times intersecting, they could not be defined as "collaborating" in any conventional sense in the manner of, say, Christo and Jeanne-Claude, or, to cite a more fraught model, Marina Abramović and Ulay. Nonetheless, there exists a powerful affinity in their different forms and modes of production, one that I have experienced in mostly uncanny ways. For instance, an idea in Kapur's writing has often led me back to an artwork by Sundaram, and vice versa, but not because of explicit cues or direct references, though such connections do at other times exist. One of this book's central propositions is that this elusive sense of affinity signals much more than the casual cross-communication of a couple who have lived and worked together in Delhi for almost five decades. It represents, rather, an integrated configuration whose disparate, yet focused, threads take the form of a shared commitment to critical consciousness at work. The result is less a coherent unity or a specific intellectual paradigm than a series of relays between dynamic, flexible points whose very shapelessness is the result of the rigorous, ongoing process that we might refer to as critical thought.

Coming to know Vivan and Geeta personally began a new phase of engagement for me in the present century. In the past fifteen years or so, I have benefited from extended conversations with each of them, engaging with one or the other informally as well as professionally—as co-panelist, discussant, reviewer, even curator—and we have met on many occasions to view art and participate in conferences and workshops in Delhi, Mumbai, Kochi, Kassel, London, New York, and Los Angeles. Over time, this interaction has also become the basis for a valued intellectual friendship. But the primary challenge of this book is not merely the issue of bias or perspective, a concern that my training in anthropology, with its embrace of "situated knowledges" over false histories of presumed objectivity, has helped assuage. It is related to the fact that my subjects, now in their mid-seventies, are both more active than ever before, producing new artwork and writing with seemingly unstoppable levels of energy and intensity, which seem to complicate, revisit, and challenge previous projects, forcefully resisting the kind of circumscription or summation one might be tempted to connect to an undertaking of this sort.

Sundaram's art is, for instance, almost unretrospective-izable. Its multifarious, at times ephemeral, performative, and site-specific forms, which the artist has repeatedly dismantled and reinvented to new ends, resists being physically collected and displayed as a single totality in the format of a conventional retrospective survey.[1] Kapur's writing, represented by an almost uncountable number of essays, is similarly difficult to harness as a whole in any non-reductive way. Its incisive essay format and interventionist spirit represent a way of knowing based in angled perspectives and contingent truth-claims, and its self-conscious dismantling of earlier ideas and analogous reinvention of old concepts to new ends also refuses arrival or summation. In both cases, every new project brings less an accumulation and more a *distillation* of core principles and long-standing concerns. I have come to understand this as a productive tension, but the reader who seeks a more conventional narrative—a start-to-finish artistic biography or a comprehensive account of five decades of work—will no doubt be disappointed.

To approach a cultural practice not as the mere collection or accumulation of knowledge but as an active and ongoing process of creative, intellectual activity that paradoxically deconstructs such a premise—this requires a method of understanding that is necessarily selective and alert to paradigmatic instances of this process. The critic Craig Owens once described the act of engagement with a critical art practice as an effort to "write alongside" rather than write about.[2] Said characterized it as a question of "adjacency," how an author "stands to the side of, next to, or between" other works, rather than in a direct relation of primordial descent.[3] Kapur has similarly described her own reflexive stance as being "side-by-side" with contemporary artists in India. Studying the way in which Kapur has turned a lifetime of proximity to the visual arts into focused and uncompromising intellectual work, without forsaking the passion, beauty, and pleasure of the aesthetic sphere and its human relations, has been—in a word—inspirational. As a scholar, it has helped me learn, for instance, how to better comprehend the shape of my investments, how to find and formulate meaningful questions, and how to strive for the integrity of truthful pursuits.

Some may object that in highlighting the output of two individuals I have hitched my horse to a single cart, so to speak; that my sustained attention to these careers is not representative of the diversity of aesthetic practice in the Indian subcontinent, or worse, that it serves to eclipse the wide heterogeneity of forms in dispersed and regional, especially non-Delhi, locations. They may be partially right. Today, there are countless artists, writers, scholars, and curators addressing the broader tapestry of creative energy in modern and contemporary South Asian art, allowing a more synthetic picture of artists and activities across the span of multiple decades beyond the known historical art centers of Delhi, Bombay, Calcutta, and Baroda, to include such places as Bangalore, Kerala, Karachi, Lahore, Dhaka, Jaffna, and Colombo, to name but a few. These accounts provide invaluable overviews and strengthen the narratives for art history through research that makes the density and discrepant complexity of the aesthetic sphere visible in new ways. My study, by contrast, constructs an account of an exemplary practice and opts for sustained contemplation of selective works as a point of entry into broader concerns. It responds, in part, to the increasing preoccupation with the rise of a globalized art world and the suspect category of "global contemporary art," a broad, generally ahistorical banner under which the great difficulties of entire societies, their particularities and paradoxical trajectories, are too often superficially treated or wholly subsumed. It does so by favoring the methodology of a deep inquiry, by presenting large ideas in conjunction with microanalyses, and by reckoning with the relationships between knowledge and power and one's personal investments in an intellectual field.

Kapur and Sundaram have been aware of my project for some time, variously bemused, flattered, irritated, or confused by the peculiar directions my interests have taken. They are somehow constantly immersed in a major undertaking and perpetually in motion between one ambitious endeavor and the next; suffice it to say, my own study did not generally make their daily priority list. Nonetheless, our open-ended discussions about aspects of this book have been extremely valuable, leading more often than not to substantive intellectual questions and concerns. Roland Barthes famously stated that the meaning of a cultural text lay as much in its destination as in its origin, a proposition that, to my mind, opens up the fraught circuits of risk and responsibility attached to any act of earnest interpretation. That Vivan and Geeta have long embraced this Barthesian principle of multiplicity within the discursive field, seeking interpretive complexity and fragmentation over authorial coherence imposed from above, has been a major motivating factor in this journey. I wish to thank them here for supporting this effort to construct a destination of sorts, for permitting its earlier, more stumbling variations, and for indulging me in this long-term project with its possible excesses of scrutiny and the gaze. Ultimately, this book is about working through an ongoing intellectual debt. It is thus part of an unfinished process that will undoubtedly continue beyond the form taken here.

In addition, I wish to acknowledge the support of several scholarly institutions that fueled the research and writing of this manuscript. I benefited from three different residential fellowships—at the Clark Art Institute, the Getty Research Institute, and the University of California Humanities Research Institute—which provided resources, friendships, and time to think and write within a dynamic community of scholars. I am similarly indebted to the accomplished team at the Asia Art Archive, the nonprofit arts organization based in Hong Kong, who digitized the personal archive of Sundaram and Kapur as part of their vast archiving and educational activities concerned with modern and contemporary art from Asia. Their resources, which are publicly available online, have been a great asset to this researcher, offering not merely information but also self-reflexive engagements that alter ways of seeing. As well, thanks are due to the Warhol/Creative Capital Foundation for a generous arts writer's grant in the book category and to the Academic Senate, the Dean of Humanities, and the Center for the Study of Women at my home institution, UCLA, for providing funds related to this publication. I am also grateful to the Fowler Museum at UCLA for hosting a solo exhibition by Sundaram, co-curated by myself and Miwon Kwon, titled *Making Strange: Gagawaka + Postmortem*, in the spring of 2015. Geeta and Vivan came to Los Angeles for ten days to oversee the installation and to participate in various programs, including a seminar, a public lecture, and an artist talk. The success of these events and the reception by the university community were immensely gratifying, the result of almost three years of work.

This project has had such a long period of gestation that there are dozens and dozens of people—friends, colleagues, and interlocutors, alas, too many to name—based in India, Pakistan, the United States, Canada, Hong Kong, Europe, South Korea, and Great Britain, who have contributed in one way or another over the years. Thank you to all of you and to the revolution of email, FaceTime, and Skype that has enabled our extended contact and exchange. I am especially grateful to Ken Wissoker at Duke University Press for his incomparable sensitivity toward this project. I also wish to thank my hosts and audiences at the following institutions (in alphabetical order), where I have presented aspects of this study over a period of many years: the Asia Art Archive (Hong Kong), Columbia University, Cornell University, the Courtauld Art Institute, the Getty Research Institute, Johns Hopkins University, Karachi University, the Museum of Modern Art (NY), the Institute of Fine Arts at New York University, the New Europe College, Bucharest, Northwestern University, the University of the Arts London's TrAIN Center, the University of Chicago, the University of Copenhagen, the University of Illinois at Chicago, the University of Southern California, and the University of Sydney, Australia.

Lastly, and most immeasurably, I wish to thank my mother, Veena, and my sisters, Punam and Bindu, who offer sustenance in every aspect of my life. This book is dedicated with all my love to Aamir and our son, Jalal, who surround me with daily nourishment and affection, and who have generously endured, embraced, and shared in every step of this meaningful journey.

RADICAL STAKES

My study constructs an account of radical art practice in India through two seminal figures: Vivan Sundaram, the contemporary Delhi-based artist, and Geeta Kapur, the theorist, critic, and curator and the most significant interlocutor of the post-1968 avant-garde generation to which Sundaram belongs. The couple (both born in 1943) have aligned themselves with the discourses of the international Left for more than four decades and are widely regarded as veterans of socially engaged art in the subcontinent. And yet the meaning of their highly individual, parallel, and at times intersecting contributions to the visual arts has yet to receive any sustained consideration by scholars. This book treats their diverse aesthetic practices as an integrated critical configuration and examines how the artist's and the critic's wide-ranging contributions to avant-garde culture in India may be seen to respond, more urgently than ever, to the specific overdeterminations of the present era.

My argument, put briefly, is that Sundaram and Kapur have enacted through their visual arts practices a rejection of a narrative of filial or civilizational descent in favor of a more radical historiographic relationship to the past that we might understand as "genealogy" in the Foucauldian sense. The goal in constructing this inquiry is thus not to offer an evolutionary story about a previous generation's advances in art; nor is it to celebrate a portrait of a family practice or to mythologize the legacy of a "great" artistic couple. It is rather to engage the radical implications of my protagonists' self-conscious rejection of precisely such narratives for modern and contemporary Indian art and to investigate the forms that their persistent probing of twentieth-century antecedents has nonetheless taken, through specific readings of selected works. When considered together, the artist and critic present a powerful constellation of critical lessons and possibilities for contemporary art on the Indian subcontinent—and beyond—and highlight many of the major themes that have functioned to redefine the field of scholarship in this area: for instance, the formation of a non-Western modernism in constant tension and dialogue with the Euro-American canon, the negotiation with colonial history, the postcolonial national frame, and the new forms of internationalism from the vantage point of the developing world, and the fundamental relation between art practice and art theory as it has been shaped by the rigors of leftist praxis. My project is thus an interpretive exercise to prod the paradigms in contemporary Indian art, a field buoyed by a thriving art market and a proliferation of art writing as a result but still lacking in substantive scholarship that prioritizes both intellectual distance and rigorous engagement with this shifting ground.

Maverick Journeys, Autonomous Tracks

The striking black-and-white photograph in figure Intro.1 was taken in London in 1969 by a lifelong friend, the renowned artist Gulammohammed Sheikh. The picture captures something of the bohemian spirit and independent stance of two maverick trajectories at a single moment in their emergence. The sixties, as Frederic Jameson argued, were more of a "historical situation" than a periodized decade, unleashing turbulent social and political forces, spontaneous engagement, and a passionate rejection of the status quo the world over.[1] Enmeshed in the zeitgeist, our young initiates began separate journeys whose itineraries would lead them through different cities, educational institutions, social circles, and ideological milieus. Reflecting on the formative experience of the sixties, Kapur has described these uneven engagements as "vagabonding," that is, embracing the bohemian spirit of studios, exhibitions, travel, and protests in places like Delhi, London, and New York.[2] At times, their autonomous trajectories will crisscross and inter-

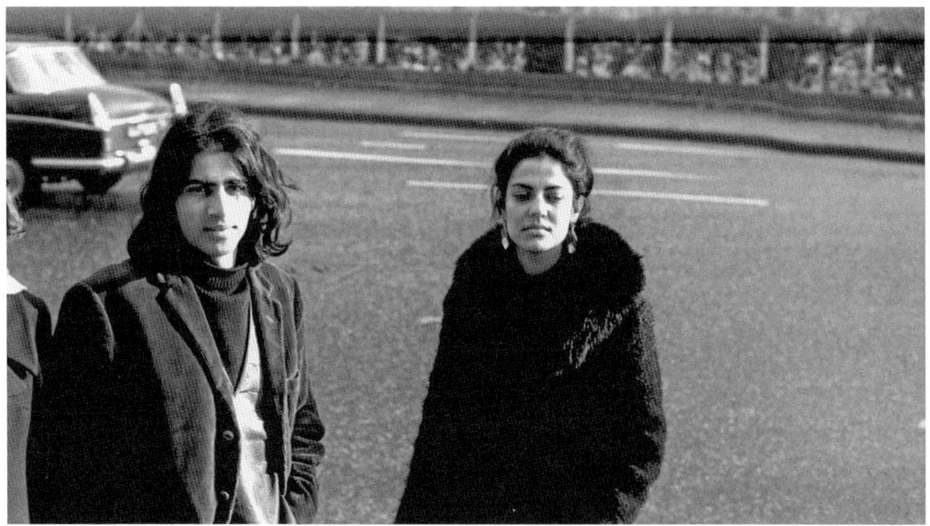

sect, leading to alternating shades of romance, intimacy, friction, and alienation. As it happens, the photograph in London records an episode of the last of these experiences: its youthful subjects, although very stylish, are also distant, noncommitted, aloof.

For his part, Sundaram, who trained as a painter in the fine arts department of the M.S. University of Baroda from 1961 to 1965 before attending the Slade School of Art in London from 1966 to 1968, had begun his political awakening. "Before I left for London," he stated, "I wasn't political at all."[3] But it was during this time that he stopped painting, took a course in the history of cinema, and developed an intense appetite for the moving image, watching hundreds of films at the Slade and at underground venues throughout the city. As well, he joined demonstrations, rallies, sit-ins, and rock concerts, becoming "so immersed in that context, [and] flowing completely in that moment."[4] Fortified by the energy of youth, the artist famously lived in a commune, protested the Vietnam War, befriended anarchists and comrades in liberation movements like the Black Panthers and women's rights, and took part in the legendary events of "May 68." After hitchhiking across North America and landing in leftist hubs along the way, he eventually found his way back to India via land four years after his departure, by hitchhiking and taking trains through Europe, Turkey, Iran, and Afghanistan. Upon his arrival in 1970, the spirit of radicalism led to new friendships in India and close personal alliances with the organized

Left (the CPI-M or Communist Party of India-Marxist)—and ultimately a stance outside the party proper as a self-identified "artist-activist."

Kapur's rites of passage took place, by contrast, more squarely within the halls of academic study, where she gained exposure at an early age to an international pantheon of mostly male artists and critics, who presented her with vital models of intellectual activity. After completing her BA in economics from the University of Delhi, Kapur set out for New York's Greenwich Village in 1963 at a mere nineteen years old to pursue a master of fine arts at NYU. Her teachers there included Irving Sandler, the critic and art historian aligned with the American abstract expressionists, and the Paris-trained African American painter Hale Woodruff, employed by the WPA (Works Projects Administration) during the Great Depression. Influenced by the polemical debates raging in American art circles at the time among critics like Harold Rosenberg and Clement Greenberg, Kapur wrote her first student reviews of key exhibitions by Andy Warhol and Claes Oldenburg, and was befriended by several Indian modernists—Akbar Padamsee, Krishen Khanna, and V.S. Gaitonde—who were also in New York as Rockefeller fellows. Returning to Delhi in 1965, she continued to "vagabond" in the bohemian world of artist studios in Delhi, Baroda, and Bombay, and she found in the senior novelist and art reformer of the Nehruvian era Mulk Raj Anand an influential friend and mentor.

In 1968, Kapur traveled to London to pursue a second MA in art criticism (awarded in 1970) at the Royal College of Art, where she was similarly inspired by the impassioned stance of the British art critic John Berger. In a recent tribute to the latter occasioned by his death at the age of ninety in 2017, Kapur shared the story of her star-crossed rendezvous with the "peerless critic" in Kensington Park in 1969.[5] It was in London, as she has stated, that she entered "more confidently into the discursive field" guided by the leftist painter-teacher Peter de Francia, "who steered her into Marxism, third-world ideology and postcolonialism."[6] On her return to Delhi in 1970, Kapur entered new kinds of liaisons, influenced by Gandhian and socialist literary circles and the world of Hindi writers in particular; one of them became a serious companion. Receiving a two-year fellowship at the Indian Institute for Advanced Study (IIAS) in 1975, she relocated to the northern hill town of Simla and immersed herself among philosophers, historians, and anthropologists, thriving amid the weekly lectures and seminars and the monastic conditions of the think tank. Later, the same would be true of a residency at Delhi's Teen Murti, the site of the Nehru Memorial Library and Museum and a center for scholars in the city. Significantly, these Indian educational institutions helped shape Kapur's identity as an *intellectual* and made her uniquely conversant with theory, scholarship, and academia from outside the conventional location of a university position.

The crises of the Emergency in the mid-1970s, which brought two years of authoritarian rule under the administration of Indira Gandhi (Nehru's daughter), led to increased disenchantment for their generation, as Kapur has reflected, and brought the embattled contest over national culture into stark and disturbing relief.[7] By the end of the 1970s, the on-again, off-again relationship between our protagonists would shift into a new kind of restlessness and synergy, driven by the ever-present crises related to secularism, civil society, and democratic politics in India and an increasingly fluid participation in shared projects (and living arrangements) in Delhi, Baroda, and Kausali. The latter was the hill station in North India where Sundaram founded the Kausali Art Center in 1976, which grew into a vital hub for artists across the disciplines through residencies, workshops, seminars, and theater experiments. In 1982, they helped launch the *Journal of Arts and Ideas*, a publication concerned broadly with leftist cultural practice and aesthetics that would assist in shaping the discourse in India for the next two decades. In 1985, they married, officially becoming comrades-in-arms. And in 1989, they joined other artists, writers, scholars, and cultural activists to form the collective known as SAHMAT (Safdar Hashmi Memorial Trust) in response to the murder of the actor, poet, and playwright Safdar Hashmi. This organization, now in its thirtieth year, continues to stand boldly for artistic freedom and secular, egalitarian values, and remains a vital platform for artistic collaboration and political solidarity across the public sphere in India.[8]

While these educational and political journeys were made possible by the privilege of a certain class background, enabling access to experiences and resources that are not available to a large swath of the population in India, it is what one *does* with this societal advantage and *how* one actively participates in the cause of social justice that drives a number of questions at the heart of this study. Significantly, the journal and the Kausali workshops, which led to numerous special issues, have attracted the attention of younger artists and scholars today seeking dynamic models for their own initiatives and an understanding of the discursive synergy that drove an earlier moment of cultural inquiry and dissent.[9] Shaped equally by the constellations of artistic discourse and leftist discussion at home and the tradition of the historical avant-garde and post-Marxist thought abroad, and still drawn to the emblematic figures of hope-filled revolutionary change, like Che Guevara, Fidel Castro, and Frantz Fanon, Sundaram's art and Kapur's criticism are ultimately a highly syncretic practice that is not reducible to a single origin or institutional location, or an individual format or space of activity, or a particular art form or art world trend, or a specific social question or political orientation.

In fact, to present my subjects' formation in this way—as a relatively straightforward articulation of intertwined historical contexts—is to neglect to confront the strange chronotopes, disruptive anachronisms, and inchoate temporalities that permeate and saturate their relation to the past. Crucially, both artist and critic approach the past not as a mere foundation for the present but as a reservoir of intellectual imagination and cultural responsibility that requires relentless demystification and rigorous reinvention and that can feed utopian confidence. More than a critical relationship to history, this is a distinctive form of time-consciousness, I suggest, in which the dependable linearity of past-present-future is disrupted to produce more discordant but no less utopic effects. These utopian aspirations, as anthropologist David Scott has argued in another context, do not belong to the progressivist teleology of historical materialism.[10] They derive instead from the dissonant temporality of aftermath, in Scott's terms, from the "disjunctures involved in living *on* in the wake of past political time, amid the ruins, specifically of postsocialist and postcolonial futures past."[11] Together, Kapur's theorizing and Sundaram's multimedia installation practice do not resolve the intractable issues of linear time or its implications for the history of art—its disjunctural relationship to history and memory, its lack of synchronicity in the world, its impossible finitude and irreversibility. Their work does, however, make temporality itself highly conspicuous in response to the conditions of our deeply unsettled present. I now turn to investigate this radical time-consciousness in more detail, for it speaks to some of the specificity and integrity of their various aesthetic projects, which ultimately "teach us how to be critical," following the criteria offered by Edward Said, rather than how to follow some predetermined path or become faithful members of a school.[12]

The Dialectics of the "Re-job"

Scholars of contemporary art have recently recognized a variety of gestures in the sphere of aesthetics that appear to dangle under the prefix "re-."[13] These heterogeneous maneuvers, represented by verbs like re-perform, reenact, reinstall, or reconstruct, have become increasingly visible in the cultural landscape and point to a certain intensification of activities involving ideas of repetition and return. Following the lessons of poststructuralism, and the Derridean concept of the "re-mark," in particular—a marking that not only marks but also redefines by marking itself as different from the first—a number of scholars and critics have linked the logic of the "re" to critical possibilities and radical aesthetic acts.[14] Nicolas Bourriaud has proposed, for instance, that the artist today functions as a "re-mixer of realities," engaged in modes of recycling and reuse that inaugurate a paradigm of "postproduction" linked to the globalized culture of the digital age.[15]

Hal Foster, in his critique of Peter Bürger's influential text, *Theory of the Avant-Garde*, has similarly prioritized the concept of return. Foster's argument is that the return by artists from Europe and America in the 1960s (the neo-avant-garde) to the artistic movements of the prewar period such as Dada, surrealism, futurism, and constructivism (the historical avant-garde) represents a more productive and elastic engagement with the past than Bürger had initially conceived.[16] In the neo-avant-garde's insistent backward glance to earlier moments of the century, Foster perceives a "strange temporality," as if "lost in stories of twentieth-century art."[17] Foster's argument is part of a broader scholarly rethinking of the avant-garde/neo-avant-garde relationship, which has served to unsettle any simplistic rendering of the relations between past and present, people and place, and origin and repetition in constructing the art history of the twentieth century in favor of a more paradoxical temporality between multiply situated avant-gardes and neo-avant-gardes and, perhaps more significantly, between the "neo" and the "now." These debates thus enable a certain freedom to stretch such concepts and historical models more firmly—as Fanon argued that Marxist analysis should be "stretched" to the situation of the colony[18]—to serve the story of artistic radicalism in much wider geopolitical contexts of the twentieth century and to challenge the enduring hegemony of the idea of the avant-garde's exclusively European provenance.

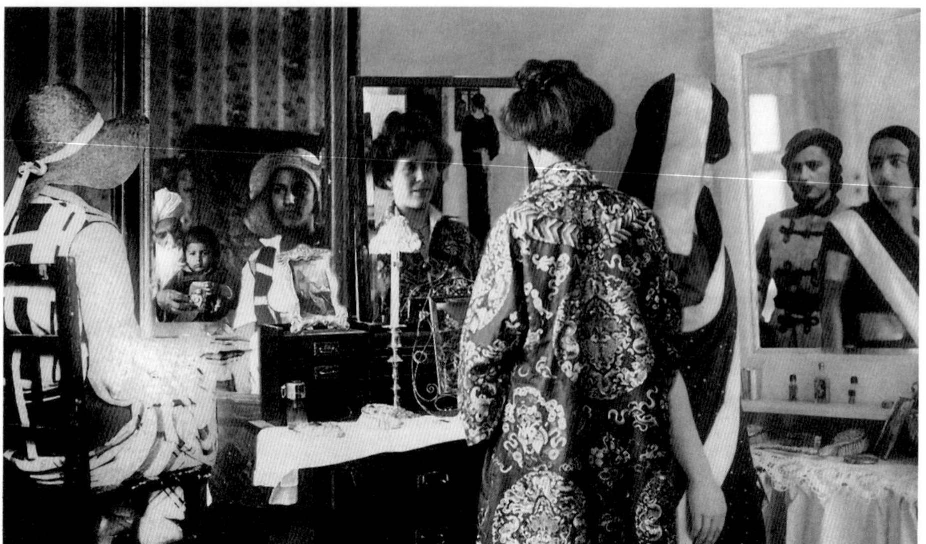

I bring these theoretical insights to bear on the particular convergence of politics and aesthetics in India represented by the careers of Sundaram and Kapur, who seem to consistently embody the "strange temporality" identified by Foster in their approaches to the cultural field. If both artist and critic appear at times to be "lost in stories of twentieth-century art," then I suggest the means to apprehending their acts of immersion rests in the theoretically informed notion of the "retake." The retake is a gesture of hermeneutic return, one that is first announced as such in the title of Sundaram's series of digital photomontages related to his maternal aunt, India's pioneering modernist painter, Amrita Sher-Gil (see figure Intro.2).

In the series, the myths and legends enveloping the biracial and bisexual Sher-Gil as a foundational figure of modernism are subjected to unique forms of subterfuge made available to the artist through computer technologies.[19] For Sundaram, the digital era enables a great deal: "You can shift to the playful, the provocative; you can lie to tell a truth. . . . There is a constant double-take or, in cinema terms, 'a retake' of the shot," he explains.[20] Thus the technique of revisitation and conversion is used to "multiply points of entry and exit" and to enter the intricate entanglements of the Sher-Gil family, the "drama of their self-appointed egos,"[21] their individual journeys and cosmopolitan life stories, through the privileged social milieus of Budapest, Simla,

Paris, and Lahore.[22] "What kind of 'genetic' maneuver," Sundaram asks, "what kinds of narcissistic relay, does this unwind?"[23]

The project is the most visible of Sundaram's multifaceted engagements interrogating the mythic structures surrounding the figure of Sher-Gil, even as they expose the artist's unique burdens and responsibilities related to the privilege gained through birthright ancestry and the personal archive of an exceptional family past. For Sundaram, the making and unmaking of kinship has taken multiple creative and intellectual forms, beginning as early as 1972, soon after his art school training, in a collection of essays he edited on Sher-Gil for a special issue of the Indian art journal *Marg*. The issue, which held contributions by Kapur, Gulammohammed Sheikh, K.G. Subramanyam, and others from the Baroda art scene, rejected the hagiography that had dominated previous accounts of Sher-Gil and demanded instead a critical investigation of what the authors perceived to be the "very uneven path of her achievements."[24] The contributors took Sher-Gil to task, at times harshly, for many things: her idealized vision of feudal life, her romanticization of the working poor, her lack of interest in India's anticolonial struggle, her unsuccessful turn toward miniature painting, and her failure to respond to the exploitation of workers at her family's sugar factory in Uttar Pradesh. In hindsight, it was the first serious treatment of Sher-Gil by working artists, and the spirit of iconoclasm that pervaded the special issue was part of the evolution of their own practices as painters, leading, in particular, to the polemical assertion of figuration seen in the 1981 *Place for People* exhibition, a landmark show that featured six artists and the critic, Kapur, seeking to retheorize the basis for historical narrative itself.[25]

In the years to come, Sundaram would continue to probe his individual relationship to his iconic aunt, turning his attention toward the family itself in a manner that drifted from these collective concerns. The absence of an actual relationship with Amrita, who died before he was born, enabled a multitude of fictive scenarios and highly creative imaginative acts. Sundaram's searching, melancholic canvas *The Sher-Gil Family* (1983–84), for example, presented a portrait of kinship within the isolation and privacy of domestic space, enhanced by the play of shadows and light. *The Sher-Gil Archive* (1995), by contrast, an installation that gathered together boxes, suitcases, closets, fabric, photographs, and videos, as depicted in figure Intro.3, invoked the spirit of

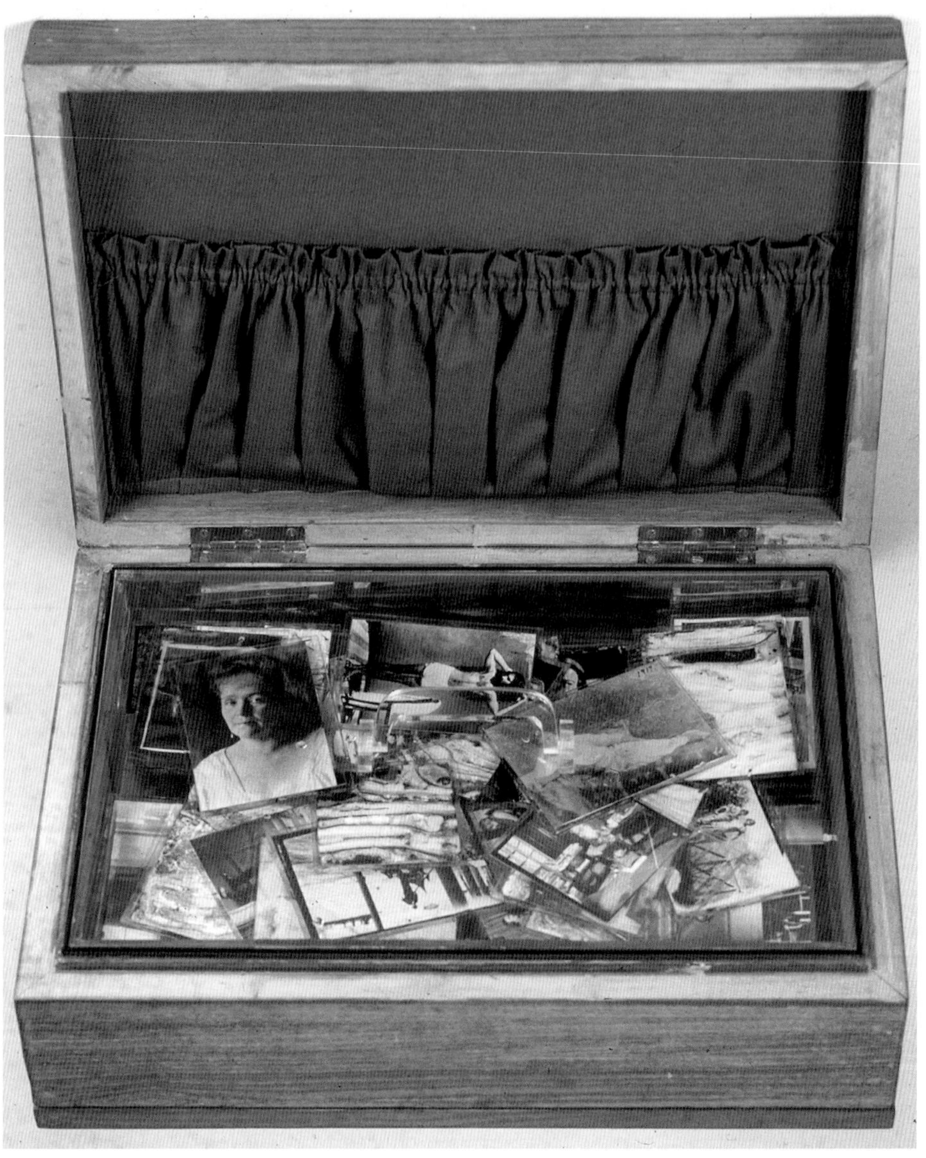

FIGURE INTRO.3 Vivan Sundaram, *Box Five: Family Album*, 2005. From *The Sher-Gil Archive* series. Teak box with plastic case, mirror, gabardine cloth, and framed photographs in water. Courtesy of the artist.

Marcel Duchamp to hint at the preciousness of a familial past.[26] Two major book projects furthered these activities: first, an edited compilation of his grandfather Umrao Singh Sher-Gil's corpus of amateur photographs, and second, a two-volume collection of Amrita's letters, which consolidated the archive of private correspondence for future research.[27] The combined output leads inevitably to the question, What is at stake in this persistent looking back, this overwhelming preoccupation with the familial scene? Does it "unwind the genetic maneuver," as Sundaram proposed, or does it assign the artist to a single, isolated, identifiable lineage? Or does it suggest a more paradoxical foray into the realm of the ancestral that somehow fixes and unfixes descent at the same time? In the pages that follow I develop an argument that supports and embraces the ambiguity of the latter. For now, I also draw attention to the title of his project, which appears to offer something of a clue. By insisting on the singular "retake," rather than the plural, more intuitive "retakes," Sundaram privileges the *process* over the product and asserts his art practice as a verb, not a noun.

The idea of the retake as a maneuver of unwinding also works, albeit more loosely, to characterize Geeta Kapur's efforts to theorize modernism in numerous essays on twentieth-century Indian art, written during the late 1980s and 1990s and collected in her influential book *When Was Modernism: Essays on Contemporary Cultural Practice in India* (2000). In Kapur's collection of essays the retake appears as a single utterance in a vast theoretical vocabulary driven toward articulating and differentiating the "unlogged initiatives" that flourish in the art-making that surrounds her in India. Thus, Kapur argued in the book that the finely choreographed photo and video performances of Bangalore-based Pushpamala N, which systematically upturn the history of gender stereotypes, offered a "retake on the arts of representation";[28] the rough materiality and existentialist viewpoints of senior sculptor N.N. Rimzon provided a "retake on the phenomenological encounter";[29] the part-human/part-animal/part-goddess forms produced by the inventiveness of sculptors Dhruva Mistry and Ravinder Reddy presented "retakes on the (classical) sculptural tradition";[30] and the emergence of radical art practice in India during the 1990s itself necessitated a "retake" of the American avant-garde.[31]

Kapur adopted, in other words, the retake into her critical lexicon to enunciate a range of strategies of revisitation and return evident in the heterogeneous field of contemporary Indian art. More importantly, the methodology of the retake was also the basis for a self-reflexive textual practice that disrupted linear chronology in favor of disjuncture, difference, and more dissonant effects. Even the rhetorical title of her book, *When Was Modernism*, evokes something of a temporal riddle and reflects the paradoxical sense of temporality that Foster connected to the critical consciousness of the neo-avante-garde. As I will argue, Kapur's preference for recursive loops, retroactive devices, and anachronistic ruptures in her narrative strategies for Indian art is more than a mere stylistic choice. Her work does not simply construct a historical account of modernism in India, it "re-marks" it in the Derridean sense.

While these activities may appear unrelated—at best reflecting a mutual concern with tradition and the past, or at worse, shoring up a privileged art historical lineage or fixing the boundaries of a hegemonic formation—I argue that the retake is precisely about unfixing such claims to filiation and descent and opening up the possibilities of the past in a tight calculation with the needs of the present. In Sundaram's art and Kapur's writing, we witness a similar rejection of certain modes of belonging—filial, evolutionary, authentic, civilizational—and a refusal of the authority of heritage schemes, in favor of a critical historical practice that upends the idea of organic development. Tropes of archaeology and excavation, repetition and relay, are thus crucial to their conceptual operations and help shape distinctive imaginative acts. These are techniques by which the substratum of stories and journeys are mined in order to bring to the surface layers of history and memory that disallow "roots" or nativist attachments. Accordingly, the past becomes less a foundation for the present than a dynamic and continually reconfigurable ground that takes shape through multiplicity and renewal. This kind of historical practice, or "genealogy," in the terms put forth by Michel Foucault, is not, as the philosopher explained, "an acquisition, a possession that grows and solidifies; rather, it is an unstable assemblage of faults, fissures, and heterogeneous layers that threaten the fragile inheritor from within."[32]

Accepting Fragility

The title of this book, *A Fragile Inheritance*, is partly derived from this formulation by Foucault, which points to the hazardous and precarious nature of any radical historical project. And yet, Foucault's reference to the "fragile inheritor" emphasizes the vulnerability of the *recipient*, rather than the fragility of the inheritance per se, and places the onus of genealogical understanding in large part on its receivers. It is no longer a question, he wrote, of merely receiving a stable set of truths for the present but "of risking the destruction of the subject who seeks knowledge in the endless deployment of the will to knowledge."[33] The destruction of subjectivity may seem a dramatic description of what it means to seek a base in an antifoundational field of knowledge; nonetheless, it is a process that by definition entails uncertainty, instability, puzzlement, and perplexity. What Foucault described elsewhere as "effective history" was composed of "entangled and confused parchments"; it required patience and a knowledge of details, and it reversed the assumptions of distance and objectivity so long held in value by professional historians.[34] For Foucault, the latter amounted to "the famous perspective of frogs," the view of those groveling at the foot of mountain peaks that focus on the highest forms, the noblest periods, the most elevated and grandiose ideas. An effective history, by contrast, "shortens its vision" to that which is near; it embraces its own proximity; it calls for more detailed contemplations and "slanted perceptions."[35] It does not follow smooth, continuous schemas of development, nor does it permit the sense of affirmation or connectedness that we associate with the idea of heritage.[36] It involves instead a "limit attitude," a critical ethos that consists of "analyzing and reflecting on the limits," an approach that is often experimental, undertaken at the limits of ourselves, and that can also imply a degree of coming undone.[37]

These are the kinds of qualities that define the radical knowledge practices of the subjects of this study and help to locate their often intense and uncompromising relationships toward the most intimate territory of the past. They are also the principles that guide my own investigation, resulting in several methodological dilemmas that further complicate the idea of a fragile quest, or bequest. For instance, how does one begin to articulate that which often resists circumscription, or to outline the contours of a critical imagination without foreclosing or collapsing on its protean lines of sight? And how does one *not* lapse into the "famous perspective of frogs" that looks upward with reverence to perceived higher forms, while negotiating the dialectics of proximity and distance that come with intimate, sustained contemplation over time? As I have suggested, Sundaram's familial, cross-generational discourse renders the notion of inheritance unstable. Similarly, Kapur's radical historiography of art rejects any complacent or naturalized reception of culture, insisting on a role for criticism to this end. In other words, there is no unambiguous transmission of ideas for any researcher who takes them seriously; thus I turn here to further probe the fragility of the framework of inheritance itself.

Uprooting Inheritance

The idea of inheritance, as a mechanism that connects human beings across generations, belongs to a spectrum of slippery concepts like ancestry, descent, lineage, and legacy. The concern with how a thing is passed on in a relay across time gives way to tensions around tradition and succession, as with, for instance, the contest over heritage. Moreover, inheritance is embedded in social hierarchies and relations of power and is often the means for inequitable distribution. One need only think of the privileged recipients of inheritance schemes—the heirs and beneficiaries of the ruling classes—to grasp how inheritance sustains systems of social stratification. In relation to the nation-form, as Étienne Balibar has argued, inheritance is invariably bound up in biologistic models of human reproduction, which open onto questions of genetics—and the reactionary domain of eugenics, inherited defects, degeneracy, and purification schemes—all under the name of a "naturalistic" paradigm.[38] Here, the histories of colonialism and slavery, with their complex regimes of racial and sexual domination, can have a role in disrupting these naturalistic frameworks by throwing the problems of reproduction and the mechanisms of transference into a new light.

As part of Salman Rushdie's "midnight's children," the generation of Indians born on the cusp of India's independence in 1947, my protagonists were historically positioned for the epic confrontation with such naturalized models of cultural inheritance. The break from colonial rule and the investment in the secular democracy of the new nation-state made the question of cultural transfer and transmission an immensely urgent project, one that was felt at the level of state- and nation-building and at the level of aesthetic experience. Significantly, both artist's and critic's earliest projects in the 1960s strained in earnestness *against* the dominant national narratives of unbroken ancient origins in an attempt to thwart such a sentimentalized inheritance. Sundaram's photo-collages from 1965, which played with found materials from ancient Hindu sites like Khajuraho and Elephanta (well before the concept of found object was part of his vocabulary), stand as iconoclastic jabs at these civilizational tropes and the official government books that serve as documents of heritage.[39] In figure Intro.4, for example, two female figures derived from classical Indian sculpture, one more slender than the other, are juxtaposed with an advertising slogan for a diet product ("stay slim with Limical") in an irreverent Warhol-esque subversion of consumerist regimes and the romanticized authority of the ancient past.[40] In a similar vein, Kapur's MA thesis of 1969, her first serious piece of writing undertaken at London's Royal College of Art, argued for the necessity of an active "*quest* for identity" for artists negotiating a postcolonial culture, as opposed to a passive bequest involving the static reception of preexisting forms.[41] Later, Kapur would challenge the organic basis of the civilizational tropes deployed in the lyrical cinema of Satyajit Ray as part of a searching stock-taking of the Nehruvian inheritance and the seductive liberal-humanist legacies of that era more broadly. In chapter 3, "The World, the Art, and the Critic," I take these early efforts in the 1960s to seek out spaces for contemporary culture beyond the predeterminations of the ancestral as a series of "beginnings" in the sense meant by Edward Said: not as a divine point of origin but rather as a "first step in the intentional production of meaning" that facilitates relationships to preexisting ideas and necessitates a practice of "beginning and beginning again" in the lifelong pursuit for an alternative collective imaginary.[42]

Such a questioning of roots does not mean less of a commitment to country or nation — and has nothing to do with being "antinational," a hostile term that has become part of the vocabulary of the Right within the reactionary context of Indian politics today. On the contrary, to critique the problematic of roots is to be entirely committed to a particular soil, but not necessarily to a logic of inheritance that derives *by default* from the family tree. The French philosophers Gilles Deleuze and Félix Guattari famously refuted the root-tree paradigm, denouncing its organic basis for systems of origin and reproduction as "arborescent knowledge," the most classical, "oldest, and weariest kind of thought."[43] For them, the model of the family tree with its roots, trunk, and metaphoric branches implied a certain fixity and solidity and embodied many of the foundationalist limitations of psychoanalytic and structuralist thought. They proposed instead the theory of the rhizome, a different kind of subterranean stem that defies the monolithic, clas-

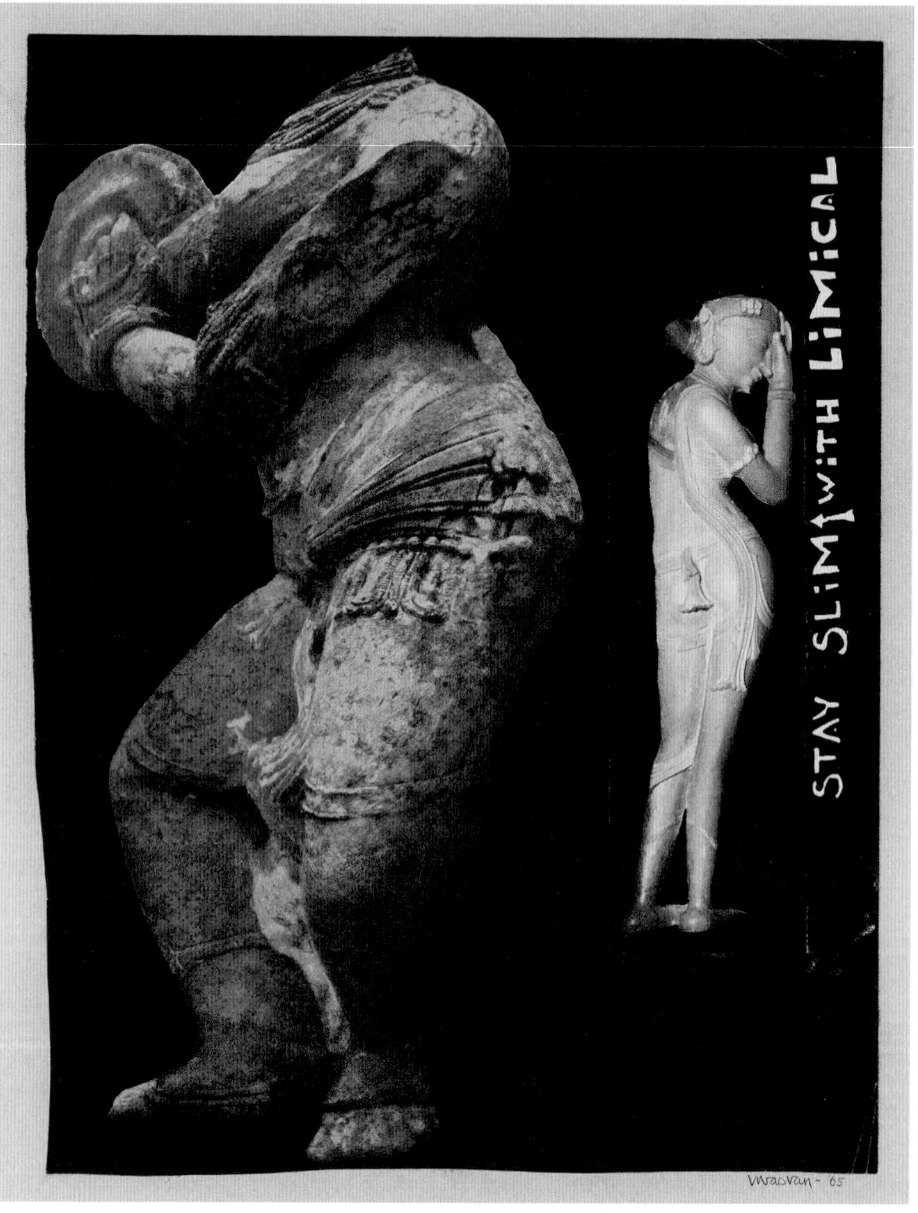

FIGURE INTRO.4 Vivan Sundaram, *Keep Slim*, 1965. Collage of ink and photograph.
Grey Art Gallery, New York University Art Collection. Gift of Abby Weed Grey, G1975.219.
Photo courtesy of Grey Art Gallery, New York University.

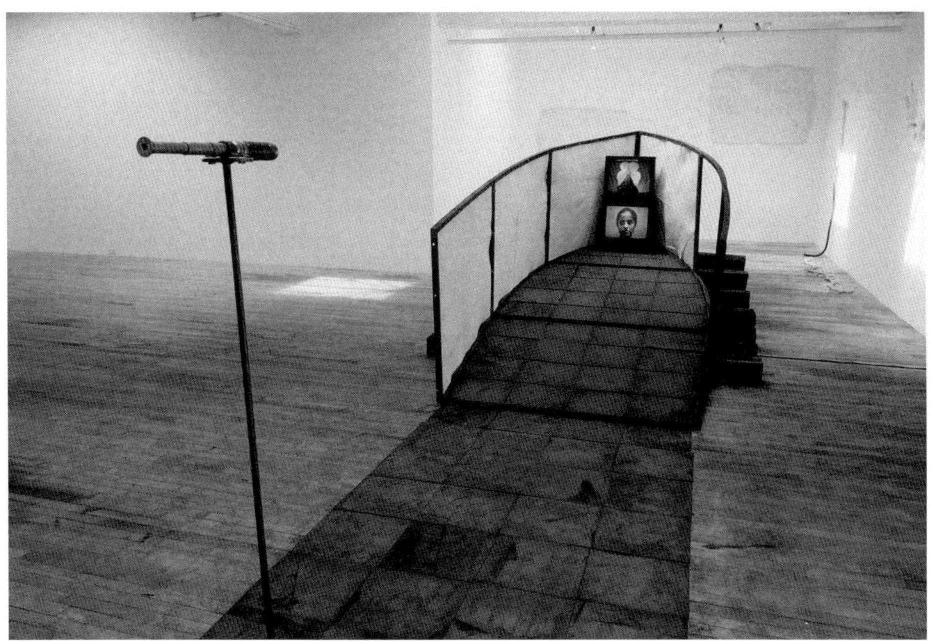

sificatory structure of the tree and is based in principles of multiplicity, heterogeneity, connection, and rupture that can "explode into lines of flight."[44] The model of the rhizome, with its amorphous set of linkages and interconnections, corresponded with the emergence of the internet in the 1990s and was quickly seized by theorists of cyberspace as the framework for the digital age. However, the philosophical distinction between arboreal and rhizomatic frameworks has relevance here beyond the issues raised by technological culture.

The subjects of my study consistently reject the kinds of thought procedures that involve planting roots as bedrock, in Deleuze and Guattari's terms; what they offer instead are a proliferation of "routes" through principles of expansion, variation, repetition, and reuse.[45] The navigational tool of the "critic's compass" and the metaphors of flotation that prevail in Kapur's writing, which I elaborate in chapter 3, are both expressions of this antifoundationalist sensibility. And these narrative devices have their counterpart in the motif of the boat that has been a recurrent feature of Sundaram's art, as seen in the example of figure Intro.5. The boat has taken a multitude of forms in the artist's painting, installation, and video/new media work over the past four decades: from full-scale architectural models to stripped-down elemen-

FIGURE INTRO.5 Vivan Sundaram, *Boat*, 1994. Handmade paper, steel, wood, and video (installation view). Courtesy of the artist.

tal parts; from fragmented forms of water-borne debris to sculptural assemblages made from repurposed parts; from boatlike abstractions and mythical vessels to actual shipping containers turned repositories of history.

As Tania Roy has argued, Sundaram's boat-works during the 1990s responded directly to the rise of sectarian violence on the subcontinent and addressed the depletion of meaning "in an unmoored present," providing allegories of violence, disruption, and dislocation but also refuge, rescue, and self-preservation.[46] Simultaneously a conceptual idiom and a visual technique, the boat in Sundaram's art galvanizes alternative perspectives and unfamiliar horizons based in liminal offshore lines of sight. At once a symbol of journeying and crossing and a space of suspension and concentration, the boat is a means of accessing *routes* (not roots) and of coping with the ongoing crises between subject and society. Little wonder then, as Roy observed, that the vessel was mobilized by Sundaram with greater urgency than ever to counter the escalating campaign for an authentic Hindu heritage based in Vedic origins and civilizational roots that found violent expression in Ayodhya in 1992, and which continues to persist, both as cultural struggle and state-sanctioned ideology, throughout the Indian subcontinent today.

The word "radical" in my subtitle, *Radical Stakes in Contemporary Indian Art*, conspicuously refers to this problematic of roots at the same time it signals a politicized orientation and a broad commitment to social change in general. Etymologically, "radical" derives from the Latin *radicalis*, "of or having roots," or simply *radice*, the root, and the term was used in this manner from the medieval era on. However, by the seventeenth century, the root under discussion became both literal and metaphorical. Eventually, the "radical" object could be the root of a plant, a language, a scientific process, a disease. One result of this expansion of meaning was that a radical by the early nineteenth century came to describe a person *who performed the overturning of roots*, as in "radical reformers." It may seem contradictory, as contemporary artist Mariam Ghani has noted, "that a *radical* can be both a root part and founding principle, and an extreme agent of change and reactions, simultaneously basic and new; but all this contradiction resolves at the root, which is both the foundation of the status quo and the natural starting point for its reform."[47]

Seizing upon these shifts in vocabulary, I use the phrase "radical stakes" to signal the fluid investments in the politics of culture that are ultimately driven by a commitment to change and to alternative moorings and social attachments. Accordingly, the subject of this book is as much a reading of *their* (the artist's and critic's) radical stakes as it is a process of articulating my own. These latter investments take the form of three broad intellectual preoccupations and self-directing goals. The first is to inhabit and continue a tradition of leftist practice and thought fashioned by an earlier generation by engaging with its intellectual presuppositions, critical procedures, and secular-humanist-democratic vision. The second is to revitalize a discursive arena lagging from overdetermined concepts and ideas, in part, as I will shortly explain, due to the professionalization of postcolonial theory in the academy. And the third is to seek in the practices of art and art writing an exemplary intellectual response to these dilemmas, one that has relevance across the humanities and social sciences, well beyond the domain of the visual arts.

The Current Conjuncture

Accordingly, the aim of the present inquiry is not merely to examine the contributions made by Kapur and Sundaram to the discourses of contemporary art in South Asia. It is also to enter and continue some of the problems and difficulties raised by such radical approaches to the aesthetic field and to begin to self-fashion a personal inheritance that could help respond to the urgencies of our "current conjuncture." This phrase was Stuart Hall's term for the new relationships and dispositions of power emerging at a given historical moment: "The condensation of forces during a period of crisis, and the new social configurations which result, mark a new 'conjuncture,'" he stated.[48] For Hall, naming the new conjuncture was a matter of political necessity, even if a given term—for him, neoliberalism—was less than satisfactory and always provisional.

Notably, Hall's vocabulary and investigative style were productively appropriated by Geeta Kapur to identify the ground of political antagonism and cultural resistance in India in the new millennium. In a widely cited essay, "A Cultural Conjuncture in India," Kapur argued that with globalization, "new factors have emerged to alter the role of artists as citizens."[49] Writing in the wake of the 2004 elections in India, which saw the centrist Congress Party return to power in an unexpected challenge to the right-wing orientation thriving among the middle classes, Kapur connected this "churning of Indian democracy" to the new modes of experimentation with video and new media precipitated by the shift from the analog to the digital and reflected on the agonistic role for "critical art" within the flourishing marketplace.[50]

If Kapur's call in that essay for "a situational analysis of cultural production within vastly heterogeneous geopolitical realities"[51] harbored a degree of skeptical optimism, the acceleration of inequality and sociopolitical crises the world over surely point to a more difficult, volatile, and regressive conjuncture today. There is no question that we live in truly perilous times in which the future seems profoundly uncertain. The resurgence of authoritarian politics—embodied by Prime Minister Narendra Modi in India and President Donald Trump in the United States but equally visible in the autocratic rulers of Brazil, Turkey, Japan, Russia, and the Philippines—points to a disturbing pattern in which principles of truth and democratic freedom, even the right to criticism and dissent, can no longer be taken for granted.

Instead, these social justice ideals appear to be increasingly threatened by the rise of xenophobic nationalism, religious radicalism, and the unpredictable pairing of disillusionment and populism unleashed by the phenomena of Brexit/Trump. The global refugee crisis, and the chilling reaction to the influx of migrants and the dispossessed in the United States and Europe, has fueled a wave of neo-fascism, anti-Semitism, and Islamophobia; the hostility toward Muslims around the world is perhaps the most pronounced of these xenophobic expressions. Battles are being waged over threatened civil liberties, women's reproductive rights, and the devastating effects of global warming on the planet; travel bans and border walls are being constructed, further destabilizing poor, marginalized, and unprotected populations everywhere. Meanwhile, Trump's notorious Twitter feed conveys a belligerent disregard of issues of the highest importance, while promising (and delivering) a kind of suspension of thinking, a rejection of historical understanding, and a refusal to face the complexity of the world. It also raises a troubling question: How should we speak truth to power when power seems no longer concerned with the truth?

And yet, as Stuart Hall stated with his unparalleled strength of intelligence and insistence on keeping open the door to the future,

What happens next is not pregiven. Hegemony is a tricky concept and provokes muddled thinking. No project achieves "hegemony" as a completed project. It is a process, not a state of being. No victories are permanent or final. Hegemony has constantly to be "worked on," maintained, renewed, revised. Excluded social forces, whose consent has not been won, whose interests have not been taken into account, form the basis of counter-movements, resistance, alternative strategies and visions . . . and the struggle over a hegemonic system starts anew. They constitute what Raymond Williams called "the emergent"—and are the reason why history is never closed but maintains an open horizon towards the future.[52]

Following in the critical tradition of Williams and Hall, the creative activities of the artist and critic provide a model of intellectual practice that prioritizes the process of *becoming* as a mode of engagement and radical thought. This kind of cultural imaginary, with its rejection of closure and finality of all sorts, and its active investment in the agency and struggle of intellectual work, is of vital importance within the current contexts of global crises and sense of intellectual impasse within the humanities. There is a broad consensus that the radical intellectual toolkit known as postcolonial theory became increasingly exhausted as a critical vocabulary by the late 1990s, either "dulled" as investigative tackle by academic institutionalization and "multicultural managerialism," or firmly displaced (Trumped?) by the shift to "the global."[53] The same has been said of the other "posts" that galvanized aesthetic debates at the end of the millennium, namely, poststructuralism and postmodernism: their depletion amounts to what Hal Foster has called our current "paradigm-of-no-paradigm"[54] and the general experience of a condition of aftermath, of living on within the fault lines of implosion and duress.[55]

Foucault warned about the inevitability of bankrupt concepts, stating they provided no more than "ready-made synthesis." The task is "to free the problems they pose," he argued presciently, looking beyond the cul-de-sac of assimilated "isms."[56] Accordingly, I seek a reinvestment in the strategies of resilience and renewal that drove an earlier tradition of leftist thought, and an engagement with a legacy of ideas *put into practice*, as the basis for a repositioned response to the challenges of our times. As we shall see, the enormous faith that our practitioners have placed in art is not because it provides solace, escape, distraction, or diversion; nor does it promise coherence, resolution, or a predetermined direction. It is because art's intelligence and intrepid investigation of the world from which it emerges presents a place for us *to go right now*; it provides ballast against the terrible unknown, resources for a continual becoming, and a means for survival, resilience, and renewal.

Filiation vs. the Affiliative Scheme

The fraught nature of the idea of inheritance and the difficulty of transmission across the generational divide were also problems at the center of Edward Said's distinction between "filiation" and "affiliation." These concepts, which first appeared in *The World, the Text, and the Critic* and were developed further in *Culture and Imperialism*, were closely linked to Said's notion of "worldliness" and his approach to the practice of "secular criticism" more broadly.[57] Few things, Said argued, were as problematic and universally fraught in the modern era as the assumption of a natural continuity between one generation and the next. If patterns of *filiation*, resulting from natal links, had served to cohere relationships in traditional society, then these were increasingly eroded and replaced by modes of *affiliation* in the modern era. Said saw this as a persistent tension in the world of high modernism and its intelligentsia and pointed to the prevalence of such tropes as childless couples, orphaned children, and still childbirths within English literature, "all of them suggesting the difficulties of filiation."[58] What Said saw in such modernist writers as T.S. Eliot, James Joyce, Joseph Conrad, and Ezra Pound was "the pressure to produce new and different ways of conceiving human relationships"[59] and a creative reimagining of social bonds that could substitute for the stability of biological connections across generations. Thus, if filiation was a form of belonging that came with birth or family, then affiliative relationships were acquired through "social and political conviction, economic and historical circumstances, voluntary effort and willful deliberation."[60] If the filiative scheme belonged to the realm of nature and biological life, then "affiliation belongs exclusively to culture and society."[61] And if filiation was based on descent and "organic complicity," then affiliation was something actively forged through "critical consciousness and scholarly work."[62]

The intellectual output of Sundaram and Kapur, as I have suggested, is characterized by a refusal of those forms of belonging based on familial or biological descent and a highly procreative and regenerative drive toward that which we might see as "an affiliative order." The couple, who have no children of their own, are also known in Delhi for their tireless attendance over the decades at the city's rapidly shapeshifting art world events, and their stamina and energy for exhibitions, openings, gallery talks, conferences across the academic fields, performances, open studios, and all manner of other, more eccentric happenings has been much commented upon. The scope and range of their activities must also be understood as reflecting the broader community of artists, activists, and intellectuals in India to which they belong, whose members stand by a principled commitment to civil society and cultural work often debated through rigorous dissensus. Such everyday activities share with their major works of art and writing a seemingly insatiable appetite for past, present, and future simultaneously. In the constant return toward twentieth-century antecedents and the active embrace of younger artists and new initiates—a pointed enthusiasm for both predecessors and successors—we see both artist and critic rejecting timeless or quasi-transcendental mechanisms of belonging, and instead activating affiliative relationships in a somewhat systematic way. And yet, such a process, as Said stated, which can involve the transformation of something personal or narrow into "a cultural act of great importance,"[63] is not systematic or easily grasped through a predetermined methodology. To begin to take such work seriously is thus to try to apprehend the many forms, positions, events, and contexts in which this contribution, defined ultimately by Said as "critical thought,"[64] takes its shape and gains its force.

Generational Frames

The idea of "generation," like the notion of inheritance, is a thoroughly temporal construct, one that is linked equally to the structure of an individual lifetime and to the experience of collective identities. Generation implies identification, belonging, and a social, even quasi-biological bond. It is at times consistent with the idea of cohort, which assumes a shared consciousness of sorts; at other times it marks the fact of social difference and the parent-offspring relation in particular. It was the Hungarian-born sociologist Karl Mannheim who first objected to the positivist's linear rendering of generation as "the curve of the progress of the human species" over time in his 1923 essay, "The Problem of Generations."[65] For Mannheim, mere chronology did not in itself produce commonality or collective identity. "Were it not for the existence of social interaction between human beings," he stated flatly, "generation would not exist as a social phenomenon: there would be merely birth, aging, and death."[66] If the quote reveals the stark dichotomy between the social and the biological in Mannheim's classic sociology of knowledge, it also displays his own investment in a more organic account of human existence and its relevance to social and historical change.[67]

Recently, anthropologist David Scott has turned to the category of generation "as a mode of thinking the continuities and discontinuities of the past in the present," and has connected this inquiry to intellectual history and to the work of criticism in particular.[68] Scott's far-reaching project of interviews with Caribbean intellectuals, writers, and political actors—most notable among them, Stuart Hall—is highly sensitive to the nuanced fabric of intellectual inheritance and to the structure of generation as a social form. For Scott, the idea of generation contains within it an essentially paradoxical temporality because generations do not merely succeed one another, they overlap and coexist. "Different generations live at the same time," he reminds us, and this fact of *co-existence* implies active participation in a continuous social process and differently located subjects who can nonetheless work toward a shared location.[69] Building on what Mannheim referred to as "frameworks of anticipation," Scott thus expands and redefines the idea of generation as "a frame in which to think of the plenitude as well as the finitude of human existence."[70]

This more synchronic, less sequential approach to the phenomena of generations—to their "successive-yet-overlapping" co-presence in history[71]—situates a more dialogical, multilocational terrain through which to conceive of creative practitioners and aesthetic forms, past and present. In relation to art history, it should also create suspicion about "modernist myths" that derive from seamless stories of generational succession rather than from the "ground of repetition and recurrence" upon which all aesthetic practice is based.[72] Over two decades ago, Griselda Pollock reflected on how generational coordinates within feminist art history (in the form of first, second, and third waves, for example) had served to flatten certain narratives about art and artists, noting that feminist discourse had—at times—been "unconsciously depoliticized" by being framed through generational and geographic differences.[73]

A quibble along these lines could be made about the recent volume *Midnight to the Boom: Painting in India after Independence* (2013), which provides a portrait of Indian art in the second half of the twentieth century, primarily from the Herwitz Collection at the Peabody Essex Museum, the most significant painting collection of its kind in the United States. Featuring contributions from top scholars in the field, the book identifies three successive generations of artists in South Asia in the twentieth century. Accordingly, the first generation, largely born between 1910 and 1930, are the "Pathbreakers"; the second, who "began to make waves in the 1970's," are "Midnight's Children"; and the third, who turned to new forms, materials, and languages from the early 1990s, are the "New Mediators."[74] Inevitably, artists who fall into more than one cohort, like Sundaram and Nalani Malani, are said to be "on the cusp between generations"; and confusingly, a younger "fourth generation," represented by Sudarshan Shetty and Subodh Gupta, is identified as having emerged through the expanding conditions of the global art market, also in the early 1990s.[75] In other words, the schema appears to strain against Mannheim's key lessons about generations—that human experience is temporally overlapping, that chronology does not in itself produce commonality, and that humanity is always coexistent but not necessarily coeval. Significantly, it also prohibits a more dialogical account of creative practice through which artists assume a multiplicity of agonistic *and* shared orientations toward the spaces of culture in their own time.

Remembering Bhupen: Intimacy and Subversion

The painter Bhupen Khakhar, an emblematic figure of the so-called Baroda generation, is an artist who demands understanding through the kind of expanded generational optic suggested by Scott. This is because until his death from cancer in 2003, this openly gay painter was often at the center of sociality and a source of creative vitality for his famed group of peers in Baroda—among them, Nasreen Mohamedi, Gulammohammed Sheikh, Nalani Malani, Nilima Sheikh, Vivan Sundaram, and Geeta Kapur—with whom he forged many different kinds

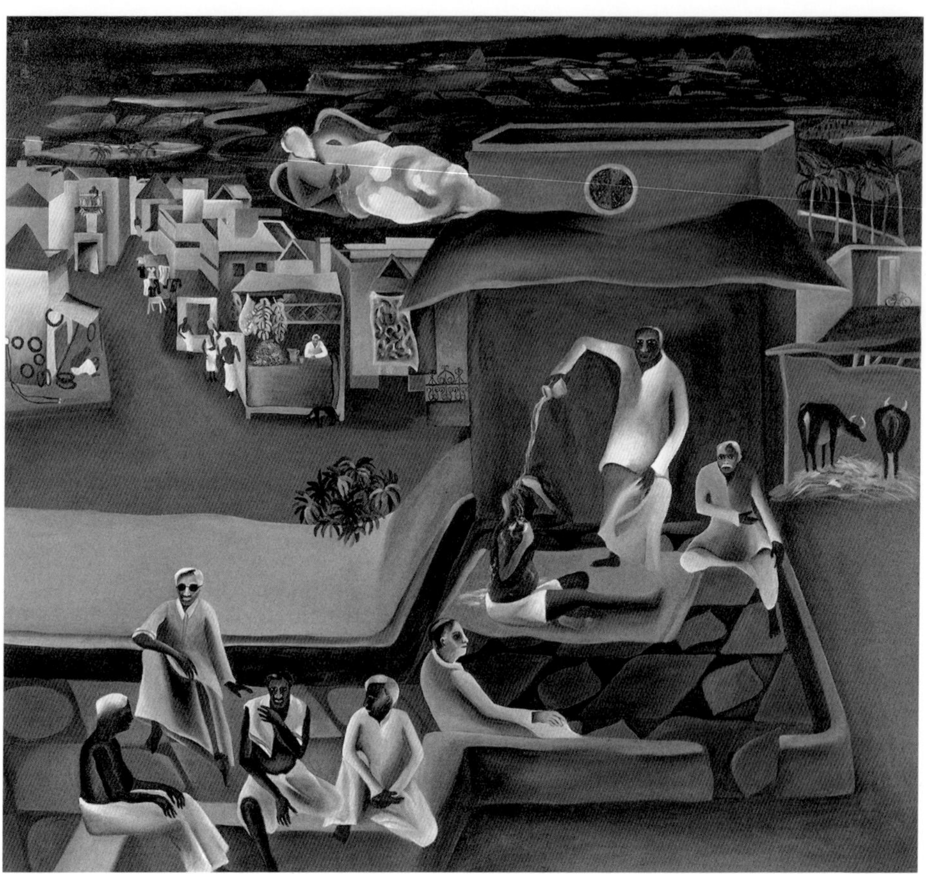

FIGURE INTRO.6
Bhupen Khakhar,
Death in the Family,
1978. Oil on canvas.
© Trustees of the
Bhupen Khakhar
Estate/Victoria and
Albert Museum,
London.

of bonds through love, humor, empathy, friendship, and artistic solidarity. At the same time, the relevance and significance of Khakhar's painting have expanded and multiplied dramatically as his work has been posthumously received in meaningful ways by countless younger practitioners. This atmosphere of reception is now certainly part of the interpretive complexity and multidimensionality of his oeuvre, as evidenced by a major retrospective exhibition of his work at the Tate Modern in London in 2016.[76] This international show dramatized the remarkable ability of Khakhar's paintings, with their elemental themes of love, sexuality, illness, and the body, as portrayed in figure Intro.6, to "speak" to differentially located subjects across a vast spectrum of social, historical, and generational experience.

Khakhar's status as an artist through which other artists converge and connect was at the heart of an earlier 2013 exhibition in Mumbai,

Touched by Bhupen, commemorating the tenth anniversary of the painter's death. The show featured twenty-five contributors, some friends and colleagues from his circle, others younger practitioners indebted to his work, reflecting on the ways the painter affected their lives: as reference, inspiration, exemplar, and role model.[77] In a memorable homage titled "Buddy," translated from Gujarati for the English-language catalogue, Gulammohammed Sheikh offered an especially intimate set of reflections about the journey of their five-decade-long friendship, speaking of mischief, mayhem, travel, and their "playful duet" in pursuit of a pictorial language through the "alternating currents of being close and being distant."[78] His first-person account about their remarkable bond narrates a certain generational experience unavailable to those outside the cohort except *by way of narrative itself*. To this extent, it builds upon the now canonical volume edited by Sheikh in 1997, *Contemporary Art in Baroda*, which included contributions by Nilima Sheikh, Ajay Sinha, and Ashish Rajadhyaksha, all practitioners in some way connected to the art school, and which remains to this day the most significant account of Baroda's distinctive intellectual and institutional milieu.[79]

If one instance of the critical consciousness I have been explicating rests in the micro-corpus of creative activity that Sundaram produced around Amrita Sher-Gil, then another exceptional instance can be seen in the artist's and the critic's very different posthumous engagements with the life and art of their peer, Bhupen Khakhar. A key feature of affiliation, for Said, was that it *converted* the anguish of familial loss into a more productive language, by means of invention, adoption, and ultimately transformation into something that others can share. As with Sheikh, this is at the potent center of several projects dedicated to the "uncommon universe" of Khakhar, which galvanize methods of mediation and interpretation to serve alternative narratives and critical self-reflection. These projects include a 2007 essay by Kapur whose title I have just referenced;[80] a second essay in conjunction with Khakar's retrospective at the Tate Modern in 2016; a double-page collage made by Sundaram, comprising photos, images, and fragments from Khakhar's letters, also for the Tate Modern exhibition; a series of works by Sundaram made with paper, pencil, and string, *Bad Drawings for Dost* (2004–5); and an exhibition titled *Subject of Death* (2012) curated by Kapur on the occasion of the tenth anniversary of the painter's passing.[81] By turning now to examine a selection of these projects, I seek to show how this creative investment in the legacy of Khakhar represents both an affectionate homage to the painter's unique social vision and a confrontation of sorts with the inherent limits of successionist narratives and generational frames.[82]

In *Bad Drawings for Dost*, for example, Sundaram revisited pictorial elements from Khakhar's paintings, by tracing over them by hand and then piercing them with a needle and thread, in a tactile operation involving returning, touching, retracing, and stitching. The resulting series of works, Nancy Adajania has stated, present themselves "like a stain of water on the tissue of memory."[83] In these rough stitches and drawings, as depicted in figure Intro.7, Sundaram turned, after a decade of installation and photo/video-based projects, to "caress" the images of his *dost* ("friend" in Hindi), "as though, by touching his paintings, he could make contact with the departed."[84] The allegory of touch is especially resonant since, as Kapur has stated, "Khakhar's figuration testified to many forms of touch," from wounding to healing to sexual incursion, to the extent that he came close to establishing a genre in this vein.[85] Indeed, several of Sundaram's titles in the series—for instance, *Petals/Five Penises* and *Two Men Please All*—seem to inhabit or "touch" the titles of Khakhar's more iconic paintings. But why is such an intimate experience of exchange through touch conceived as a set of "bad drawings" by Sundaram? If the term "bad" is a measure of quality, then what does it mean, it seems reasonable to ask, to make *bad* drawings for a *good* friend?

One answer could be that the gesture stands as a form of recognition of Khakhar's own self-conception as an artist. "I draw badly," the painter once confessed to his friend, the British artist Timothy Hyman, in his characteristically irreverent manner toward aesthetic codes and conventions.[86] And yet, in an interview published in the *Indian Express*, Sundaram offered another response. They were called "bad drawings," he said, "because the images were traced, but I worked on them by dislocating parts of the original painting. It added a certain complexity to the image."[87] Adajania has suggested another explanation, similarly connecting the notion of "bad" to the rough, unfinished aspect of the work. In Sundaram's pictures "there is no urgency," she observes, "to reach for the closure of the perfect composition."[88] Their accounts would seem to confirm, then, that a "bad" drawing is something defined by its rudimentary form. It is minimally composed or technically improvisational, like a rough sketch or a traced line. A "bad drawing"

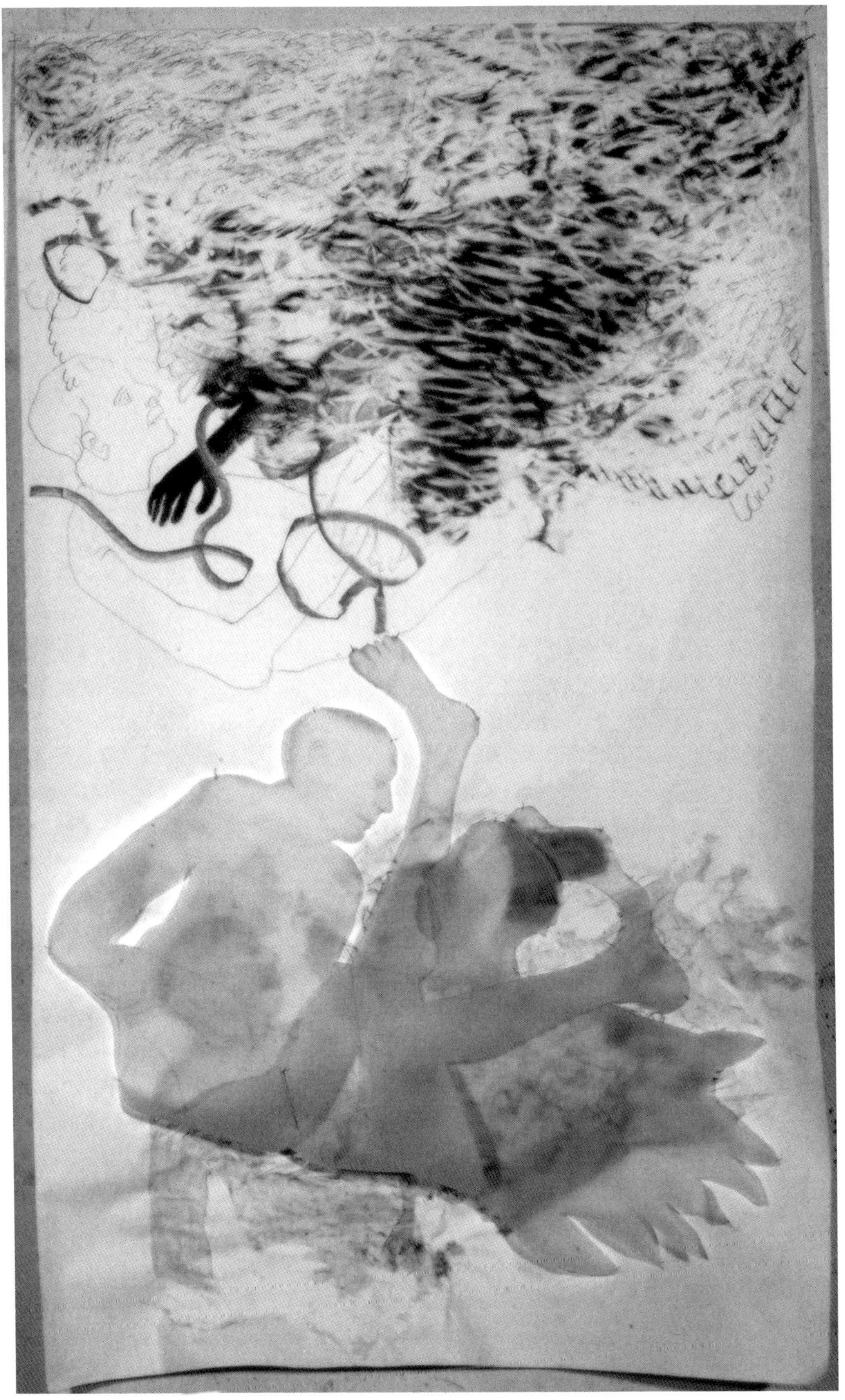

is partial and ongoing, a quick offering, perhaps, among many, in the process of remembering a friend.

Kapur's writing and curatorial projects point to further layers of meaning in relation to the aesthetic hierarchies and social norms that might attach themselves to a word like "bad." In her account of Khakhar, included in the volume *Pop Art and Vernacular Cultures* (2007), edited by Kobena Mercer, Kapur emphasized the painter's rejection from the outset of dichotomous designations, for instance, between avant-garde and kitsch or between high art codes and the realm of the popular. "Khakhar was a vanguard figure who thumbed his nose at high art," she explained. Moreover, "his love acts remained on the *edge* of respectability." For Kapur, this becomes an important basis from which Khakhar staked "a counter-claim for an avant-garde based on marginal and eccentric sources."[89] "Through a trickster's intransigence," she stated, Khakhar ultimately subverted all manner of conventions relating to male bodies and homosexual desire, and this connects, at least implicitly, to the artist's own interest in "bad drawing." Thus Khakhar's investment in bad drawing supported "a vulnerable form of representation."[90] Another viewer, Emilia Terracciano, appears to confirm this sense of vulnerability: "Khakhar's sketches are open about their faults," she observed in a 2013 review of an exhibition of his drawings in London, but his deft, swift pencil sketches remain refreshingly spontaneous and ultimately lend support to his highly individual representational project.[91]

What should we make of this puzzling vocabulary of "badness" surrounding Bhupen Khakhar? Does it have any relation to the 1978 exhibition *Bad Painting*, curated by Marcia Tucker at the New Museum of Contemporary Art in New York? There, the term came to stand for a predominantly figurative and purposely raw style of painting being developed in America in reaction to the dominant minimalist and conceptualist schools of the era.[92] As it turns out, there is probably no connection; Khakhar himself had little interest in the fickle immediacy of art world trends. The point, for our purposes, is to observe how such questions sustain and activate ambiguity and illegibility, effecting an *interpolative* intellectual practice that disallows shortcuts and instantaneous access and demands instead high levels of engagement from its audience. Such a practice often splinters and multiplies frames of reference, leading to additional questions and further research. In the case of Khakhar, we are left with no bottom line or final word, and no definitive way to characterize his art. We apprehend, instead, different points of entry into the multidimensional hierarchies operative in the painter's life and work—sexual, aesthetic, societal, behavioral—some of them resonating with the notion "bad." One effect is that the word "bad" no longer functions as a Kantian sign of judgment and objective value. Instead, these modes of engagement push the term into the service of Khakhar's own conditions of marginality. If anything, such interventions come to stand for the societal *costs* (not worth) that were evident in his life and art.

If the phrase "for dost" in Sundaram's title suggests a friendship that was forged at least partly outside the boundaries of the English language, and hints at Khakhar's own relationship to the vernacular realm, then Kapur's reference to "Saint Bhupen" is even more dense with nuance and intertextual citation. Here, the critic performs the same "trickster's intransigence" that she identified in her subject, the artist. This is because Kapur's declaration of sainthood appears, upon first glance, as the ultimate act of veneration and canonization, and it seems therefore a sign of reverence distinctly at odds with the kind of critical retake I have suggested. However, her title "Saint Bhupen" is a reference to "Saint Genet," the name of the book by Jean-Paul Sartre about the French writer and political activist Jean Genet, who was also openly homosexual. Significantly, Sartre's title, *Saint Genet*, has proven resonant for scholars and thinkers in queer studies, who have appropriated the philosopher's paradigmatic attempt to link Genet's marginality and homosexuality to the "greatness" of his art as a model for queer historiography. David Halperin's book *Saint Foucault*, which argues for a reading of Michel Foucault, who died of AIDS in 1984, as a gay intellectual, is an excellent example. But Kapur's nomenclature, "Saint Bhupen," does more than invoke the complex psychology and morality that is at stake in the gender positioning of gay men, which Sartre and Halperin set out to grasp in their major studies of Genet and Foucault. It also invokes the precarious position of the critic in this operation, recalling, in particular, Susan Sontag's objections in *Against Interpretation* to the "thick encrustations" of interpretation that surrounded important artists in her now classic set of reflections about criticism and her harsh indictment of Sartre's book on Genet.[93]

"*Saint Genet* is a cancer of a book," "exasperating" and "grotesquely verbose," wrote Sontag in her memorable 1966 review of Sartre's six-hundred-plus-page tome. For her, it broke "every rule of decorum established for the critic" and epitomized the problem of over-interpretation.[94] Sontag viewed Sartre's book as an "indefatigable act of literary and philosophical disembowelment practiced on Genet"; at best, it was an indulgent exercise intended to prove Sartre's own investments in existentialism and psychoanalysis.[95] Félix Guattari would later agree with Sontag's general assessment of the situation: "It was wrong for Sartre to project onto Genet" his own psychogenetic schema, he stated.[96] And yet, Guattari's attempt to "regain" Genet from Sartre's oppressive analysis in the book, which he viewed as both a "colossal and sumptuous monument" and a "mausoleum," similarly reflected his own interest in developing an antipsychiatric theoretical argument. Thus, in addition to foregrounding gay subjectivity, *Saint Genet* may be seen to stand for some of the most essential challenges to interpretation itself as they have been articulated within the Franco-American philosophical tradition since the 1960s.

Kapur's retake on this inheritance for India in her fertile moniker, Saint Bhupen, thus compels us to recall some of the major lessons of this tradition—for example, to challenge the stultifying separation between form and content; to struggle with the dilemma that knowledge is power; and to seek, as Sontag argued, "a descriptive, rather than prescriptive, vocabulary" for art.[97] As well, this loaded reference invites us to consider in philosophical terms the significance of the space between the critic and her subject. Kapur has acknowledged cutting her teeth on this intellectual tradition, explaining in a recent interview how the debates surrounding interpretation launched by Sontag's text helped her to develop a more critical approach in her writing. "I was already aware that interpretation was a problematized area," she stated. "But the interesting thing was to work out how one actively problematizes it."[98]

Kapur's ingenious act of commemoration in the exhibition *Subject of Death* portrayed in figure Intro.8—to hang Saint Bhupen "resplendent" in the gallery among friends—sustains this process of active problematization and represents another instance of the "working out how" that is crucial to her critical praxis. Her retake on Sartre's epithet points to a contested history of theoretical frames—existentialism, psychoanalysis, and poststructural critique—and cautiously navigates the crowded intersection of theory's lapse into dogmatic excess. Kapur's return to Sontag (this time the text is *Illness as Metaphor*) in her later essay on Khakhar concerned with the tensions surrounding mortality in his final

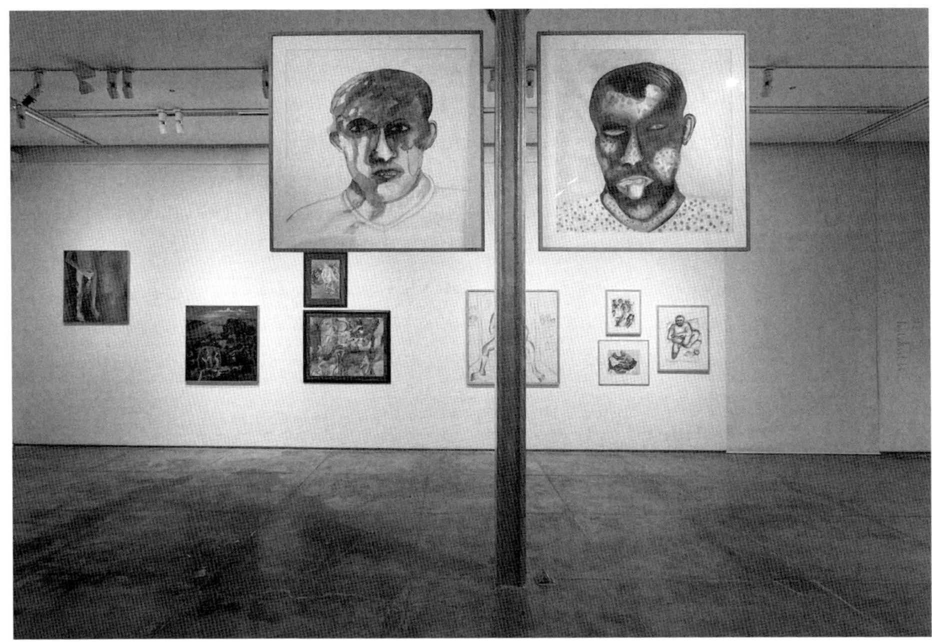

paintings, when the artist was suffering acutely from cancer, appears to have been compelled by the same consideration: "I needed to remember how language—its descriptive powers and its follies in the way of metaphors—can cause offence to the person actually suffering from a disease," she stated.[99]

Accordingly, the luminous language of this essay, which Kapur describes as both a continuation of her 2007 text and an "epilogue to his heretical oeuvre," confronts the morbidity of Khakhar's illness and affirms painting's agential role within the devastating conditions of disease and death. Khakhar's late works, she writes, do not so much "out-maneuver death"; they turn *the objective indifference of death's gaze into aura.*[100] For her, the act of writing must attempt to retrieve the body of the lost friend "from the curse of eternity" and secure for him instead "a place in active memory."[101] What is striking is not only Kapur's dedication to protecting Khakhar from the excesses of language, an artist who—it should be recalled—"thumbed his nose" at theory's high ground; there is also something of a devotional quality, reminiscent of Khakhar's own performative (and mischievous) relation to the sacred. And yet, Kapur's is a firmly *secular* consecration in the end, drawn entirely from the philosophical or "affiliative" field. And this returns us

FIGURE INTRO.8 *Subject of Death* (installation view), exhibition curated by Geeta Kapur, 2013. Photograph by Anil Rane. Courtesy of Chemould Prescott Road.

to some essential questions about the relations among language, philosophy, and the arts: namely, what *should be* the role of interpretation and explication—what forms and registers should it take, and when? Where are the lines between knowledge, possession, and the needs of the self? How can a loved friend's creative life be recalled with corresponding levels of love and creativity? And how should language and the space of display be effectively put to this valiant task?

Problem-Spaces: The Shape of the Inquiry

This trail of activity in the wake of Bhupen Khakar's death conveys something of the *work* that Sundaram's art and Kapur's writing and curating demands from its viewers and readers. Taken together, the former's drawings "for *dost*" and the latter's essay investigations and *Subject of Death* exhibition do not qualify as a "collaboration" in any conventional sense; nor do these projects exist on an equal footing, given the varying registers and depths of engagement that distinguish the critic from the artist here. Nonetheless, through their textual and visual allusions and techniques of tracing, translation, interpretation, and display, we apprehend a sophisticated play of language and signs, as well as meanings that reverberate across heterogeneous forms. This is not to say that the outcome is always successful; on the contrary, the struggle toward that which is often beyond grasp involves persistence, difficulty, and, at times, mixed results. As Said cautioned, affiliation was itself a fragile thing, always fraught with doubleness and at risk of collapsing from the critical to the uncritical: "Affiliation sometimes reproduces filiation, sometimes makes its own forms."[102] The key was to recognize the subtle difference between the two and the continual negotiation on the part of artists and writers to seek that "potential space inside civil society . . . [of] alternative acts and alternative intentions" conceived as a fundamental intellectual obligation.[103]

Said also pointed to the possibility that the drive toward difficulty might "take the joy out of one's heart," as if pleasure was somehow antithetical to the insistent skepticism of critical thought.[104] This final point serves to highlight several intangible qualities—beauty, love, pleasure, and hope—that seem to float freely, indeed reliably, across my subjects' creative output over time. Sundaram's aesthetic forms are frequently beautiful, often breathtaking, even sublime; similarly, Kapur's writing is full of compassion, moments of bliss, and modulations of love and hope. And yet, these various affective registers are never at odds with the sharpness of their societal critiques, nor do they reflect a momentary lapse of judgment or a dilution of one's critical concerns.

"To be truly radical," Raymond Williams stated with unwavering conviction, "is to make hope possible, rather than despair convincing."[105] For him, hope was a pragmatic asset, the antidote to disaffection and despair; the loss of hope could lead to fatalism and complacency and become a self-fulfilling route to the misery it foresaw. In a similar vein, the beauty and joy that come uniquely from the aesthetic sphere offer a calibrated politics of hope for our subjects. More than sentimentality or a facile sense of optimism, this is a constitutive feature of their affiliative practice, rooted in the analysis of societal forces, fueled by the processes of participation and engagement, and linked to the expansion of the political imagination. This aspirational, yet firmly secular, quality exists in many of their major projects, and it speaks to that which Walter Benjamin attributed to the otherwise metaphysical space of the aura: an aesthetic quality that is fundamentally unassimilable and that resists being wholly recuperated in the end.

The points of intersection that occur between Kapur's writing and Sundaram's art-making in the examples of Khakar and Sher-Gil also stand as an exemplary case of criticism's possibilities in relation to art. Suffice it to say that Kapur's own writing about the Sher-Gil family, which began with a skeptical essay in 1972, assumes a relationship of critical distance and studied *adjacency* to the activities of this unusually creative clan. Subsequent engagements have included an essay on women artists in India that considers (among others) Amrita Sher-Gil and a text addressing Umrao Singh Sher-Gil's corpus of amateur photography alongside Sundaram's digital journey through the "labyrinthine tunnels of the family saga."[106] Her writings on Khakhar, by contrast, extend much further backward and forward, spanning a period of fifty years as already noted, accompanied by several curated exhibitions that featured Khakhar's work.[107] Meanwhile, Sundaram's iconic 1981 painting seen in figure Intro.9 of Khakhar's lively studio, *People Come and Go*, which captures, as Homi Bhabha has recognized, the atmosphere of "citationality"[108]—the hospitality and ease of intercultural experimentation that characterized India's art world at this juncture—reveals a similar kind of sustained energy and intellectual concentration over time.

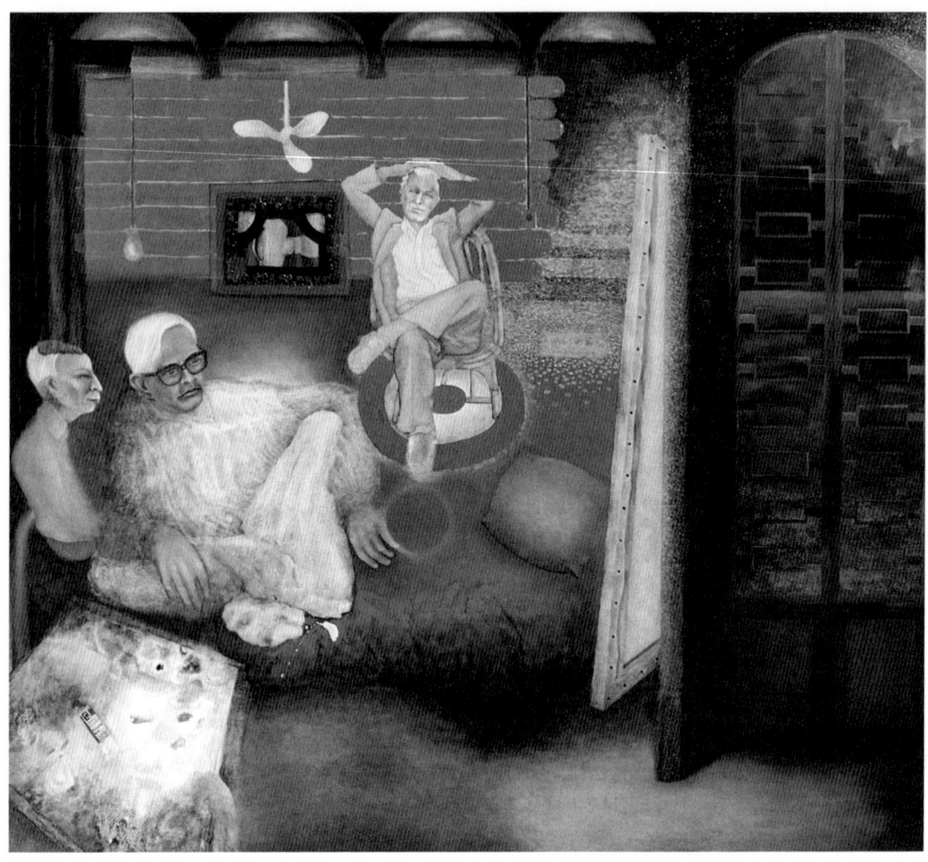

Taken together, we apprehend a lifelong interface of creativity activity, defined by overlapping interests and permeable connections. This corpus, I have suggested, *converts* filiation into affiliation; that is, it *opens out* the sphere of immediate kinship dictated by birth and marriage to a much wider arena of cultural engagement and forms of belonging. These activities further point to the possibilities inherent in the production-reception-display matrix, or put differently, they affirm and activate the dialectical space of *discourse* in contemporary art. One result is that Sher-Gil's and Khakhar's twentieth-century projects become "problem-spaces" that can serve to animate our own. A problem-space, according to David Scott, is "an ensemble of questions and answers around which a horizon of identifiable stakes (conceptual as well as ideological-political stakes) hangs."[109] It is as much a context of rival views, a space of tension and dispute, as it is a creative context where "the conventions of the language-game" are put into play.[110] For Scott, a problem-space offers the means to rethink the postcolonial critical imagination after the exhaustion of the dream of anticolonial utopias and to "refashion futures" through the politics of the present.[111]

Accordingly, in this book, I discern and enter into a variety of problem-spaces that take shape through the work of the artist and the critic. Each of the chapters that follow take the form of detailed examinations of individual projects, articulated and analyzed on their own terms. In chapters 1, 2, and 4, I investigate the dynamic status of Sundaram's art-making, its intrepid uses of different mediums and formats, and its self-conscious strategies of engagement with diverse audiences and interpretive contexts, both in India and on the international stage. In many ways, Sundaram is a quintessential "semionaut," in Nicolas Bourriaud's terms: an artist who "produces original pathways through signs."[112] By selecting three projects that span a fifteen-year period—*Works in Engine Oil and Charcoal* (1991), *History Project* (1998), and *Trash* (2005–8)—my concern is not only to comprehend how the method of hermeneutic return embodied in the digital retake becomes articulated in other forms, in his installation, video, site-specific, and multimedia work. I also explicate the meaning of this for Sundaram's socially and politically engaged art practice by attending closely to the artist's investments in democracy, social justice, and ecological concerns. Three aspects of his art, in particular—the relentless recycling of forms and materials and images, the insistence on dialectical exchange and discussion, and the constant compulsion for historical revision—provide a powerful basis for this social engagement.

Chapter 3 is devoted to the separate projects of art history and criticism undertaken by Geeta Kapur during roughly the same period. It is positioned, both literally and symbolically, at the center of the book. This is in part because the chapter represents the first essay-length analysis of Kapur's seminal contribution to art criticism in India since the emergence of her voice in the late 1960s, and traces her relationships to the politics of decolonization and the nation and to intellectual antecedents in India and Britain through such figures as K.G. Subramanyan and Raymond Williams, in particular. But it is also, crucially, where my own argument gets tested, across the divergences and points of contact between art-making, on one hand, and the writing and thought practices of the critic, on the other. Forging a passionate alliance with the working artist in India, while pushing at the limits and possibilities of language itself, Kapur's distinctive knowledge practice is, I suggest, a highly synthetic intellectual constellation that sustains multiple lines of sight.

As Kapur has argued, the "uneven/anomalous nature of third world modernisms," the subject of her book *When Was Modernism*, is linked to "differently periodized, differently theorized, variously located avant-garde moments" and to different strategies of style and exposition.[113] I thus examine Kapur's own strategies of style and exposition, attending to the texture and density of her prose—its changing modalities, its ethical commitments, its distinctly strategic, partisanal voice—in selected essays from a five-decade-long period. Beginning with the early formations of Kapur's intellectual project in the pages of the now historical journals *Vrischik* and the *Journal of Arts and Ideas* and proceeding, by the end of the chapter, to an examination of her most current writing, I seek to follow not only the shape of Kapur's theoretical models but also how she has fashioned a practice of *critique*, understood as the self-conscious activity of thought upon itself. Extending Theodor Adorno's insights about the essay as a form to Kapur's forensic, investigative deployments of the essay, this chapter thus attends to how art history and art criticism in India have been modeled by Kapur and points to some of the larger implications at stake in this progressive tradition of intellectual critique.

My final chapter turns to numerous recent projects by the artist and the critic and uses the concept of "late style" to approach the digitization of the couple's personal archive in 2010, as well as the energy and intensity of creative activity that ensued and that continues without pause even as I write. For Said, following Adorno, late style characterizes the mature phase of a creative career but not as harmony, serenity, and resolution, or as a process of aging and wisening as in the ripening of a fruit. It signals, instead, an outpouring of almost youthful energy in the advanced stages of life that strains against the forces of normalization and assimilation into history, pointing toward difficulty, contradiction, and a lack of reconciliation. These kinds of qualities can be discerned in Kapur's recent activities, in particular the series of five exhibitions she curated in 2013–14, titled *Aesthetic Bind*, at the Chemould Prescott Road in Mumbai, one of the oldest commercial galleries on the subcontinent. This complex, five-part narrative conveys Kapur's profound attempt to reckon with the conditions of her own interpretation within a curatorial platform, without any clear resolution (or any singular definition) of "the bind." Moreover, the gestures of return to familiar artists and ideas in this project are echoed in several new texts, in which the critic returns recursively to figures she has studied for decades, for instance, M. F. Husain, Bhupen Khakhar, and Nasreen Mohamedi, or revives earlier categories and ideas, like the notion of the "citizen-artist" or the concept of the avant-garde, that have long been prominent in her writing.

Following Derrida's notion of ellipsis, I argue that this *elliptical* modality is equally discernible in several recent projects by Sundaram, namely, *Gagawaka* (2011–12), *Postmortem* (2013), *Memorial* (1993–2014), and *409 Ramkinkars* (2015), in which the artist revisits and repurposes his own earlier work and/or reanimates specific modernist predecessors in Indian art. What distinguishes the late style of both Kapur and Sundaram, I propose, is not merely this creative and intellectual agility, this capacity to condense and calibrate a half century of activity in response to every new change and reverberation around them. It is also their unwillingness to resolve the difficulties or to arrive at the satisfaction of synthesis at the end. What they offer, instead, and what this book seeks to historically understand, is an increasingly powerful lack of synchronicity; a sense of being meaningfully at odds with the times; an untimeliness, in Said's terms, "fully conscious, full of memory," and in possession of a vision that is absolutely vital to how we participate in the here and now.

EARTHLY ECOLOGIES

The idea of a "desert trail," with its associations of hiking and exploration along natural pathways of the land, may well be a by-product of the American imagination. We can trace it back to the myth-making effects of early Hollywood westerns, where a desert trail was essentially a wagon trail, as in the 1935 film *The Desert Trail*, which featured the iconic actor John Wayne as a rodeo cowboy. A desert trail, in this sense, is also a "*gringo* trail," signaling the tracks of a foreign, Anglo presence in the landscape. Vivan Sundaram's *Desert Trail* (1991) in figure 1.1, a diptych made with engine oil and charcoal on paper, is definitely a picture in the spirit of the latter. It depicts a material trail, in the form of archaeological remains and petrochemical debris, in the aftermath of the first American invasion of Iraq. We are presented here with spillage, wreckage, shrapnel, fumes, and shell-shocked desert creatures in a shattered food chain. It is a portrait of an ecosystem ravaged by war, a corroded landscape of toxic remains, where unexploded ammunition settles into the soil alongside bones and (future) blasted limbs. This is certainly not the rambling desert trail of the John Wayne-as-rodeo cowboy sort. It is rather the hideous trail of a storm in the desert, or more precisely, the trail of Operation Desert Storm.

Sundaram's diptych is part of a series consisting of forty-some works on paper in engine oil and charcoal undertaken by the artist in 1991 in response to the first Gulf War. Occupying a place in between drawing,

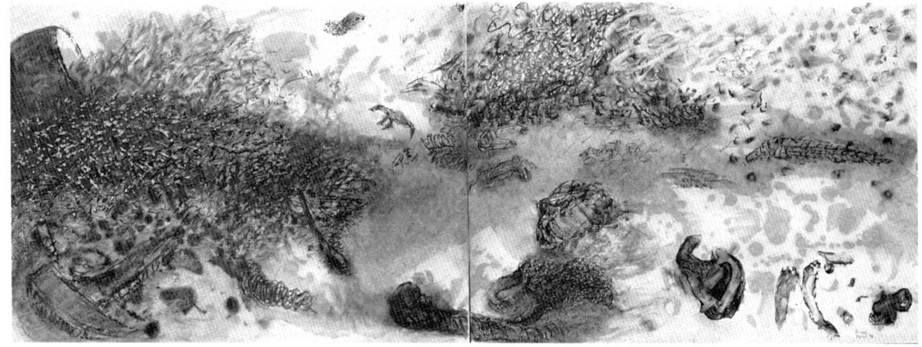

painting, and installation, these compositions, which were not exhibited outside of India until recently, mark a pivotal moment in the artist's practice at a crucial historical juncture. Here, for the first time Sundaram abandoned conventional painting and allowed his pictures to slide out of their frames and off their walls to generate alternative forms and relationships to the gallery space. The series thus marks Sundaram's transition to the installation, video, digital photomontage, and multimedia work that would define his art-making from 1991 on, a formal shift that was driven by several historical conditions of crises, namely, the international crisis of the first Gulf War, the collapse of the former Soviet Union, and the rise of communal violence in India, leading to the destruction of the Babri mosque in Ayodhya by organized gangs of Hindu extremists the following year.[1] Moreover, the economic reforms implemented by the Indian government in 1991 marked the beginnings of a new era of liberalization in the country, leading to the simultaneous phenomenon of India's neoliberal turn, which—for many—has had similarly cataclysmic effects. As Sundaram stated in response to these conditions in an interview, "Changed circumstances and new experiences required a new articulation."[2] Elsewhere he reflected, "I began using unorthodox media, and then I started the process of breaking out of the easel format, such as by stitching sheets of paper together, which allow[ed] one into a space outside the frame, allowing me a greater flexibility."[3]

In this chapter, I suggest that Sundaram's engine oil works, and his understated search for "greater flexibility" in 1991, represent something of a major constellation, the kind of coalescent gesture that T. J. Clark once described in the context of modern French painting as "supercharged with historical meaning" around which significance clusters.[4]

"The more we look and enquire" into such works, Clark stated, "the more facets of social reality they seem to touch and animate."[5] Situated at the vanguard of the formal experimentation that radicalized Indian art in the 1990s, Sundaram's engine oil compositions were an important effort to grasp the new configurations and have proven to have an enduring relevance to the contemporary, even as they have refused to conform to the preservationist imperatives of archival conservation. The status of the materials in this project—oil, handmade paper, charcoal, and zinc—stands in marked contrast, for example, to those used by the British artist Richard Wilson, who also turned to recycled engine oil for his 1987 installation in London. Wilson's site-specific work, 20:50, filled the gallery to waist height with petroleum to produce a perception-altering reflective sea and remained permanently installed in the Saatchi Gallery in a custom-built room for over two decades, in a sense, fully absorbed into the commercial gallery space. By contrast, several of Sundaram's drawings with oil have become fragile artifacts in their own right, growing more brittle, discolored, and faded over time, reflecting the reality of eco-historical change that is itself of crucial concern in the work.

As I will show, the multiple and intertwined meanings of oil in Sundaram's series—at once a geological resource, a global commodity, and a painterly medium with its origins in Euro-Western high culture— point to the interconnections between vastly different histories of oil (ecological, art historical, economic, and political) and present a powerful indictment of the violence generated by American militarism in the Middle East. On one hand, Sundaram's images of falling bombs, cataclysmic explosions, and carcinogenic fumes work to expose the spectacular forms of military destruction unleashed by the "smart bomb" in two successive wars in Iraq and anticipate the expanded use of the aerial drone by the American military in Pakistan, Afghanistan, Somalia, and elsewhere. On the other hand, his mysterious oil-drenched images of fallen Babylonian soldiers and Akkadian kings point to a less visible, more elusive, and open-ended sense of devastation, a form of violence upon both culture and the land whose effects are distinctly linked to the passage of time.

The latter is a portrait of what literary critic Rob Nixon has defined as "slow violence," that which "seeps long term into ecologies," both rural and urban, and for generations to come, and whose hidden forces and protracted processes contrast sharply with the spectacle of high-speed global capitalism in our era.[6] For Nixon, slow violence involves delayed effects, deferred victims, and the microprocesses of erosion and erasure; it refers to the "long dyings—the staggered and staggeringly discounted casualties, both human and ecological that result from war's toxic aftermaths" and penetrate the substratum of our planet.[7] In what follows, I discuss how Sundaram's turn to certain materials, motifs, and techniques in this series—in particular, his embrace of archaeological detritus, petrochemical debris, and oscillating underground and overhead views—makes legible these new regimes of violence and vulnerability and provides the basis for a critical perspective linked not to abstract universals but to the materiality and logic of the concrete. Moreover, the radical temporality on display in these works, linking a fossilized, geo-civilizational past to a technological present and environmental future, will come to define many of Sundaram's later and more ambitious endeavors, for instance, the vast material landscapes composed from rubble and debris that form the basis of his project *Trash* (2005–8), which I analyze in chapter 4, and *Black Gold* (2012), which I discuss at the end of this chapter. I thus turn briefly here to lay some conceptual ground for grasping the persistence of this particular configuration in his work.

The Rubric of Ruination

In recent years, artists and intellectuals across the humanities and social sciences, often drawing upon the seminal insights of the German critic and theorist Walter Benjamin, have turned to the tropes of ruination, rubble, waste, and debris to reflect on the contingency and fragility of certain sociohistorical configurations associated with modernity.[8] In his "Theses on the Philosophy of History," Benjamin famously posited progress as a storm that "keeps piling wreckage upon wreckage," leaving "a pile of debris" in its wake.[9] Writing on the eve of the Nazi genocide of the Jews during the Second World War, the philosopher was drawn to these signs of material excess, accumulation, and decay to develop his critique of the ideology of progress and the forward march of European civilization. In his account, the romanticized classical and neoclassical topoi of the ruin, representing the rise and fall of glorious empires, came to signal a disenchantment with modernity and its myths of progress and civilizational glory. The account has helped to stimulate, as anthropologist Gastón Gordillo has explained, a shift away from the type of ruins studied by classical archaeology, "such as vestiges from an ancient past or sites associated with heritage and tourism, and toward modern, contemporary, industrial forms of decay and destruction, the physical and social detritus created the world over by capitalist, state and imperial projects and conflicts."[10] Benjamin saw in ruins ambivalent "allegories of thinking itself,"[11] providing the basis for an expanded, more paradoxical, and less sentimental approach to ruination as a critical analytic for the modern era. The recent turn by anthropologist Ann Stoler to ruins as "epicenters of renewed claims, as history in a spirited voice, as sites that animate new possibilities, bids for entitlement, and unexpected political projects" is an impassioned effort within the social sciences to activate such a critical imagination.[12]

Sundaram's turn to the physicality of detritus — to engine oil figured as petrochemical spill, to archaeological rubble in his installation *Black Gold* (2012), or to actual garbage from Delhi in *Trash* (2005–8) — involves a similar rejection of the grand narratives of civilization and a purposeful reappropriation of the materiality of debris. In these projects, as we shall see, refuse is simultaneously a hazard and a resource, a framework for historical understanding, and a powerful lens onto human subjectivity, for it defines those subjects who must survive its proximity and whose vulnerability and marginality are bound up in that fact. In Sundaram's art, ruins are left in the wake of wars and sectarian conflict; but they also result from other kinds of societal processes, for example, the excesses of consumption and accumulation arising from rapid and uneven urban expansion and growth. In the ruin-landscape of *Black Gold* (2012), moreover, a large-scale model composed of 2,000-year-old terra-cotta shards, there is no singular culprit or agent of destruction. Here, the more elemental processes of time, wind, and water lead to sunken places and forgotten pasts, as temporality intersects with human activity, and the aerial perspective summons not the mechanisms of imperial surveillance but a more abstract fantasy of history itself. Equally important in Sundaram's oeuvre, however, is that such motifs of degradation and decay are simultaneously images of renewal and regeneration. In other words, a productive dialectic between the material and the social is opened up through these frameworks of ruin and repair. This chapter thus investigates how three interlocking themes introduced for the first time in the engine oil series — the sophisticated semiotics of oil and debris; the place of archaeology, landscape, and the ruin; and the visual optic of the aerial perspective—converge in a powerful portrait of our human ecology in crises that is more relevant today than ever before.

The Epistemology of Oil

Figure 1.2, titled *Land Shift*, an exemplary piece from the series, depicts twelve pieces of paper stitched together—beginning on the wall and stretching onto the floor—in front of which is a flat zinc tray containing a small black pool of engine oil. The dark swirls make the work distinctly geological; it is like a profile cut from the substratum of the land depicting a microecology of indiscernible processes. Here, accumulations of oil point to an elusive dynamics of metabolic exchange. We sense movement, mutation, and disruption as petroleum insidiously mingles with earth. But what is the nature of the "shift" in *Land Shift*? Is this a picture of a "natural" mineral deposit in the soil bed being subjected to processes of sedimentation and flow? Or is it a portrait of an unnatural thing—of contamination—that speaks to the formlessness and terrible irrevocability of the hazardous leak or toxic spill? Here, as fossil fuel meets the fossil record, we sense an ambiguous new ecological order where chemicals are literally inseparable from the soil and where it becomes difficult to discern what is unjust or out of place. At the same time, a number of associations with oil are established: "oil" is simultaneously an artistic medium, a geological entity belonging to the land, a commodity that is dredged from the earth (hijacked, collected, and contained), and a substance released back into the land as industrial waste or hazardous spill.

Another picture shown in figure 1.3, titled *Approaching 100,000 Sorties*, reveals that oil in Sundaram's series is also at the contested center of American militarism in the Persian Gulf. The phrase in his title, like that of *Desert Trail*, highlights the cruel vocabulary produced by the American political elite by playing on those perverse sets of military euphemisms like "Desert Storm," "Enduring Freedom," "Shock and Awe," and the "War on Terror," designed to conceal the violence inherent in their operations. Like the previous work, this one also constructs a profile of a landscape, but now as a series of explosive collisions or—as the title suggests—as an act of violence on the landscape of Iraq. These and other images mimic explosions, or more accurately, they propel you

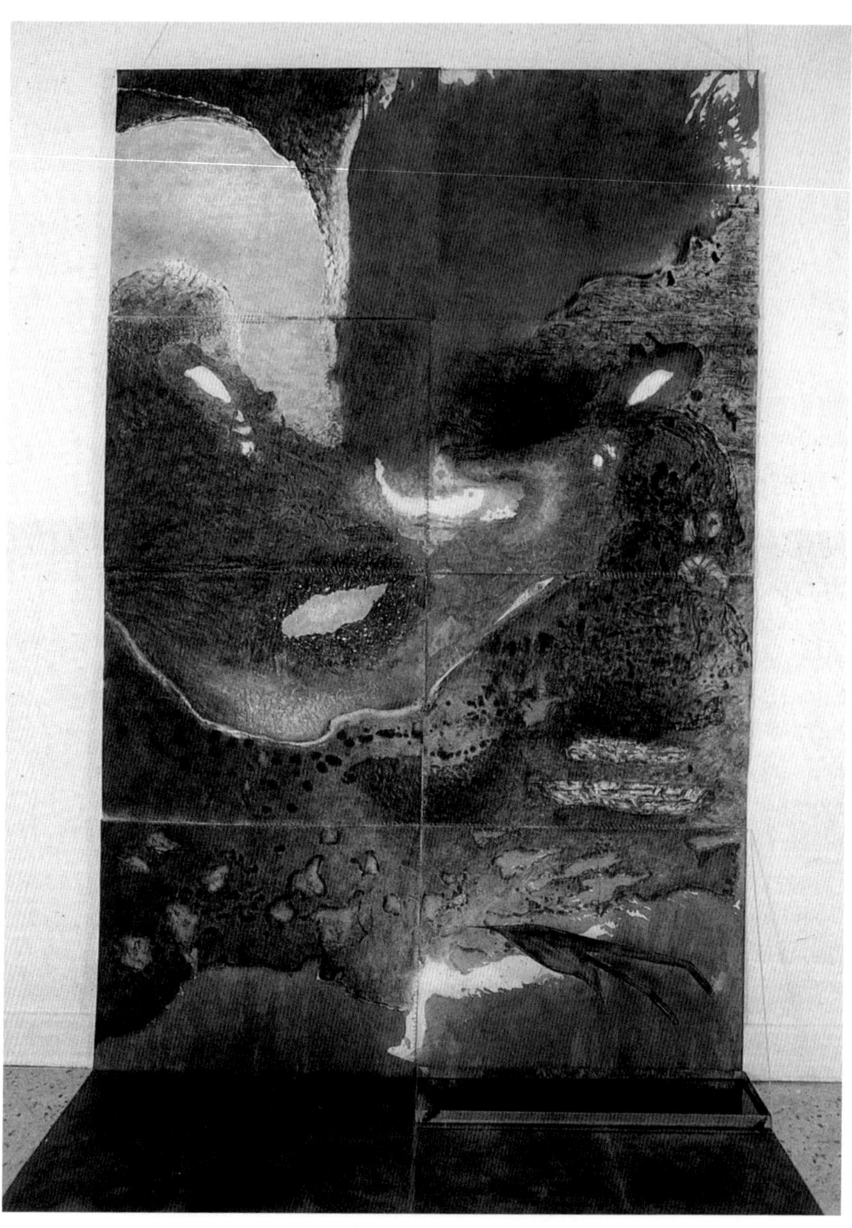

FIGURE 1.2 Vivan Sundaram, *Land Shift*, 1991. Stitched paper on wall and floor with engine oil in zinc tray and painted acrylic sheet. Courtesy of the artist.

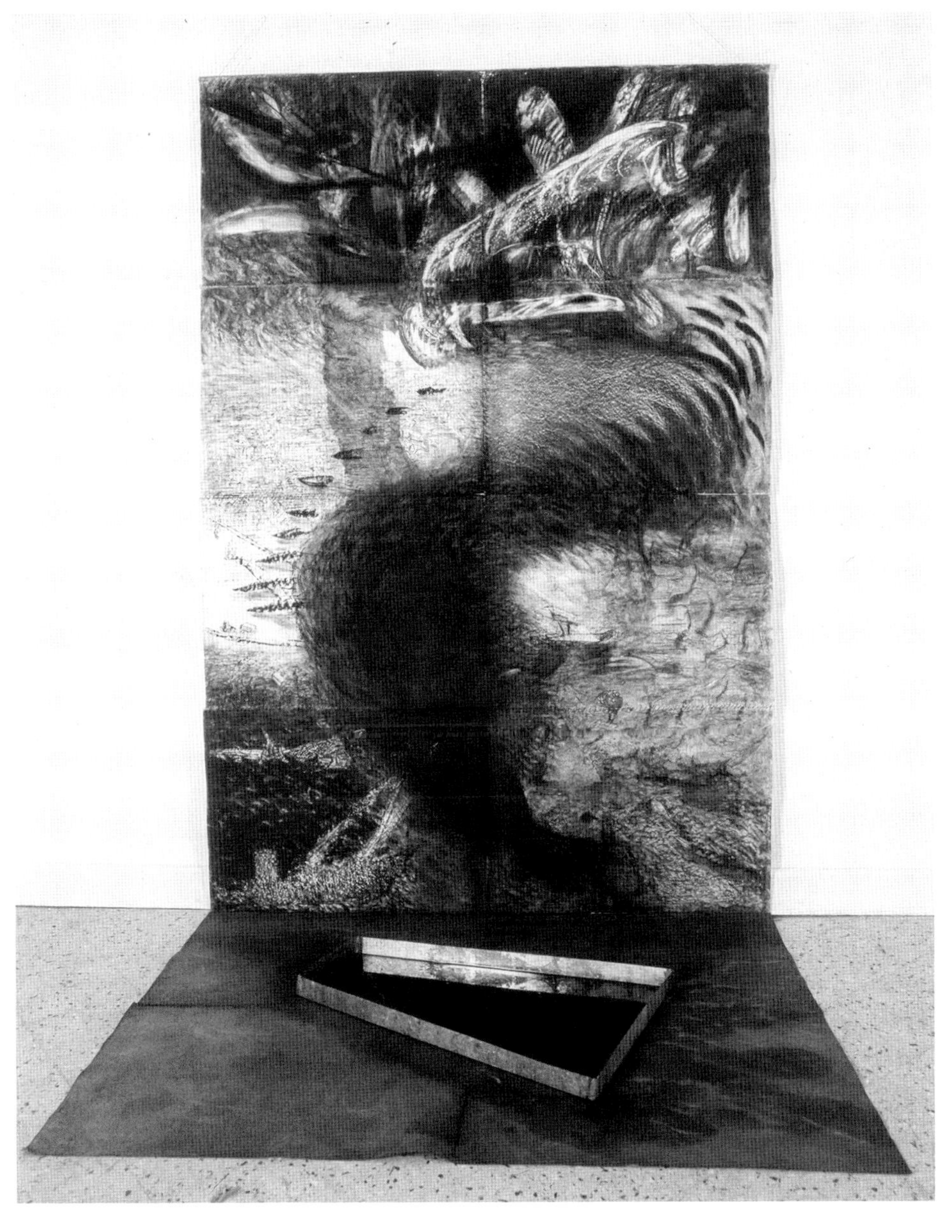

FIGURE 1.3 Vivan Sundaram, *Approaching 100,000 Sorties*, 1991. Stitched paper on wall and floor with engine oil in zinc tray. Courtesy of the artist.

into the moment of an explosion: we are presented here with a formation of bombs dropped from above, a swirling cloud of black smoke, vortexes, chaos, and general fallout and debris. On the floor again is the zinc tray of engine oil, this time like a miniature boat docked in front of this great picture of destruction, or—as you move closer to the piece—like a black glass mirror through which the viewer adds their reflection to the whole alienating scene.[13] It is the voracious historical appetite of modern warfare for petroleum, the deadly complicity between oil and war, that these oil-saturated images of combustion and destruction evoke in a particularly haunting way.[14]

"Petroleum resists the five-act form," Bertolt Brecht stated in his 1929 response to a play about the effects of an oil strike in Albania. "Today's catastrophes do not proceed in a straight line but in cyclical crises."[15] Brecht's comments, emerging from the fraught conditions of modernity in Weimar Germany, express the necessity of grasping modernity's catastrophic effects in a nonlinear, dialectical way and speak to the difficulty of presenting oil's industrial realities within the conventions of traditional aesthetic forms. "Petroleum creates new relationships," he argued, which are immensely complicated and "can only be simplified by *formal* means" (emphasis in original).[16] The formal challenge of representing the twentieth century's oil experience was similarly the subject of a short essay by the Indian novelist Amitav Ghosh, titled "Petrofiction: The Oil Encounter and the Novel" and published in 1992, a year after the start of the first Gulf War and Sundaram's own formal experiments with oil.[17] Ghosh's essay was a review of the "immense significance" of Jordanian writer Abdelrahman Munif's *Cities of Salt*, the first of five novels in Arabic dealing with the history of oil, and it questioned the lack of creative writing on the subject and decried the "barrenness" and "imaginative sterility" that had characterized this epic story until then.[18] For Ghosh, the history of oil, with its principal protagonists—America, on one side, and the peoples of the Arabian Peninsula and Persian Gulf, on the other—had been a devastatingly painful story, "a matter of embarrassment verging on the unspeakable, the pornographic."[19] The world of oil, he argued, with its "bafflingly multilingual" communities "lived out within a space that is no place at all," is "intrinsically displaced, heterogeneous, and international" and challenges the novel's comfortable relation to the settled boundaries of nation-states; "it tends to trip fiction into incoherence."[20] Ghosh's account pointed toward the dispersed spatial, temporal, and geopolitical coordinates of the twentieth century's experience with oil, and it emphasized—in contrast to Brecht—the specifically postcolonial character of this slippery terrain.

In recent years, numerous scholars, reflecting a transformed environmental awareness based in the urgent effects of carbon emissions and the depletion of fossil fuels on a planetary scale, have embraced Ghosh's text as marking the beginnings of a new interdisciplinary formation dubbed "eco-criticism" or "energy humanities."[21] These scholars have sought to confront the history and cultural centrality of oil over the last century—it is "not just a commodity; it is *the* commodity," according to one writer[22]—and have called for fresh intellectual and political imaginaries to confront oil's slippery status and terrible ubiquity in our late-capitalist industrial modernity. The cultural theorist and Left activist Imre Szeman, a leading critical voice in these discussions, for instance, has positioned the question of "how to know oil" as a crucial challenge for "energy epistemologies" and political futures.[23] For Szeman, the significance of oil is *both* in its material realities and in the cultural narratives that shape our understanding of it, hence the value of an interdisciplinary approach integrating art, literature, and cultural studies. One consequence has been the proliferation of a new vocabulary (though not always precise), marked by numerous neologisms that begin with "petro"—like "petro-fiction," "petro-modernity," and "petro-melancholia" (the sense of loss and grief that comes with the end of humanity's love affair with oil).[24] Accordingly, scholars have begun to articulate oil's relationship to a vast spectrum of topics: issues of carbon emissions, climate change, and global warning, on the one hand, and the escalation of militarism, the rise of political Islam, and the will toward democratization embodied by the 2011 uprisings of the Arab Spring, on the other.[25]

Sundaram's images represent an early instance of Szeman's call to *know oil differently*, and they appear to support his account of oil as a "periodizing" substance, a material that can absorb and reflect the major conditions of crises of our times. *Land Shift* provides an unusual vision, for instance, of a status that the oil industry has implicitly denied: the state of crude petroleum beneath the surface of the earth. This rather basic fact about oil—that it remains largely invisible in its subterranean form—is at the heart of Timothy Mitchell's approach to the phenomenon he refers to as "carbon democracy." Mitchell, a political theorist and scholar of Egypt, argues that because oil (unlike coal) comes to the surface by pressure and pumps, its workers remain entirely aboveground, disassociated from the physical attachments and earthly ecology of the liquid form.[26] These conditions provide the basis for the unusual labor politics of the oil industry and for its elusive material realities of production and distribution. Those working with oil do not descend into the ground, an encounter that produced decisive advancements in the history of labor and major works of literature and art—from Émile Zola's classic novel about a French miners' strike, *Germinal* (1885), to Steve McQueen's contemporary exploration of the claustrophobic conditions of a South African mine, *Western Deep* (2002). Sundaram's embedded geological portrait of oil represents, by contrast, a strictly imaginative encounter that defies and departs from this figural tradition of depicting human industry and work. At the same time, the little zinc tray recalls the relative fluidity and lightness of oil, the properties that have made it a uniquely seaborne fossil fuel. In this way, Sundaram dispenses with the archetypal image of labor embodied by the figure of the coal worker in favor of a more Mitchell-like focus on extraction and transportation. Drilling, pipelines, oil tankers, export, blockade, shortage, war, militarism, and spills: these are the associations in *Land Shift* that form the basis for the radical complexity of oil's politics and situates its democratic potential within an international arena.

The series bears a strong affinity, in this sense, with Allan Sekula's *Fish Story*, the American photographer's exploration into the elusive spaces of a networked global economy undertaken at a parallel moment, between 1989 and 1995.[27] Sekula's photographic investigation of the global circuits of shipping, simultaneously panoramic, expansive, claustrophobic, and bleak, was similarly concerned with ports and harbors, with the phenomenon of transport and "containerization"—which he described memorably as the "victory of the rectangular solid over the messy contingency of the Ark"[28]—and with a micro and macro view of an interconnected world. Growing up in a harbor surrounded by supertankers and container ships, Sekula stated that he developed a heightened awareness of "the primacy of material forces." Far from a sentimental perspective, "this crude materialism is underwritten by disaster. Ships explode, leak, sink, collide. Accidents happen everyday. Gravity is recognized as a force."[29]

Although there are clearly formal differences between Sundaram's intrepid experiments with oil and Sekula's efforts to revitalize the tradition of documentary photography, both artists sought a materialist engagement with the emerging effects of globalization in the 1990s and a renewal of a Left perspective to this end. And yet, Sekula's masterful maritime portrait, involving years of research and travel, steered clear of the ports of the Persian Gulf, even as he acknowledged that such locations exist as "fulcrums of history," more powerful and unpredictable than others.[30] Nonetheless, *Fish Story*—as Benjamin Buchloh argued—strove for "the possibility of understanding history in the age of electronic media" and the new contingencies of visual information, in particular, the "fallen facticity of the world," the forms of concealment and clandestine cover-ups that belong to the operations of capital but never quite cohere into a graspable whole.[31] Several of the images in Sundaram's series, as I will elaborate, reveal a similar challenge to the changing forms of consciousness of the digital era and an attempt to grasp the new configurations through "the primacy of material forces."

Oil, Painting, Politics

What makes Iraq special, stated the neoconservative hawk Paul Wolfowitz flatly when he was deputy defense secretary in the second Bush administration, is that "the country floats on a sea of oil."[32] Though it is beyond the scope of this chapter to recount the history of American involvement in Middle East oil,[33] Wolfowitz's statement is a powerful reminder of the role of this history in defining the agendas of the various "petro-politicians" in or close to the White House in our time: Dick Cheney, the former CEO of the energy giant Halliburton; George W. Bush, a former CEO of his own oil and gas company in Texas; and Rex Tillerson, the CEO of ExxonMobil and short-lived secretary of state in the Trump administration. Their identities appear to derive in part from the mythic heroism of American oilmen at the beginning of the previous century, the heyday of economic and political expansionism for America, embodied by the triumph of the 1893 World's Columbian Exposition in Chicago. That event brought the promise of advanced technology, mass consumption, and economic prosperity to its spectators—the roots of the American dream—and consolidated the nation's vision of itself as the vanguard of social, cultural, and civilizational progress.[34] Significantly, the Chicago World's Fair of 1893 was also the space where the "high" arts of Western oil painting were separated from the "ethnographic" exhibits of painters from the colonies, establishing oil at the center of yet another social hierarchy, also implicit in Sundaram's work. It was there in Chicago that Raja Ravi Varma, for example—the first professional artist in India to adopt the Western techniques of oil and easel, and widely acknowledged as the father of modern Indian art—received two gold medals for his "well-executed portraits" of Indian women, launching his success on the international stage and further cementing his popularity in India. However, Varma's paintings did not make it to the venerable fine arts pavilion at the Chicago World's Fair in 1893. Instead, his pictures, along with those of the Indian photographer Deen Dayal, were relegated to the ethnographic section, not admired as works of fine art but rather commended by judges for their "ethnological value" and held up as evidence for the continued success of the British civilizing mission in India.[35]

Although the medium that Sundaram employs in the series is burnt or used motor oil (it has actually been run through the engine of a car and is preferred by the artist for its dirt and discoloration effects), the material with its murky impurities evokes some of the prejudices and enduring hierarchies confronted by the first generation of oil painters in India. The example of Varma represents some of the paradoxes that have resulted from oil painting's complicated journey to the Indian subcontinent: the medium was introduced to Indians in the eighteenth century by Europeans, promoted by the British throughout the nineteenth century in their museums and art schools as part of the so-called civilizing mission, rejected by nationalists in the early twentieth century as a "foreign" medium belonging to the colonizer, and then seized by modern artists throughout the twentieth century with varying degrees of ambivalence, mimicry, appropriation, and/or subversion, often at the same time.

It is significant that Sundaram is both personally and professionally linked to these emblematic moments of modernism in India: as previously noted, he is the nephew of the charismatic female painter Amrita Sher-Gil, who went to Paris in the 1920s to train in post-Impressionist circles before returning to India in the 1930s. I have argued elsewhere that Sher-Gil's extraordinary 1934 painting titled *Self-Portrait as Tahitian*, where her own nude body occupies the romantic space of Gauguin's Tahitian females, is a fascinating subversion of the dominant tropes of Western primitivism and an expression of the entanglements of Indian painters within modernism's powerful representational dilemmas.[36]

Similarly, Sundaram's return to the hybrid and cosmopolitan legacies of his famous aunt in the digitally manipulated photomontage series *Retake of Amrita* discussed in my introduction exposes the stylish, yet distinctly melancholic, mix between European and Indian social milieus within which oil painters in India, like Sher-Gil, confronted the perennial problem of "Indianness" in their art (see figure Intro.2).[37]

From such a vantage point, oil is not an innocent art historical material but one that is dredged through a long history of power and infused with inescapable paradoxes and predicaments. And it is the multiple meanings of oil in Sundaram's images, as I have suggested, that point to these several different historical phenomena simultaneously: the perception of oil as both commodity and contaminant, the connection between oil and imperial violence, and the postcolonial consciousness brought to oil as an artistic medium with its origins in the West. Such a "politics of the palette"[38] may not belong exclusively to artists from the formerly colonized world; critical perspectives on the history of oil can derive (and have derived) from a range of physical locations and material practices. But it is not surprising that at the same time that the formal consideration of the relationship between oil as an artistic and geopolitical commodity, which Sundaram undertook *at a time of war*, emerged from an artist so critically positioned within the intertwined histories of West and non-West, and across the power differentials of the first and third worlds. I will return to elaborate these structures of inequality shortly by way of a particularly forceful image, *From the First World/From the Third World*, in addition to other examples from the series, which provide a view of discrepant experiences in an inextricably connected and intertwined world.

Archaeology, Politics, and the Iraq Museum

If Iraq "floats on a sea of oil," as Wolfowitz noted, it also sits on a bedrock of antiquities, since there are more than 10,000 known archaeological sites in the country, of which barely one-fifth have been excavated—making essentially *all* of modern Iraq an archaeological site. Moreover, the story of archaeology in the country begins at approximately the same time as the story of foreign interest in its oil: at the height of European imperial expansion in the nineteenth century, when Western nations believed it was their right to possess the raw materials and cultural property they uncovered in the non-Western world. By the early twentieth century, however, both oil and archaeology became inseparable from the cultural and economic nationalism emerging in Iraq at the time and became important arenas through which Iraq's anticolonial struggle was staged. One of the greatest challenges for Iraqi nationalists in the early decades of the twentieth century was to regain control of the resources, both natural and cultural, being extracted from the new nation-state.

One can imagine how the world was stunned in the 1840s when British, French, and German archaeologists first encountered, rather suddenly and unexpectedly, the vast ruins of the Assyrian empire and its capital city, Nineveh, in the northern part of what was called Mesopotamia, as well as the great walled city of the Babylonian kingdom to the south. True, Mesopotamia had long been an exotic referent for European culture, perhaps best embodied by Eugène Delacroix's famous painting of 1827–28 depicting the fall of the Assyrian king, *Death of Sardanapalus*.[39] However, the survival of its material culture, which represented for Euro-Western audiences the physical proof of events depicted in the Bible, was indeed a momentous revelation. In fact, for over a hundred years, from approximately 1810 to 1910, almost all excavations in Iraq by Europeans and Americans were conducted at pre-Islamic sites like Babylon and Nippur, a source of fascination because of their relation to the Bible, while Islamic sites — not to mention the contemporary Islamic inhabitants of the area — were largely overlooked.[40]

When British administrators first drew up the boundaries of modern Iraq in 1918–19, it was not an accident that they included the ancient sites of Sumer, Akkad, Babylonia, and Assyria within the new geopolitical entity. The British had deliberately followed the contours of these long-dead ancient cultures, which was easier than outlining the current realities of the region with its Arabic, Persian, Kurdish, and Turkish speakers and its mixture of Muslim, Jewish, and Christian populations.[41] This was at the heart of the paradoxical project of establishing a new nation-state in the ancient space deemed the "cradle of civilization." Gertrude Bell, one of the most famous Englishwomen in the British empire,[42] who established the Iraq Museum in Baghdad, served as Iraq's first director of antiquities and assisted in drawing the boundaries of the new nation, reflected upon this paradox at the time: "History," Bell wrote, "suffers an atmospheric distortion. We look upon a past civilization and see it, not as it was, but charged with the significance of that through which we gaze, as down the centuries shadow overlies shadow, some dim, some luminous, and some so strongly coloured that all the age behind is tinged with a borrowed hue."[43]

The distortion of modernity's view of the past was perhaps best embodied in the particularities of the museum inaugurated by Bell in 1923 — the Iraq Museum, conceived in part to help protect the archaeological remains of Iraq from the insatiable appetite of the Western museum. Paradoxically, Bell had also implemented antiquities regulations during these years that allowed for extensive exporting of artifacts based on assumptions about their "universal" significance and the Western museum's rights to ownership.[44] Bell nevertheless promoted the institution tirelessly in its early days: she organized makeshift displays, coordinated lectures from visiting archaeologists, and eventually managed to find a permanent space. "It will be a real museum rather like the British Museum, only a little smaller," she stated with pride in 1926.[45]

Although Bell's model may well have been the grand institution of the Victorian metropolis, the museum she created in Baghdad was an altogether different event. It did not boast an imperial collection or a "universal art survey" like its European counterparts; nor did it emerge from the impetus or initiatives of Iraqis themselves. On the contrary, it was the British who saw the necessity of a national museum for their nation-building efforts during the indirect rule of the Mandate period, a new identity created by the League of Nations for a country still unable to "stand alone" requiring the tutelage of the "advanced nations."[46] Nevertheless, by the time of Bell's death in 1926, the museum had moved to a new location in northern Baghdad, and its collection consisted of some ten-thousand-plus objects. With inexplicable optimism (in view of her suicide shortly afterward), Bell wrote to her father, "I burst with pride when I show people over the Museum. It is becoming such a wonderful place."[47]

That Bell's museum reflected a European imaginary somewhat at odds with the politics of the new nation would become increasingly clear. Sati al-Husri, the nationalist leader who replaced Bell as Iraq's director of antiquities by the 1930s, did not include, for example, visits to the museum in the pedagogy of the new Iraqi school curriculum.[48] He focused instead on the arrival of Islam in the region from the seventh century AD and on, generating a collection of Islamic objects for the museum through large-scale excavations of Islamic archaeological sites, like the great mosques and imperial architecture of the Umayyad and Abbasid Caliphates, 661–750 AD and 750–1258 AD, respectively, or the second Abbasid capital at Samarra (836–892 AD). One result was that the museum continued to grow, acquiring a new role for itself as a nationalist repository of a shared relationship to an Islamic and a pre-Islamic past for Iraqis.

As many scholars have argued, the museum in general as a cultural institution has long helped to consolidate the "imagined communities" of the modern nation-state, from its earliest inception in the post-Enlightenment era to its contemporary expressions in a multicultural world.[49] The tragic destruction of the Iraq Museum resulting from the unchecked frenzy and violence of looters—who pillaged government buildings and businesses after the fall of Baghdad and, for several days in early April 2003, also targeted the museum—cannot be viewed therefore as a marginal aside to the real battlefield of the US-led invasion, as the Bush administration and the mainstream media repeatedly attempted to claim. We might recall Donald Rumsfeld's dismissive response to these events: "Stuff happens," he said at a press conference, shrugging. "Freedom's untidy, and free people are free to make mistakes and commit crimes and do bad things." Visibly irritated by the media's "exaggerated reports" of the damage, Rumsfeld stated at the same press conference, "It's the same picture of some person walking out of some building with a vase and you see it twenty times. And you think, my goodness, were there that many vases?" He paused before delivering his punch line: "Is it possible that there were that many vases in the whole country?"[50] Rumsfeld's hubris and flat indifference toward the products of culture and humanity in Iraq was unacceptable for many reasons; for our purposes, it expressed a contemporary imperialist ethos in which the material reality of violence was connected to the symbolic materiality of the archaeological past. To understand this kind of cultural violence as a specific form of destruction in the present, in contrast to generalized clichés about "culture-in-ruins," I return once again to Sundaram's art.

An Artist's Vision

When the drill bore down toward the stony fissures
and plunged its implacable intestine
into the subterranean estates,

and dead years, eyes of the ages,
imprisoned plants' roots
and scaly systems
became strata of water,
fire shot up through the tubes
transformed into cold liquid,
in the customs house of the heights,
issuing from its world of sinister depth,
it encountered a pale engineer
and a title deed.

Pablo Neruda, excerpt from *Standard Oil Co.* (1940)

There are strong correspondences between Pablo Neruda's anti-imperialist poem of 1940, which condemns the international oil companies for the "drill that bore down toward the stony fissures" plunging its "implacable intestine" into the ground, and Vivan Sundaram's engine oil works undertaken by the artist a half century later. The Chilean poet's sense of violation to the "subterranean estates" of the earth, which manifest the "eyes of the ages"—namely, the collective experience of human history—resonates with Sundaram's visual renderings of deep petroleum deposits and sunken ancestral figures, as in *Soldier of Babylon I*, figure 1.4. Similarly, Neruda's reflection on the moment when the substance breaks through the surface of the earth and meets, unhappily, "a pale engineer and a title deed," conveys the spirit of Sundaram's Gulf War critique of foreign oil interests and the enduring imperial paradigm of possession in Iraq. The resonances further call up a much earlier project by Sundaram, *The Heights of Macchu Picchu* (1972), which was inspired by Neruda's epic poem of the same name. In a gesture of homage to the Marxist poet and recent winner of the Nobel Prize in Literature, that series of twenty-four ink drawings on paper included a portrait of the stylish Neruda depicted in his signature beret.

Sundaram created the Macchu Picchu pictures at another important conjuncture: upon his return to India after his political awakening as a student in London, also the year before Neruda's death in Chile. The drawings testify, in part, to the lively reception of Neruda by intellectuals and artists on the subcontinent at the time as a model for revolutionary thought, third world politics, radical consciousness, and aesthetic ideas.[51] By 1976, Sundaram had established the Kasauli Art Centre at

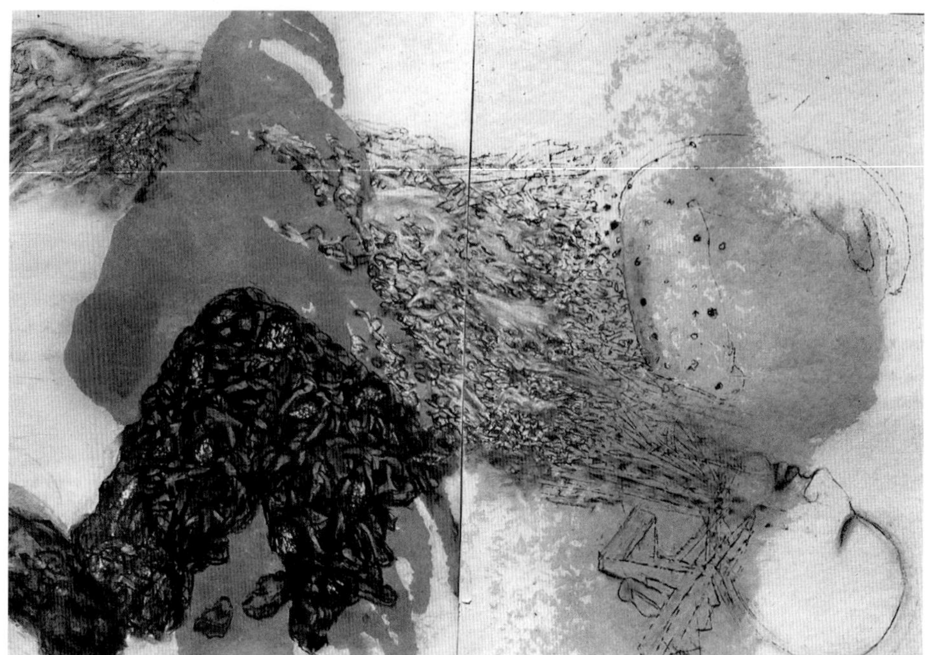

his family's hill station home in Himachal Pradesh, which held artist residencies, workshops, seminars, and performances throughout the late 1970s and 1980s, and became an important site for the evolution and advancement of these discourses of Marxist aesthetics. Sundaram has said about his work from the early seventies that he "tried both to illustrate the Marxist position and to find formal equivalents for the ideological struggle."[52] Accordingly, in *The Heights of Macchu Picchu*, the artist followed Neruda's journey into the ruins of the ancient Incan city and juxtaposed—as the poet did—the beauty and splendor of its stones with the tragic fate of its bones, in the form of the forgotten bodies of the Incan slaves that toiled and perished on the site. The series, as Ajay Sinha has described, "traces the topography of human ruins inch by inch. In one, dead men and women, drawn like little notations, tumble forth to evoke trenches with piles of dead bodies in Hitler's Germany. In another, a monolithic image of Marx seeps from a swarm of root."[53] Generally viewed as belonging to a youthful, more polemical, phase of Sundaram's career, the series contains, I suggest, a number of themes that cannot be dismissed as merely ideological. The sediments of the ancient past; the ecology, topography, and memory of ruins; and the

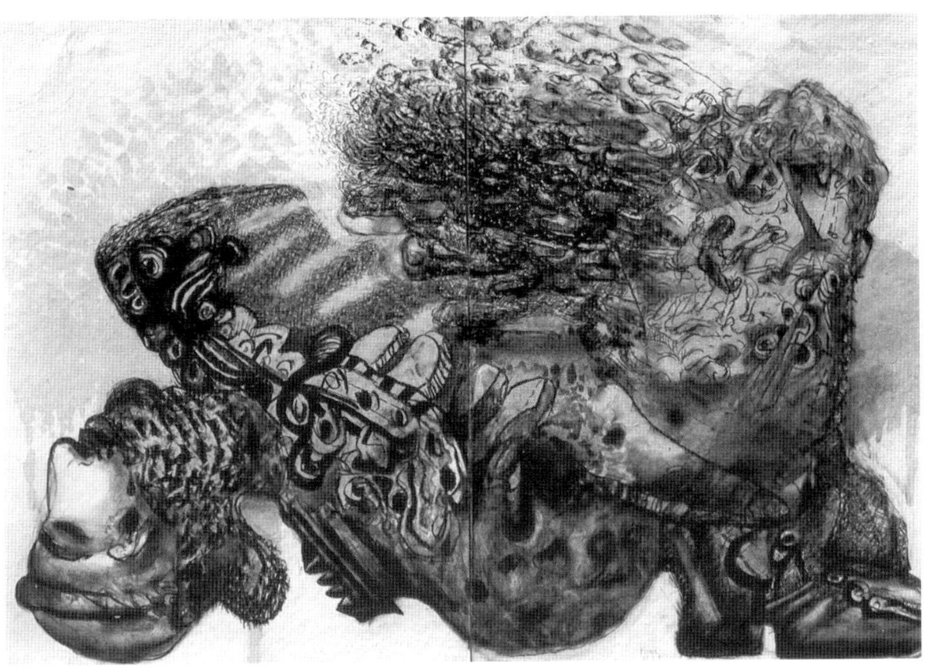

living, breathing geology of the earth: these tropes all return in the engine oil work and will persist throughout the artist's career.

First exhibited in India in 1991, the engine oil compositions were in part inspired by a visit to Iraq two years earlier, when Sundaram participated in the Second International Art Exhibition in Baghdad and won one of the five gold medals that were named after Saddam Hussein and awarded at the time. But Sundaram also traveled during this 1989 trip to a number of historical and archaeological sites that have since been either looted or destroyed. Indeed, the extent to which his 1991 series anticipates the crisis of civil society and threat to archaeological heritage in Iraq by 2003—or the ongoing wars in Syria, Afghanistan, Yemen, and elsewhere with their devastating impact on ancient ruins, like Palmyra—is a tragic thing to have witnessed in the new millennium. Sundaram could not have predicted, for example, that the iconic press photo of a beheaded sculpture lying amid the rubble after the looting of the Iraq Museum would render so literal the carnage he envisioned a dozen years earlier in his majestic portrait of heroic tragedy depicted in figure 1.5, *Death of an Akkadian King*.

This diptych and others appear to foreshadow the events of the sec-

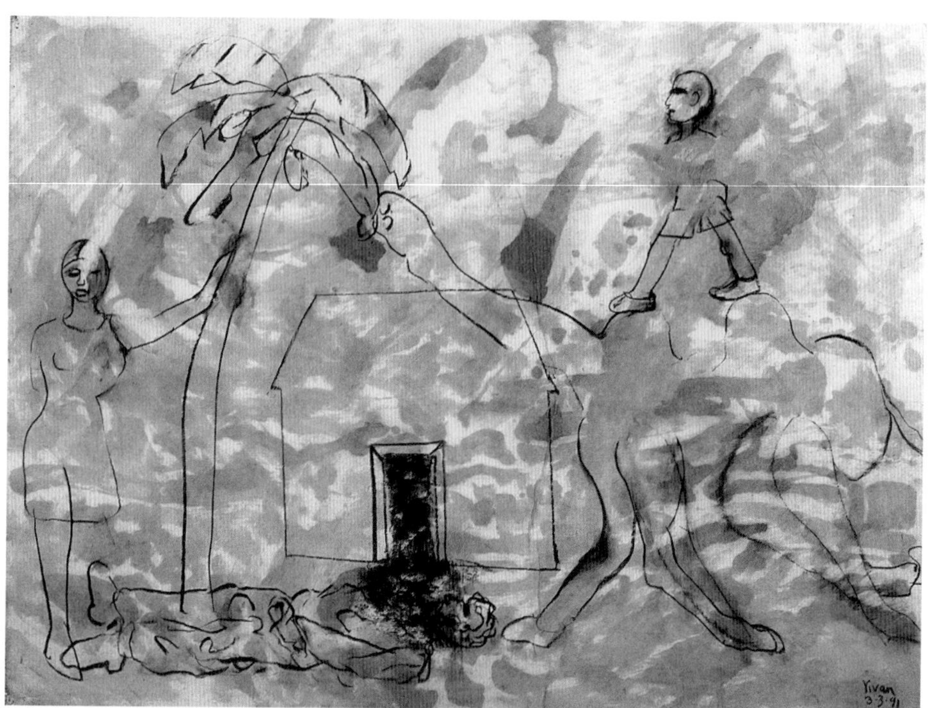

FIGURE 1.6
Vivan Sundaram,
*Mesopotamian
Drawing II*, 1991.
Engine oil and
charcoal on paper.
Courtesy of the
artist.

ond Gulf War and the entanglements of oil in the escalations of violence in the region, a fact that adds to their haunting temporal effects. In these images, we see not the contemporary people of Iraq but rather the great figures of an ancient civilization lying executed on the floor, bound or buried, limbs distorted or dismembered, heads tilted back, eyes closed in death, shrouded in angry clouds of black and gray. In figure 1.6, *Mesopotamian Drawing II*, the outline of a house and other timeless imagery (a camel, a Babylonian figure, a woman, and a palm tree—reminders of the once fertile crescent) appear together on paper stained with oil, presented as if in a dense veil of smoke. In the foreground is a man lying dead on the ground, apparently choked by black sludge. Here, oil's blackness and slimy fecal qualities open onto a realm of abject associations. The substance thickens and becomes, in the words of a former Venezuelan president, "the devil's excrement," connected to foul smells and suffocating forms, the embodiment of evil itself.[54] "The representational problem oil presents to the committed artist," Stephanie LeMenager stated in her book *Living Oil*, "has to do with oil's primal associations with earth's body, therefore with the permeability, excess, and multiplicities of all bodies."[55] We might view Sundaram's response to this problem in his play with the indeterminacy of the medium itself. Newly liberated from painterly formats, the artist's experiments with the slippery material are anything but slick; they produce dense ecological and organic associations, at times with unpredictable effects.

The Aerial Perspective: Sundaram's View from Above

The images of "techno-warfare" that were first promoted by the US military during the first Gulf War in 1991 depended upon a view from afar. As Susan Sontag wrote, those televisual images of "the sky above the dying, filled with light-traces of missiles and shells," served to illustrate America's absolute military superiority over its enemy.[56] The so-called smart bomb—a bomb with a camera attached to its front—allowed the television viewer to participate directly in the military triumph and in effect constituted the television screen and its viewer as an extended apparatus of the bomb itself. Sundaram is acutely conscious of these disembodying visual acts, the kinds of involvements and detachments they enable and permit, and their role in the construction of the Western viewing subject.[57] In several pictures he constructs a CNN-type aerial view that tends to obscure the specific details of a scene into a vague or blurry haze—in figure 1.7, for instance, the outline of a human figure is smudged into the fallout. We see forms that transmute and metamorphose as the present seems to explode the past: elsewhere, as in figure 1.8, old cuneiform-like shapes are smeared and eroded, and new ones have not yet acquired their shape.

The series was no doubt shaped by another set of Sundaram's drawings that deal thematically with the Second World War, a series that the artist created in 1988 after visiting Auschwitz and Birkenau for the first time. In those dark charcoal sketches, reminiscent of William Kentridge's drawings of apartheid South Africa, the artist confronted the destruction of the Holocaust through landscapes of loss and social devastation. But it is the aerial or overhead view, along with the radical transformation of waste into medium—burnt engine oil repurposed as paint—that marks the biggest difference between the two series and anticipates the increasingly sophisticated organization of aerial perspectives over landscapes of debris in subsequent projects like *Tracking* (2003–4), *Trash* (2005–8), and *Black Gold* (2012).

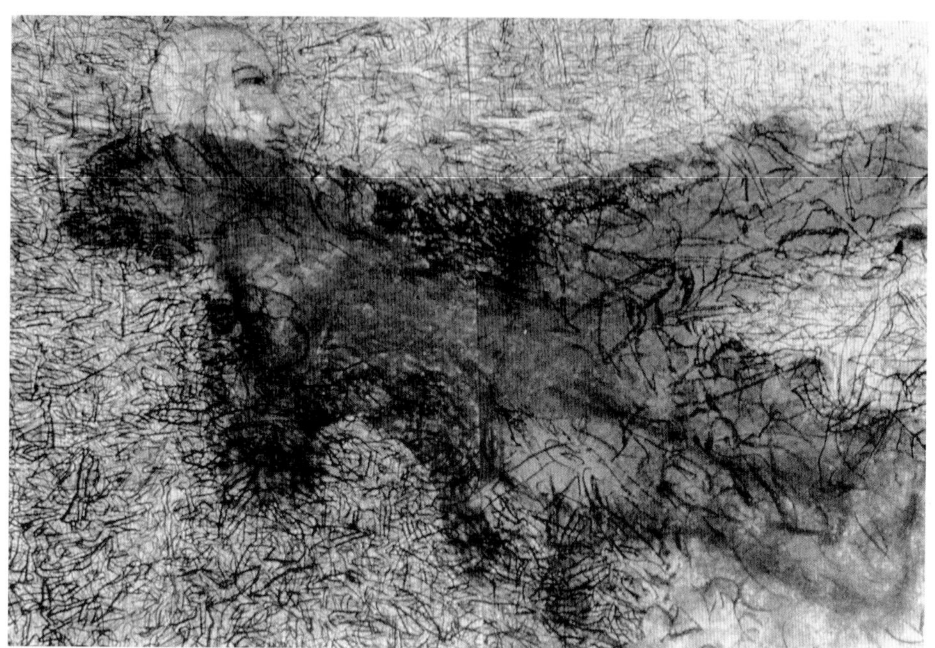

Sundaram's frequent use of an aerial optic or overhead view contrasts sharply with what the writer W. G. Sebald viewed as a lack of engagement, the ominous silence, that characterized Germany's relationship to the massive aerial bombing campaigns of the Second World War. The war in the air, Sebald stated, was "war pure and undisguised."[58] This was because the strategic leveling of some 131 German towns and cities by the Allied forces represented a wholesale annihilation of the enemy aimed at "his dwellings, his history, and his natural environment."[59] Such a reality of total destruction, "incomprehensible in its extremity" according to Sebald, led the German people "to overload, to paralysis of the capacity to think and feel," resulting in a kind of collective amnesia or shell shock that epitomized Germany's condition of material and moral ruin following the war.[60] Sebald was thus concerned with the dialectics of devastation and denial, in particular, Germany's failure to produce a literature that responded to the suffering caused by the air wars. Throughout his writing, Sebald, following Benjamin, turned to the image of the ruin as a sort of master trope for the traumas of the twentieth century, a material form through which to grasp precisely what was most unassimilable for humanity.

Sundaram's repeated use of the aerial perspective in multiple registers and formats suggests a similar consciousness of the catastrophic effects of militarized violence unleashed from above. In his hands, however, the format of the overhead view also invokes new scopic regimes, in particular, the forms of subjectivity, surveillance, and spectatorship associated with the age of "precision" warfare and late twentieth-century aerial technologies like the smart bomb and the drone. Even Sebald, who died prematurely in a car accident shortly after 9/11, may not have imagined the more ominous modalities of aerial violence introduced in the digital age and the expansion of warfare in the twenty-first century through means of what the US State Department calls "unmanned aerial vehicles" (or UAVs).[61] The novelty of such aerial technologies, increasingly part of everyday life in the form of navigational devices like GPS and Google Earth, is countered by the paradoxical invisibility of the violence resulting from UAVs deployed in Pakistan, Afghanistan, the Persian Gulf, and North Africa, where the US government has continued to expand its controversial drone warfare program in "undeclared wars." It is this dramatic tension between vision and obfuscation—the perception of the world through Google Earth, on one hand, and the terrible secrecy of the covert operation, on the other—that Sundaram's furtive oil smudges and blurred contours (as per figure 1.8) anticipate in an uncanny way.

In his dual projection video of 2003–4 titled *Tracking* (included in the New York exhibition of *Trash* in 2008), Sundaram elaborated upon these new conditions of perception and control in the period of America's response to the 9/11 attacks. In the video, a spotlight hovers over a mysterious geography of moving shadows and indiscernible forms, vaguely illuminating what appear to be clandestine spaces and unfamiliar acts. Here, the mythology of precision in a remote-controlled war is countered with ambiguity, dimness, and shadows. Secrecy and concealment lead to an ominous sense of fear; strategies of surveillance produce existential unease. *Tracking* can be connected to the work of several radical artists—for example, Trevor Paglen, Hito Steyerl, or the late Harun Farocki, who have sought to denormalize the phenomenon of "drone vision," the unnerving perspective of the automated drone, which fatally constitutes subjects as targets through (inexact) processes of algorithmic recognition. "The view from above," as the German artist and filmmaker Steyerl has asserted, "is a perfect metonymy for a more general verticalization of class relations … seen through the lenses and on the screens of military, entertainment, and information industries.

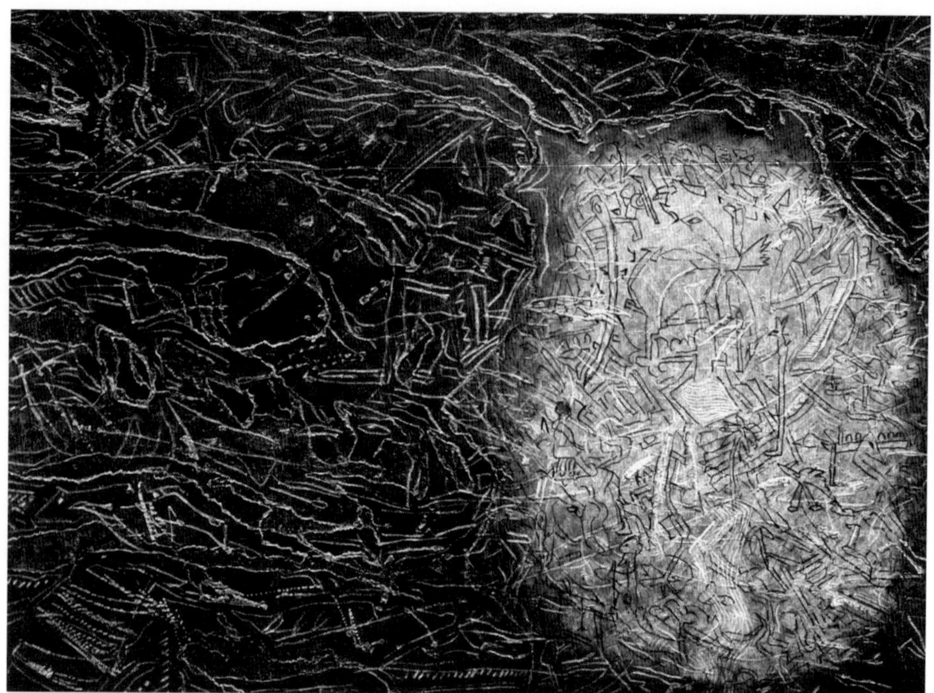

It is a proxy perspective that projects delusions of stability, safety, and extreme mastery onto a backdrop of expanded 3-D sovereignty."[62]

What kind of human agency is possible within the "proxy perspective" of these new visual conditions of high-tech warfare? And what kinds of practices of observation could help counter the chilling sense of alienation and lack of empathy that emerge in the shift from horizontal to vertical war? While artists like Steyerl often seize the new technology using, for instance, web-based platforms, GPS navigation apps, and social media such as Instagram and Twitter to forge a counter-politics in the public sphere, Sundaram returns us ultimately to the land, and to the traces of human history in the land, as the location from which to address the crises and politics of perspective itself. The way in which these preoccupations further intersect with the materiality of the ruin is best seen in yet another of Sundaram's major projects, his installation *Black Gold*, a site-specific work for the Kochi-Muziris Biennale, India's first international biennale of contemporary art held in Kerala in 2012.

Black Gold: Ruins, Rubble, and the View from Above

Separated by more than two decades, the engine oil series and *Black Gold* resonate with one another in more than just name. The latter represents a mature point in a formal process that dramatically expands the scale, medium, and perspectival techniques first witnessed in Sundaram's Iraq war series. The black gold here refers not to oil but to another legendary commodity—pepper—well known for its central historical role in the ancient spice trade in India, and Kerala in particular. "Pepper it was that brought Vasco da Gama's tall ships across the ocean," explained Salman Rushdie's narrator in the novel *The Moor's Last Sigh*, a saga about four generations of family who claimed "wrong-side-of-the-blanket descent" from the famous Portuguese explorer, the first European to reach India by sea.[63] The location of the biennale in the southern state of Kerala, known *both* for its ancient spice trade routes and its radical Left politics in the modern era, was thus especially significant for India's first effort at an international survey exhibition of this sort. Cofounded and curated by the artists Bose Krishnamachari and Riyas Komu, the biennale sought to harness "the historical cosmopolitan legacy of the modern metropolis of Kochi, and its mythical predecessor the ancient port Muziris,"[64] said to have been destroyed by flooding in the fourteenth century. The event brought together some eighty artists from India and the rest of the world for several months to display their work in various venues and dispersed sites, among them the historic warehouses of Aspinwall House and Pepper House, names that evoke the circuitry of past colonial trade. There is by now a degree of consensus within the intense discussions surrounding the biennale phenomenon that the form has emerged as one of *the* most significant platforms for contemporary art in the past three decades.[65] The success of the Kochi-Muziris Biennale in India, soon approaching its fifth edition, is that it seized the well-known flexibility and strengths of the biennale format—its orientation toward site-specificity, intercultural dialogue, local publics, and non-market forces—in ways that have proven to redefine and reinvigorate the platform for both local and international audiences once again.

Sundaram's *Black Gold* installation at the Kochi-Muziris Biennale was a vast physical landscape, in his words "an imaginary habitation,"[66] composed of discarded terra-cotta shards from an actual archaeological excavation near the biennale's coastal site. It depicted, more precisely, the mythical topos invoked by the biennale's co-organizers, the ancient port city and trade center of Muziris. The obtainment and deployment of archaeological shards, defined as prehistoric fragments, usually broken pottery or stone—like the artist's use of engine oil—carried rich semiotic effects. The etymology of the word "shard," from the Old English *sceard*, is connected to the idea of breakage, but a shard's existence is paradoxically related to resilience—to its resistance to forces of destruction over time. Sundaram gathered these potent symbols of ruination, fragmentation, and survival into a large-scale accumulation: a multi-perspectival, three-dimensional landscape that could be apprehended from different angles and viewing positions around the installation. The result was a large-scale "rubble model"; whether it was seen from above or at eye level, the viewer encountered a complex terra-cotta terrain, as seen in figure 1.9, of patterned swirls, pseudo-architectural forms, and whimsical details with seemingly infinite horizons. Part relic, part memorial, part fantasy, part ruin, it depicted the endless social relations encoded into the built environment rather than an actual city per se.

The technique of the aerial view was apparent in yet another component of the *Black Gold* installation: a multichannel video projected onto the floor, which showed the rubble model, along with accumulations of black peppercorns, being relentlessly subjected to the forces of the sea. Here, the viewer could further inhabit, by literally stepping onto, the abstract rendering of a forgotten place. The projection resembled a marine oil spill, but it was also a portrait of sluggish erosion: the viewer is reminded not of sudden catastrophe but of the way that natural forces like wind, water, or time itself can also gradually undo human achievement or weaken the edifice of civilization. Once again, as in the engine oil series, landscape and the materiality of debris (now terra-cotta remains) converge with the aerial view to allow us to reflect on the past and to imagine the possibility of unknown futures. They also point to Sundaram's preoccupation over decades with a certain microeconomy of ruination and repair, with sunken spaces, exploited lands, nameless victims, and forgotten pasts. The point of *Black Gold*'s relationship to the "fallen city" (it is literally a mock-up of this archaeological conceit) is not to evoke the memory of former greatness but to build a different economy out of its rubble. And if the ruin, undoubtedly a thing of beauty that has been romanticized for hundreds of years, cannot escape the problem of aestheticization, it is nonetheless, in Sundaram's hands, also a supple trope for self-reflection and awareness.

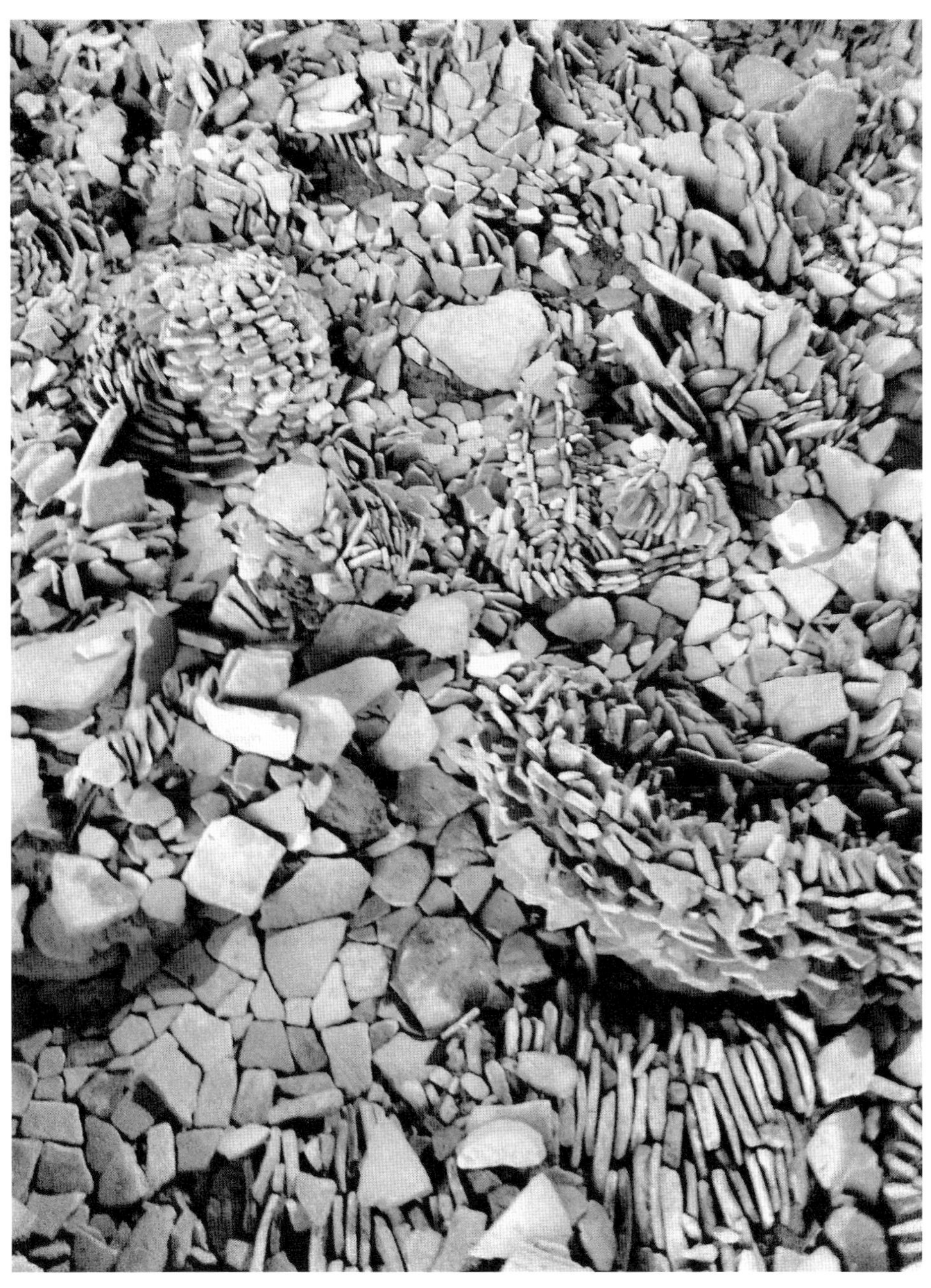

FIGURE 1.9 Vivan Sundaram, *Black Gold*, 2012. Detail of installation with ancient terra-cotta shards. Photograph by the author.

Conclusion: Ruination and Inequality

Ann Stoler, in considering the Caribbean poet and Nobel laureate Derek Walcott's account of "the rot that remains," observes that the writer's language is poetic, but what he looks toward is not. Sundaram's non-verbal discourse of debris is similarly beautiful, even elegiac, but focused on that which is most difficult to grasp. What the artist depicts, to borrow Stoler's words, are "intimate injuries that appear as only faint traces, or deep deformations and differentiations of social geography that go by other names."[67] Figure 1.10 presents a final image from the engine oil series, titled *From the First World/From the Third World*, as a powerful closing example. It is a Rorschach-like composition, which seems at first glance more abstract: the top contains the phrase "from the first world," the bottom bears the label "from the third world." Yet implicit in this hierarchy of forms (are they figures? bodies of water? landscapes?) is a strong political message about different and unequal worldviews. If they are landscapes, they are not the kind of landscapes in oil that dominated European art history in the nineteenth century, a genre that was itself bound up in the discourses of imperial representation and the "imagined geographies" it charted.[68] Instead they are the kind of landscapes that make visible the processes by which culture and geography are inflected in the self and by which competing social identities are shaped. Like the Manichaean separation between the settler and the native in Fanon's formulation of the colonial city, this is a world cut into two compartments: these "first and third world" views exist unequal and apart; they do not converge or mix; they dramatize in short the politics of global space.

Does this image, then, convey the same polarities as Samuel Huntington's "clash of civilizations" or America's infamous "you're with us or against us" statements on the world stage? Does it stage, in other words, the irreducible division between "us" and "them" in pictorial terms? It is important to recognize how it does *not*, and to distinguish such strategies of the Left from the Right. What Sundaram depicts is not a universalist account of primordial cultural difference, nor a moral "clash" between good and evil, itself a symptom of the self-righteous religious thinking that has typified the discourses of the Right. Nor is it a simple demonization of the other, so pervasive a strategy at times of war. It is, rather, a positioned and geopolitical response to a different set of stakes altogether: to the unequal distributions of global power

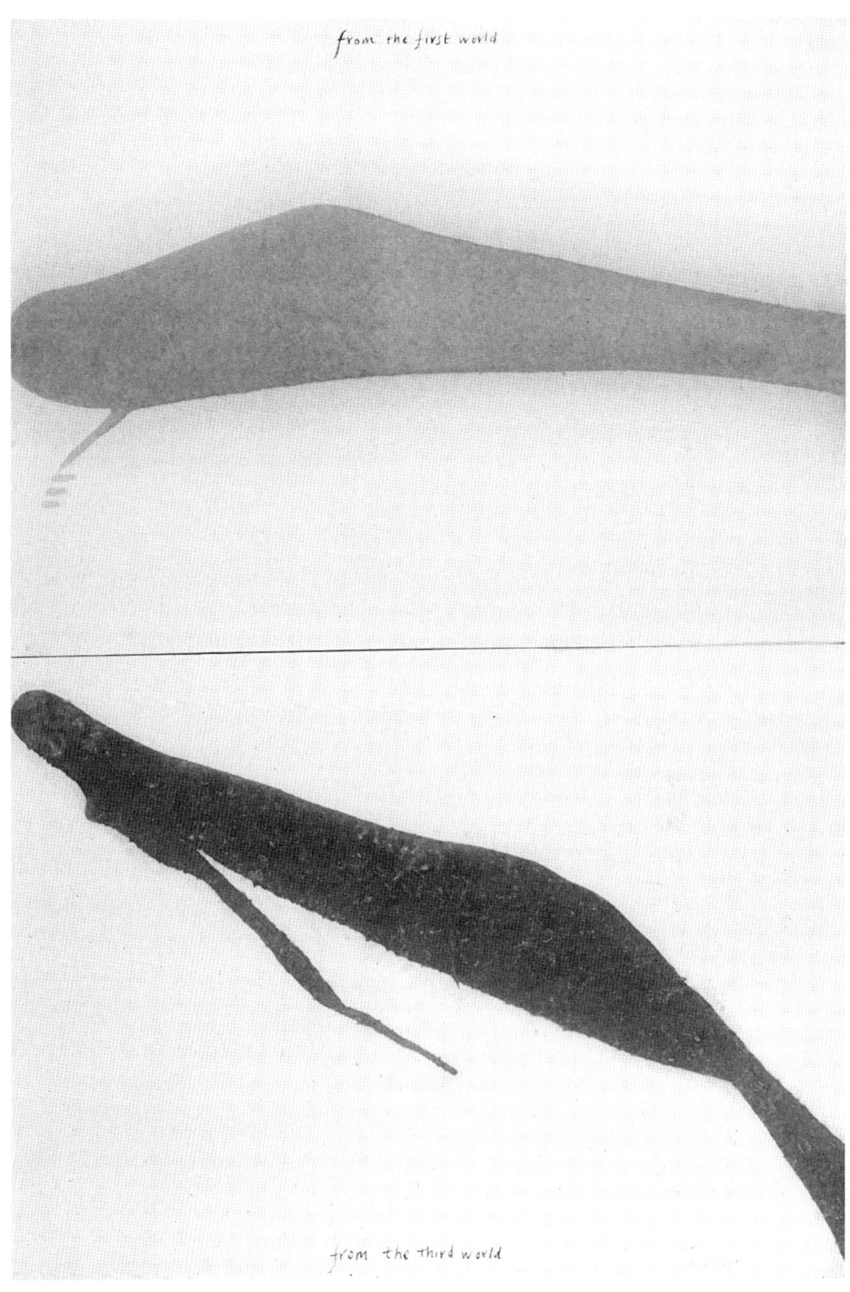

FIGURE 1.10 Vivan Sundaram, *From the First World/From the Third World*, 1991. Diptych made with engine oil and charcoal on paper. Courtesy of the artist.

today, the realities of third world social and political struggle, the histories of colonial humiliation and injustice, and the continued problems of underdevelopment in spite of (and because of) economic globalization. It is therefore not merely the connection to antiquity, or the particular relationship of belonging to an ancient past that India and Iraq appear to share, that gives this series by Sundaram its critical charge. It is, rather, the shared experience of subjugation within empire, in particular the modern formation of the British Empire, through which the most powerful connections between India and Iraq are foregrounded in the work.

Gertrude Bell was, in fact, repeatedly drawn to the lessons and experiences of British imperial rule in India, and she visited the subcontinent in 1903 to attend the viceroy Lord Curzon's Delhi Durbar—a "gorgeous fantasy" in her view.[69] After all, the British were interested in Mesopotamia because of its strategic position as a corridor to India. However, by the time Bell was sent to "pull things straight between Delhi and Cairo," the contradictions, failures, and prejudices of empire had been increasingly exposed to its participants and observers. Bell was both concerned by what she called "Britain's colonial arrogance and vision of supremacy"[70] and driven by the larger, ill-fated project of the late-Victorian "civilizing mission." Similarly, Lord Curzon, the enthusiastic promoter of traditional Indian art, who argued that "it is equally our duty to dig and discover [antiquities], to classify, reproduce and describe, to copy and decipher, and to cherish and conserve,"[71] concluded his career as the chief architect of the Anglo-Persian agreement of 1919, which cemented the interests of the Anglo-Persian Oil Company (later British Petroleum) in Iraq. As Curzon stated at the time, "we possess in the south-western corner of Persia great assets in the shape of oilfields . . . which give us a commanding interest in that part of the world."[72] Oil and antiquities were thus perceived as assets within the broader benevolence of the civilizing mission for the first generation of modern empire-builders like Curzon. And, as Sundaram's images serve to make visible, such perceptions and equations continue to shape the deadly strategies of the Western powers today.

Some may argue—as indeed Donald Rumsfeld did—that against all the other disasters of war, the destruction of an art object or an archaeological site is a trivial matter, a frivolous concern of intellectuals alone. But the archaeological record, like oil, is a non-renewable resource, and violence upon the historical memory of a place, as we know in the case of Native American populations, is directly related to the scale of human suffering and to the crises confronted by future generations. By using elemental, indeed ancient, materials (oil, handmade paper, charcoal, zinc), Sundaram's work returns us to the land as a kind of bedrock in which oil, antiquities, and the past reside—and upon which economies, nations, and wars are built—and it reminds us of the devastating impact of war on the physical and historical environment of a region. But his images are neither wholly apocalyptic nor entirely pessimistic in the end. They point instead toward the utopian possibilities that emerge from the dialectics of fragmentation and repair. "Somewhere within this annihilated world," he has stated in another context, "there is this ground plan of nature, somewhere underlying this uprooted terrain there is a need for order."[73] Sundaram is not alone in searching for a basis for a less unjust world or in responding to our new era of perpetual and undeclared wars; he is of course accompanied in this enterprise by countless other artists in India and around the world. But his experimentations with form, his historical consciousness, and his assertion of a specifically situated identity within the contemporary contours of global power offer us a picture of the beleaguered present that it is no longer possible to ignore.

THE EDIFICE COMPLEX

When the viceroy, Lord Curzon, announced his plan for the Victoria Memorial Museum in Calcutta in 1901 in the grief-filled days following Queen Victoria's death, he called for a building "stately, spacious, monumental and grand" where "all classes will learn the lessons of history."[1] If "memorial" evokes mourning and loss and "monument" signals greatness and valor, then they exist in equal measure here in Curzon's ambitious imperial museum: it was one part a copy of the great Mughal-era memorial, the Taj Mahal; one part didactic history museum; and one part brute monument to British rule—triumphant, glorious, patrician, and great. The recipe, however fraught, nevertheless produced an inaugural moment in the genre of the modern memorial museum in India. But Curzon's bid was like the last gasp of the Victorian era as it peered into the uncertainty of the twentieth century, and the building was not realized until 1921, after some two decades of construction delays. Indeed, his vision of British sovereignty in India would prove to erode much faster than the actual physical structure itself, which remains one of Calcutta's most iconic landmarks today.

That the Victoria Memorial Museum has had a robust afterlife in the twentieth century is indisputable. The building and its expansive gardens seen in figure 2.1 continue to serve as an important public center for the present-day megacity of Kolkata, renamed as such by the state government in 2001 to reflect the original Bengali pronunciation. This

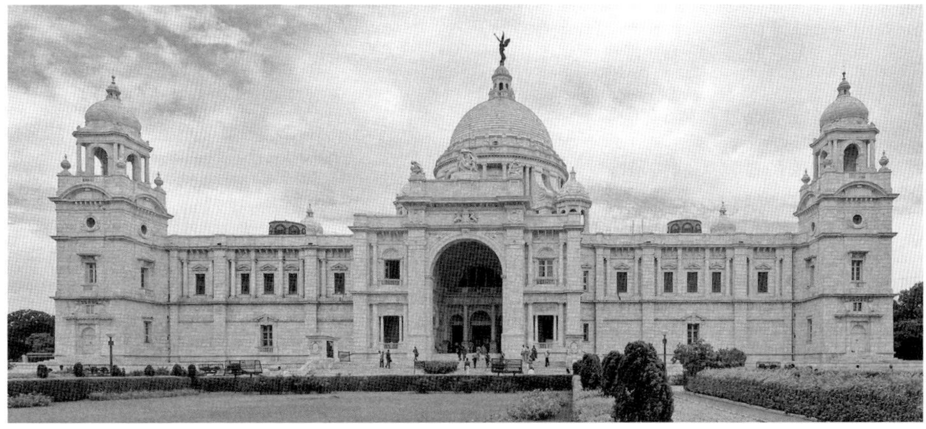

awesome urban landscape has sprawled in every direction and appears to be constantly redefining itself without ever eliminating its relationship to the peculiar *memorial-museum-monument* form standing at its core. I take as a point of departure this idea of the dynamic afterlife of things, the capacity of works of art and architecture to accrue meaning through invention and reinvention, in order to situate and critically consider the afterlife of Vivan Sundaram's contemporary art project mounted inside the Victoria Memorial Museum in 1998.

Sundaram's site-specific installation *History Project*, commissioned to mark the fiftieth anniversary of India's independence from British rule in 1947, was part of the broader turn toward installation and site-specificity that transformed art practice during the 1990s, and it remains an exemplary instance of such experimentation in India, unprecedented in both scope and scale. The artist's highly self-conscious installation, presented in figure 2.2, comprising some two dozen component parts, occupied the vast domed space of Curzon's building with all manner of found and made objects — cabinets, vitrines, photographs, texts, and audiovisual media — in a way that firmly displaced the fixed taxonomies, grand narratives, and didactic paths of the latter. If Curzon's memorial museum was defined by its rigid theatrics and moralistic tone, reflecting an imperial reality increasingly under threat, then Sundaram's associational and multisensory infrastructure broke down its presumptions of self-importance from within by privileging impermanence and "openness" in the phenomenological sense.[2] In other words, the artist's aesthetic strategy of porous and interconnected mini-conversations signaled a break from the building's pre-

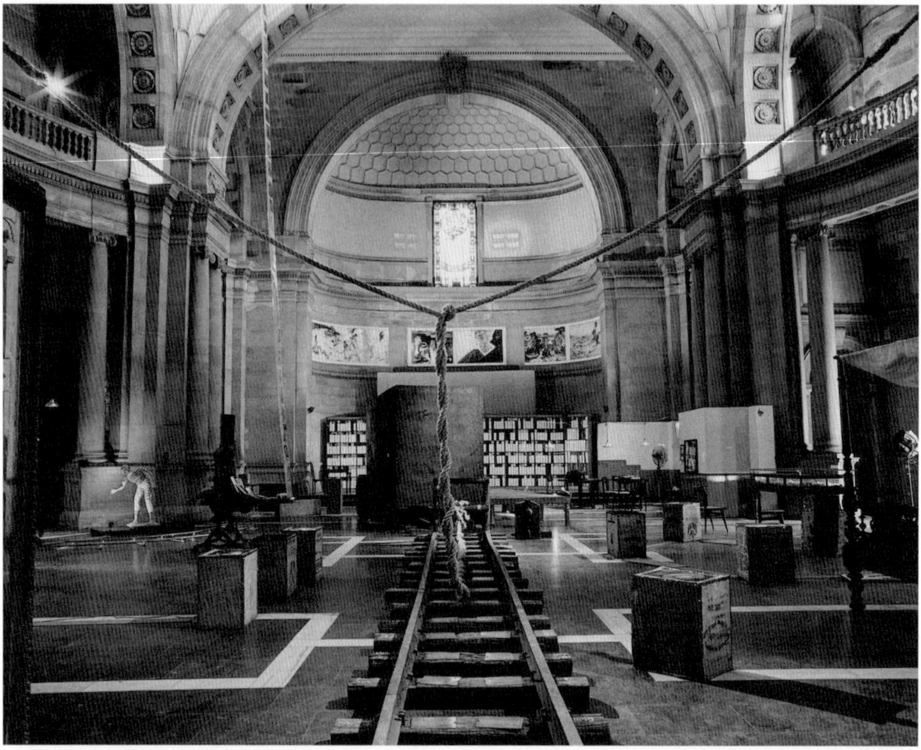

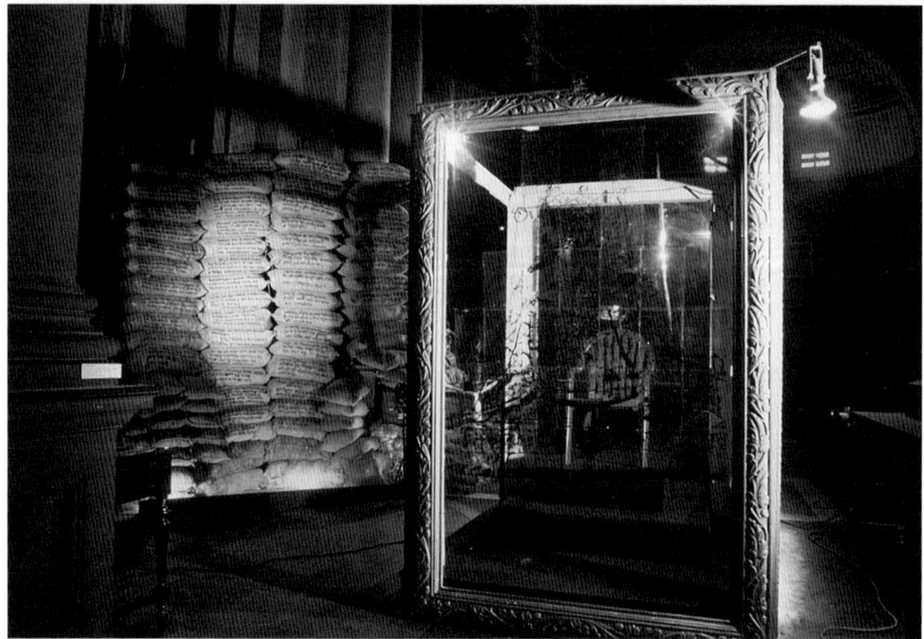

vious epistemological stance and had the effect of corroding, at least temporarily, the former foundations of the imperial site. And this raises the question of how site-specificity, which has been increasingly adopted by artists internationally as a method of engagement with museums, monuments, and other institutional sites, became the basis for a distinctly "counter-monumental" gesture at the heart of Sundaram's ambitious work.

Sundaram's sited intervention in urban Calcutta brings to mind many other contemporary art practices around the world that have prioritized site through institutionally specific work. *History Project* could be positioned, for example, alongside the transgressive acts performed by artists in Europe and America upon or against the institutions of display, whereby the relocation of the aesthetic project to a given symbolic site becomes a historical, aesthetic, and political provocation. These wide-ranging activist interventions launched by artists like Hans Haacke and Michael Asher in the late 1960s, and then reworked and reassessed in the 1980s by American artists like Andrea Fraser, Renee Green, and Fred Wilson, have come to be known, largely after the fact, as the aesthetic movement called "institutional critique."[3] Sundaram claims no direct connection to this tradition, even as he shares some of the social and political concerns of such artists, shaped by his own post-1968 avant-garde formation and four decades of a socially engaged art practice in India. At the same time, his gesture of intervention into the physical and intellectual space of modern Bengal departs in significant ways from the adversarial content of some of the earlier practitioners of institutional critique, who sought at times to confront, expose, and even embarrass or shame the high-powered players of the New York art world. His work also speaks to the inability of the first generation of these artists to understand the museum as a colonial form, and thus it exposes the limitations of institutional critique's conception of "institution" in the broadest sense. And yet, the basic premise of this aesthetic movement—that artists and museums exist in an ambivalent yet dialectical relationship to each other—also underlies *History Project* and can serve to orient some larger questions emerging from Sundaram's specific encounter. How did *History Project* engage and activate the interrelationships between such ideas as museum, monument, and memory, on one hand, and nation, public, and civic site, on the other? What happened to the museum, and its monumentality, under the conditions of Sundaram's occupation? And what is at stake in revisiting this project some twenty years after its making, given its deliberate and carefully crafted identity as a short-lived, ephemeral, and site-specific event?

Like the majority of readers of this book, I suspect, I did not see *History Project* during its three-month display in 1998, having visited the site only after its parts had long been disassembled and carted away. Fortunately, Sundaram's impermanent installation, in the manner of a great deal of contemporary art, has also had an afterlife of sorts: first, in the form of the artist's video about the project, *Structures of Memory* (1999–2000), and second, in the form of a volume of essays and photographs aimed at documenting, reexamining, and reinterpreting the event.[4] These reproductions immediately challenge and throw into disarray the art historical requirement of a firsthand encounter with a thing, whose meaning rests in its immediacy and primacy and whose value resides in its presumed authenticity, the resilient legacy of Enlightenment thought. The ephemerality of *History Project*, by contrast, makes it stubbornly immaterial: it can no longer be visited as it once was; it is available only by means of memory and documentation; it survives solely through acts of mediation and representation. To revisit the work some two decades later is thus to enter the vertiginous field of historical and museological dilemmas that were thematized in the project itself: namely, that the past is linked to the materiality of things; that history becomes legible through replay, recall, records, and representation; and that all of this is subject to the mechanisms of distortion and the erosion of human memory over time. Sundaram's *History Project* is thus simultaneously a historical work, one that has served to archive a range of historiographic and epistemological dilemmas, and a studied view of *how* history works; and the way these themes and issues echoed together off the soaring domed spaces of the Victoria Memorial Museum was surely part of its beauty and complexity.

In fact, the work of art called *History Project* actually included within its parameters a constellation of media and modes of address, including workshops, performances, video, photography, collaboration, dialogue, and *adda*—the Bengali institution of intellectual exchange— both before and after the ephemeral event, involving primarily the local intelligentsia, and often in situ in the city of Calcutta. Significantly, these activities and events are not the same as the artist's "research" or "preparation" for the project, nor do they necessarily function to reify the primacy of the original work. Rather, this extended field of social activity should be understood as formally constitutive of Sundaram's practice, which points to a further redefinition of the aesthetic process, its goals, results, and ongoing effects. Here, the emphasis is moved away from the autonomy of the art object and toward an engagement with people, ideas, and communities of interaction; away from the aura of the original piece and toward that which can be gained from documentation, reflection, and intellectual exchange. In other words, at its core *History Project* was, and continues to be, a social intervention, envisioned by the artist as a catalyst for discussion, and it underscores Sundaram's unique model of politically engaged artistic praxis.

As scholars have argued, site-specific art, which emerged in the wake of minimalism and other conceptual art movements of the 1960s, is a practice that is "discursively determined."[5] It is frequently more about process than product; it is "a movement, a chain of meanings and imbricated histories; a place marked and swiftly abandoned," and it places Sundaram in direct correspondence with the broader response by contemporary artists at the global level to the conditions of late capitalism of the 1980s and 1990s.[6] In what follows, I reflect on Sundaram's method of engagement with the hybrid institution of the memorial museum and consider the specifically Indian contexts of colonial and nationalist consciousness for historical memory and the museum itself. I then locate several of his concerns in the project within a post-Marxist intellectual tradition in India, and the discussions within Indian historiography generated by subaltern studies, in particular. At the end of the chapter, I contrast Sundaram's project with another site-specific project commissioned in 1998 undertaken in Europe—Hans Haacke's installation at the Reichstag in Berlin—in order to consider more broadly the relationship of contemporary art to the expanding discourse of museums, monuments, and memorials and their increasingly spectacular forms and functions at the beginning of the twenty-first century.

Colonialism's "Edifice Complex"

Monuments, memorials, and museums are slippery, convergent, and at times interchangeable categories, as the very name "Victoria Memorial Museum" suggests. For the American art critic Arthur Danto, the distinction between them was related to the question of intention: "We erect monuments," he wrote famously, "so that we shall always remember, and build memorials so that we shall never forget."[7] Danto's emphasis on these didactic functions is what links the monument and memorial to the museum: together they represent "a species of pedagogy" given to the instruction of posterity about the past.[8] The body of interdisciplinary scholarship that emerged in the 1990s under the banner of the "new museology" has privileged this pedagogic role in its extensive account of the connection between the emergence of museums and the rise of the modern European nation-state.[9] But it has largely ignored, by comparison, the unique pedagogic conditions and historical formation of the museum in colonial and postcolonial societies.

In India, when the British introduced the first museums at the beginning of the nineteenth century (in 1814 in Calcutta, followed by those in Madras, Lahore, and Bombay, respectively) it was to support their plans for "cultural improvement" of the colony. Colonial museum builders sought to replicate, for instance, the model of the British Museum, with its didactic survey approach, in their efforts to spread civility and rationality to the ranks of the native population. If these efforts were frustrated from the outset by a perceived failure on the part of the recalcitrant Indian masses, who often refused to follow the museum's cultural script—by touching, worshipping, and bowing to objects, for instance—then the role of the museum in the civilizing mission was besieged by a larger sense of crises: it failed, in the eyes of colonial officials, to replicate the Victorian pedagogic project of its metropolitan counterpart, and it failed to create a loyal population out of a generally thankless subject society.[10]

If a sense of failure continued to haunt the members of India's so-called Museum Movement in the decades following independence in 1947, it was related at least to the era of decolonization and different kinds of epochal problems. The challenge for these enlightened nation-builders, who inherited—as the writer Mulk Raj Anand once complained—a "bunch of half-dead warehouses from the British," was to "confront the stranglehold of an obsolete system" and to reassess the museum's responsibilities to its newly formed national public.[11] Although they rejected the lavish, costly model of museums designed, according to Anand, for "showing off the might of the nation, with domes and minarets to overawe the people," and called instead for a "new functional attitude" toward museums, the visions of this first generation of museum professionals in India, as in Europe, were constrained by their unself-conscious consolidation of a bourgeois public sphere.[12]

What Sundaram's Victoria Memorial project exposes is thus not merely the tired edifice of the museum's imperial performance, in this case, the archaic and already empty space of Curzon's pretentious last-gasp bid. The more significant focus of *History Project* is Indian nationalism's usurpation of the colonial project, a battle staged partly on the museological front, as Sundaram's superb selection of site reminds us, through the operations of memory put into play through collections, archives, and material display. In other words, an important difference in Sundaram's work, one that distinguishes *History Project* from other site-specific museum works, is that it stimulates and critically engages both the history-making echoes of the colonial museum and the way in which history was remade through Indian nationalism's epic response to the latter.

Reframing the Monument

At the entrance to Sundaram's exhibition inside the space of the Durbar Hall, a huge picture frame, one of numerous frames throughout the installation, announced to the viewer that the artist's eye was on the historical frame itself. There, on a rather unimpressive pedestal apparent in figure 2.3, Sundaram had placed a red plastic chair, a kind of *anti-throne* throne, presented to the viewer behind a large glass pane bearing a shadowy image of the former empress upon it. This peculiar arrangement stood in stark contrast to the actual monumental statue of Victoria, shown in figure 2.4, mounted on a massive stone pedestal at the entrance to the building. Originally commissioned from the British artist George Frampton (1860–1928) to commemorate the Diamond Jubilee of 1897, and later incorporated into Curzon's project, *that* statue of the aging Victoria is the very definition of an aggressive bulk. Upon its arrival in Calcutta in 1902, it was unveiled amid a grand military ceremony on the open plaza featuring hundreds of soldiers on horseback. Years later, it would assist in securing for the sculptor, Frampton, another symbolically resonant commission: the imperious pair of recumbent lions that guard the north entrance to the British Museum. In an act of dematerialization one hundred years later, Sundaram's diminutive counter-statue seemed almost to vaporize the stubborn presence of the original into something of a ghostly trace.

Upon further scrutiny, the reflection of Victoria through the large

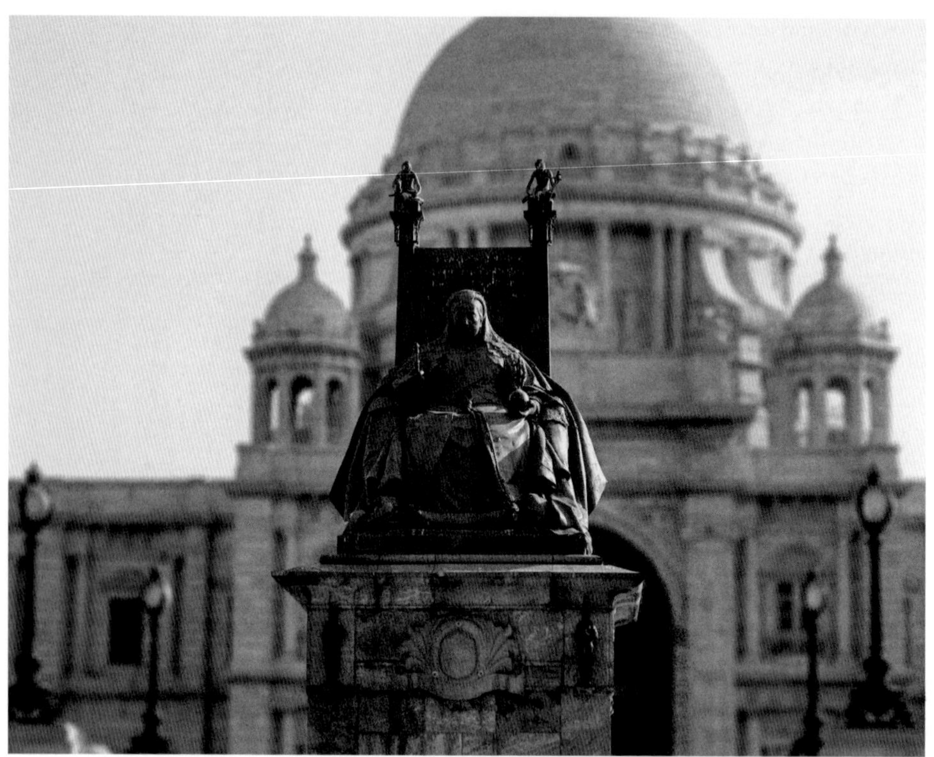

glass pane—simultaneously transparent, palimpsestic, and refractive—recalls the legendary treatment of these perceptual quandaries by Marcel Duchamp in his inscrutable 1915–23 work, titled *The Large Glass*, or *The Bride Stripped Bare by Her Bachelors, Even*. For Duchamp, in this immeasurably complex piece from the heyday of the historical avant-garde, these materials and motifs spoke to the question of desire, the boundaries of its attainability, and the abstract forces involved in human sexuality, and they connected, in his words, to "the rehabilitation of perspective."[13] However, if Duchamp's "bride" was the one who controlled the encounter and left her suitors frustrated by an array of obstacles, contrary to the purposefully deceptive title of the piece, then Sundaram's "bride"—the Victorian empress—is, by contrast, more literally "stripped bare," her physical form reduced to a spectral and powerless presence.

Sundaram's deliberately suspect shrine thus formally acknowledged the exhaustion of a Victorian memorial practice of figural representation in favor of an antiheroic, more ironic encounter by placing the

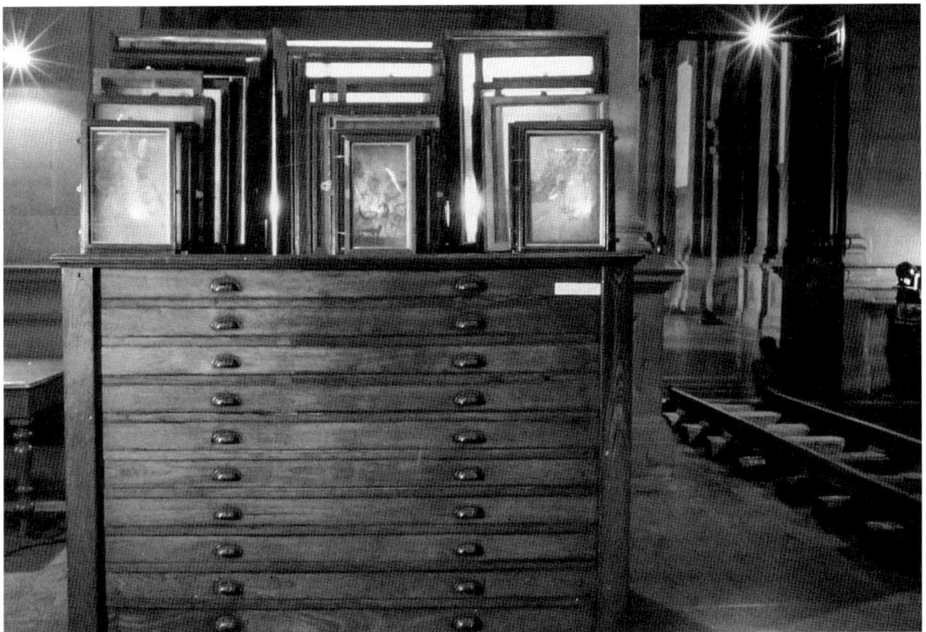

frame in the service of a range of different mnemonic functions. The reference also reveals Sundaram's own identification with the politics of the historical avant-garde by recalling the space of critical reflection first opened up by the Duchampian maneuver and the spirit of disruption and intervention associated with this aesthetic tradition. At one level, the recurring motif of the frame, seen again in figure 2.5, serves to remind the viewer of the essential function of the frame as a receptacle or container for memory. Here and elsewhere, Sundaram's frames did not claim to serve a single historical reality; they were emptied of their indexical capacity, and they pointed to "the structure of memory," not its content per se. At another level, they evoke Jacques Derrida's seminal investigation of the frame in his collection of essays *The Truth in Painting*, perhaps the French philosopher's most significant contribution to discussions in the visual arts.

It was in this text that Derrida skewered the tradition of Kantian formalism and, more broadly, philosophical discourse which grounds itself in absolute principles, "from Plato, to Hegel, Husserl, and Heidegger,"[14] by dispelling the idea that truth and beauty are somehow intrinsic to the work of art. For Derrida, the problem lay in the presupposition that we can rigorously distinguish between inside and out-

FIGURE 2.5
Vivan Sundaram,
History Project, 1998.
Stacked picture
frames on wooden
cabinet. Courtesy
of the artist.

side, between that which is internal and external to the object, between the *ergon* and the *parergon*, in Kantian terms. Derrida's redefinition of the *parergon*, as something that "comes against, beside, and in addition to the *ergon*, the work," acting from the sidelines but not wholly outside, connected to and cooperating in its operations,[15] thus served to denaturalize the work of the frame and make it complicit in the construction of meaning: "There is no natural frame,"[16] but there *is* framing, and framing "always supports and contains that which, by itself, collapses forthwith."[17] If, for Derrida, philosophy had failed to examine this "truth" about the frame, that it "puts everything to work in order to efface its effects,"[18] then deconstruction could at least make this visible through its subversive method of rhetorical undercuts, linguistic puns, and vertiginous wordplay.

Sundaram's frames in the Victoria Memorial are thus *parergonal* in the Derridean sense. They subvert the essential truth value of art and dramatize the hierarchies through which signification works to naturalize and privilege certain discourses over others. Here, the contrarian techniques of Dada are deployed to achieve what Derrida described as "a certain repeated dislocation," one that "makes the frame in general crack" through the corners of its angles and articulations and dissolves its internal and external parameters.[19] The correlations between the Derridean and Duchampian frameworks, although separated by some fifty years, have been embraced by a generation of artists and thinkers, who have found in the density of their challenges to linguistic and pictorial truth a radical relation between images and texts, or between works of art and their discourses.

Sundaram's method in *History Project*, his overall conceptual and material approach, lies somewhere deep in the folds of these critical lessons and philosophical discussions and in the creative possibilities they present. To enter this work is to enter into an arena of serious and sophisticated play, deconstructionist and Dada-esque in spirit, whereby the artist has seized command of the signs in order to undercut, pun, collide, and contradict in versatile and often destabilizing ways. What we leave at the door of the Durbar Hall is the comfort of a legible, unambiguous text or the certainty of a linear historicist path. Instead, the installation's distinctive spatial format glimpsed in figure 2.6, involving corners, domes, distortions, echoes, and the interplay of all these effects, presents a diversity of devices for breaking up the traditional and time-honored structures of meaning, knowing, and representation

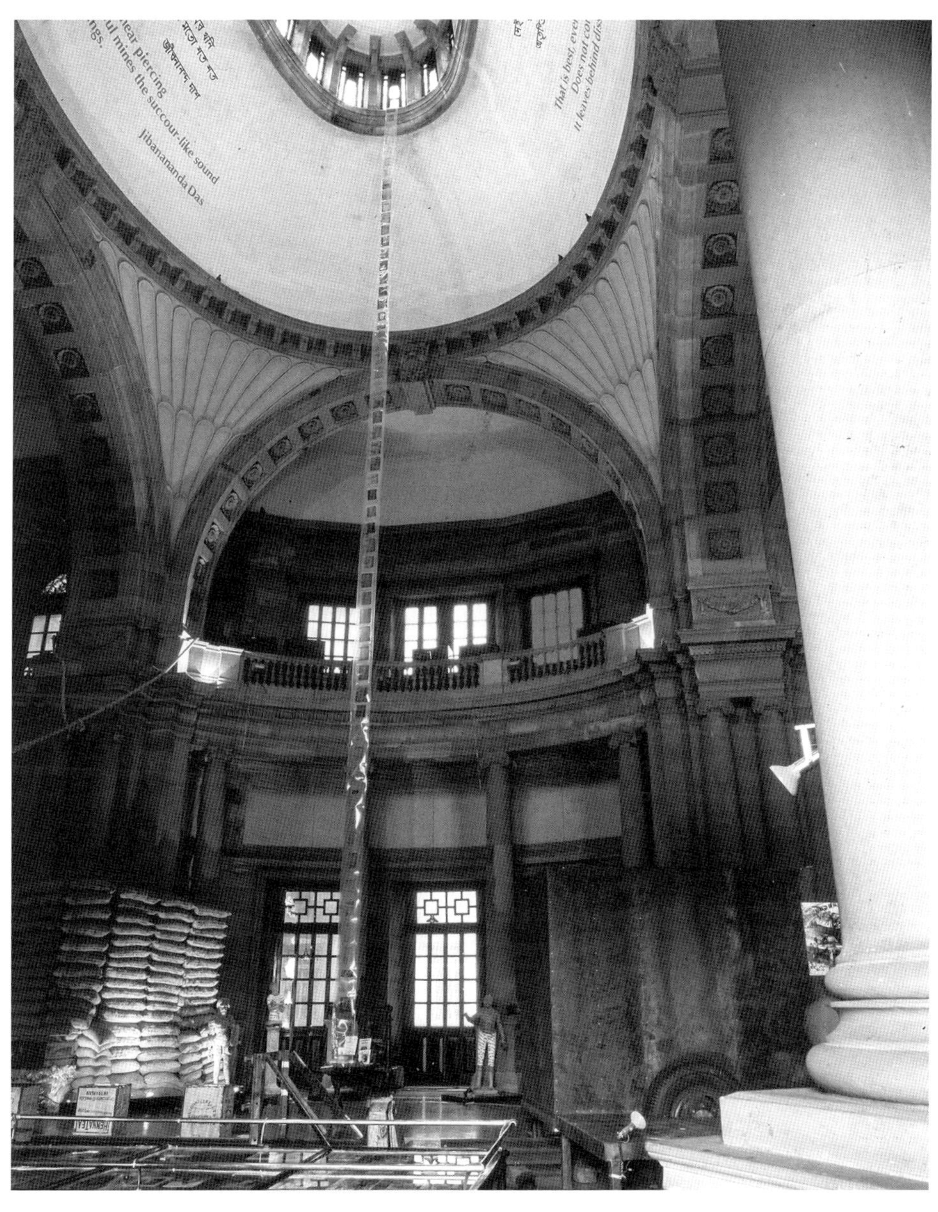

FIGURE 2.6 Vivan Sundaram, *History Project*, 1998. View of poetic verses on domed ceiling. Courtesy of the artist.

itself. What Sundaram sets out to dismantle is no less than the entire conglomeration, simultaneously philosophical *and* material/architectural; his target is the "edifice complex" in this widest possible sense.

Modern Bengal: Nationalist Imaginings

These heterogeneous and open-ended formal strategies come to converge on the particular sociohistorical event of Indian independence in multiple and (perhaps inevitably) uneven ways. For instance, next to the hologram-like throne in the hall was a tall and bulky mass of materials that contrasted sharply with the dematerializing visual effects of the former. Here, Sundaram had installed hundreds of heavy jute sacks of grain, each inscribed with the dates and descriptions of various moments in Bengal's labor history—peasant uprisings, workers' strikes, and the people's insurgencies of modern Bengal. The significance of this jute bag barricade, visible in figure 2.7, and its gesture toward a subaltern history of the period, will become clearer as we encounter the wider network of themes and interactions that Sundaram mounted elsewhere in the space, and I will return to it shortly. For now, a large wall of five hundred file boxes, each dedicated to an individual involved in India's freedom struggle, presented the weighty materiality of an archive; elsewhere a Victorian cabinet with many drawers evoked the history of collecting. All of these forms pointed to an abiding concern with history, or more precisely, with history's acts of legibility: that is, how history is made through the collection and storage of material records, how it is written, archived, and given material form. The writing desk and library of Bankim Chandra Chatterjee, one of the preeminent poetic voices of Bengali nationalism, announced further that Sundaram's theme was India's response to imperial history, in particular, the rejection by nationalists of James Mill's audacious bid to render the entire subject of Indian history "a portion of the British history."[20]

Thus, a central theme that emerged in the exhibition was the place of Bengali culture, represented by the arts, literature, theater, cinema, and photography, within the battle for the appropriation of India's past. Around the apse of the Durbar Hall, Sundaram had mounted various landscapes and figural paintings by the legendary artists of Santiniketan, recalling the great experiments with wall murals in Bengal, a preferred genre for national self-imagining. On the ceilings were pas-

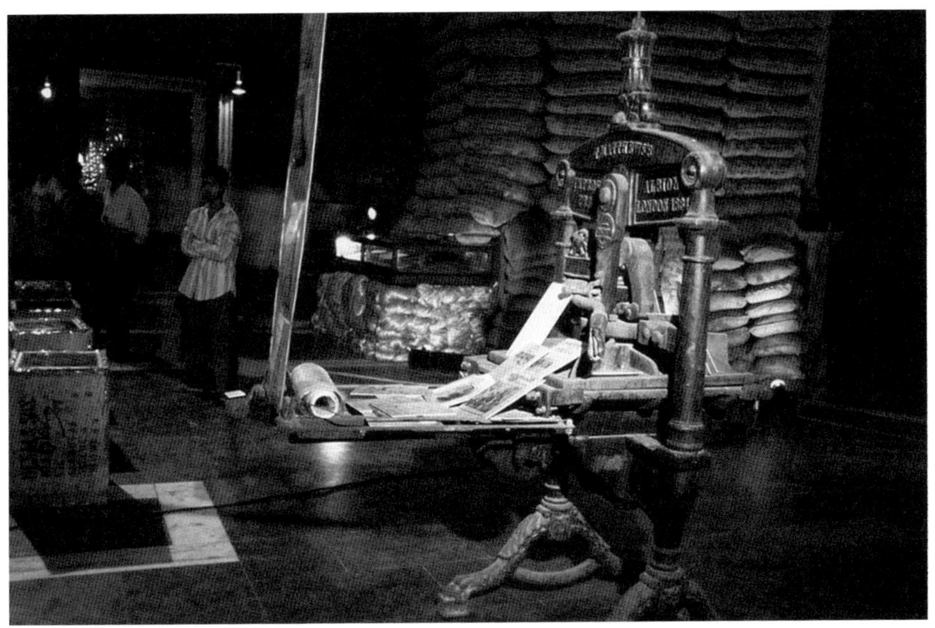

sages of translated poetry by Rabindranath Tagore and Jibanananda Das in a graceful nod toward the heavens and the sky. Figure 2.8 shows the neon phrase *Joto moth, Toto poth* in Bengali and in English ("many views, many paths") by Ramakrishna Parahamansa elevated above, as a pluralist, even utopian, ideal. Down below, an elegant old printing press placed the emphasis on the role of print culture in disseminating the literary and political writings of the period (see figure 2.7), and clay mannequins in theatrical poses, inscribed with prose from Bengali theater, offered a kind of mini-performance on the ground (see figure 2.9).

The national figures being commemorated here—if indeed these disparate quotations, artifacts, and oblique references amount to "commemoration" in any conventional sense—are not the usual generals and statesmen who get honored in public sculpture, and whose sad fate, as Andreas Huyssen has noted, is "to be toppled or to become invisible."[21] Instead, *History Project* directs us to poets, thinkers, writers, and intellectuals and celebrates the unsung (or less sung) history of Bengali ideas. One might expect the format of "words on a dome" to point toward a transcendental narrative, but Sundaram's inscription-plus-neon mix, in the manner of the glowing neon sculpture of the American minimalists of the 1960s and 1970s, suggests a more radiant,

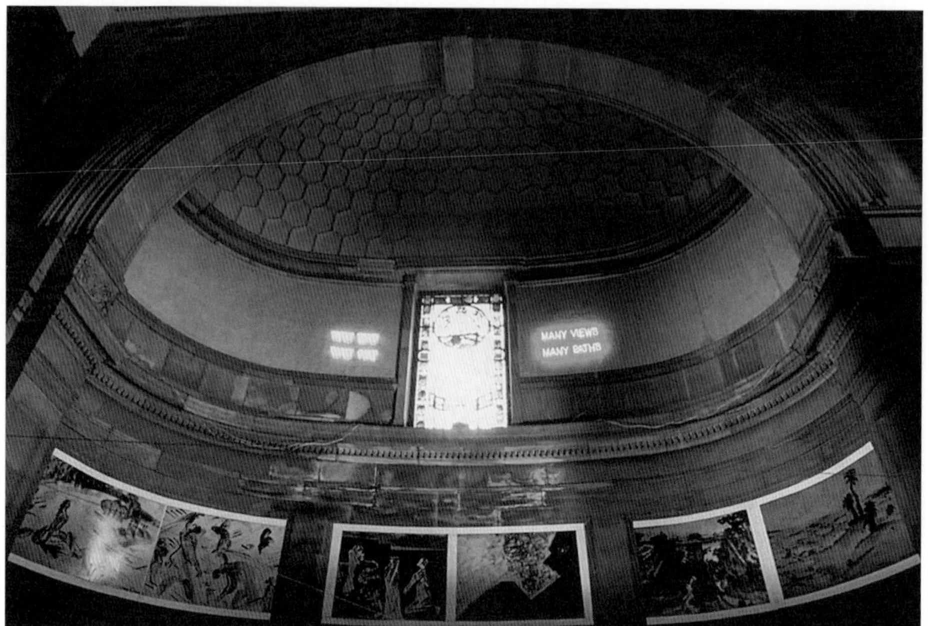

open, or immanent horizon. Like the Swiss artist Thomas Hirschhorn's fugitive street altars to philosophers, or "anti-monuments," Sundaram's memorial gestures to various Bengali intellectuals are intimate, partial, impermanent, and selective. They do not "explain" the importance of the figure being honored or impart to the viewer some predetermined truth. Instead, they offer ideas and thoughts for interaction rather than reverence, designed to feed into an ongoing discussion or to become part of a larger chain of meanings and symbols.[22] Together, these invocations of a specifically Bengali intellectual history return us repeatedly to the question of language, and to the space of a vernacular Bengali tradition in particular, a paramount and principled concern of Sundaram's, a non-Bengali speaker who nevertheless elected to grapple with the problems of access, interpretation, and translation this presented.

At the heart of Sundaram's treatment of language, and the prominence given to Bengali in the installation, is the question of the relationship between language and imperial power. In what the theorist and historian of South Asia Ranajit Guha has called "the shotgun wedding between language and colonialism," we know that an Anglophone education became synonymous with prestige and social importance, while the indigenous languages, and Bengali in particular, marked a signifi-

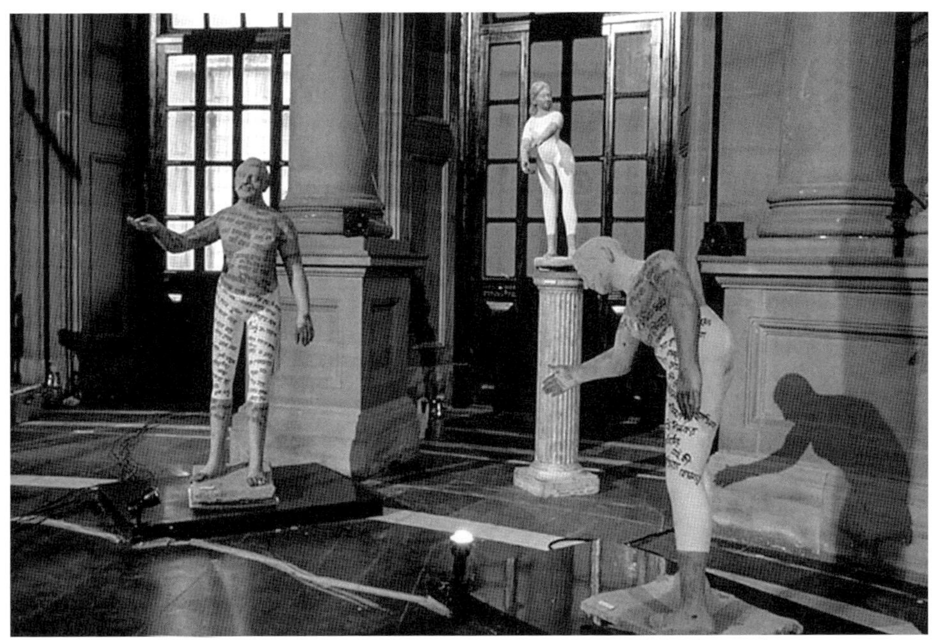

cant and in some sense autonomous domain of creative possibility. As Guha has stated, the Bengali language "grew up" in a way through its encounter with English; every semantic slide, every nuanced linguistic acrobatic generated by the needs of translation, was evidence "not only of what Bangla could *not* do, but also of what it could."[23] In other words, the intrusion and assimilation of English into Bengali could not be mistaken for mere "Westernization." The Bengali language, as a sign of the culture itself, was involved in far more complex strategies of adaptation and innovation, which gave rise to a struggle often waged at the limits of translatability into Euro-Western concepts and codes.[24] Sundaram's representation of the nationalist struggle was thus inseparable from the question of language; *History Project* depicted how resistance was staged in part through the mechanisms of language, the expressions of a shared linguistic tradition, and the idioms for conceptions of self and society drawn from outside the realm of colonial authority and reason.

What emerged from the installation, in short, was a dynamic encounter with the culture of modern Bengal as it led the struggle for Indian independence. And yet, "modern Bengal," as Arindam Dutta has noted, is really "a topos in the cultural politics of Indian nationalism, a term redolent with both pleasant and noxious aromas," like the way the phrase "antebellum Low Country" marks the American Deep South or "Louis-Philippe furniture" summons nineteenth-century France.[25] It evokes, in other words, a field of associations that were *simultaneously* historically very significant and drenched in the structures of gentility and class privilege. The new society of progressive thinkers that Sundaram's work was at pains to acknowledge was composed of the native elite. And while they ushered in a robust intellectual culture of debate and dissent, powered by a revolution in print culture, the era was plagued by repeated famines, agrarian poverty, and a relentless exploitation of the laboring poor.

One contentious feature of Sundaram's installation was the way it sought to respond to this particular dilemma, which returns us to the jute bag barricade seen in figures 2.3 and 2.7. The representation of this alternative history of political resistance places the entire project into conversation with contemporary efforts to rethink the historiography of nationalism by a host of Bengali intellectuals and their interlocutors in South Asia and beyond. What was omitted from the nationalist response to imperial history, taken to task by Ranajit Guha as an "unhistorical historiography," was "the politics of the people," the disruptions and generative forces that lay beyond the parameters of bourgeois consciousness and the representational practices of the indigenous elite.[26] The challenge to recuperate that elusive space of subjectivity and political consciousness—the "subaltern"—has become, as we know, a powerful intellectual constellation and the basis for a great deal of ongoing debate within the arena of postcolonial theory and criticism. But it is unusual to witness these ideas take form within the realm of the visual arts in quite this way and, more significantly, within the space of a public art project.

Sundaram's attempt to reveal, instead of conceal, the social distance between elite and subaltern and between women and men, as well as the structures that have erased these inequalities in the archive within the context of a civic monument, points to an understanding of public space itself as a radically heterogeneous and intersubjective arena. This is not to say that the project was *by definition* more democratic or emancipatory because it repositioned art in a public locale; on the contrary, the installation pointed to a greater uncertainty about the issue of art's democratizing effects. Rather, the work presented social inequality in modern Bengal as a condition of democratic public space, not as the basis for its ruin or demise, and it refused to indulge in the fiction of a harmonious collective unity. The artist asked of us instead, "Who is the public?" and "How do its unequal constituencies lay claim to collective identity and history?" and then called upon the viewer to "imagine community" through a self-conscious engagement with its ruptures and pluralities.

We should ask, however, a critical question: Did Sundaram's piece ultimately paint a heroic portrait of the ascendance of the Bengali bourgeoisie? Or did it abide by what Guha called "the lack of heroism" of this class, its "failure to measure up to the heroism of the European bourgeoisie in its period of ascendancy"?[27] Guha's reference is to what Marx also called, perhaps paradoxically, the "revolutionary" aspect of the bourgeoisie, their role in driving industrial expansion, their cosmopolitanism, the enormous transformations they made to society, which were also the basis of their own demise. For Guha, the Indian bourgeoisie, born as they were out of colonialism itself, lacked this heroic relationship to society; they were instead "pliant and prone to compromise," and therefore represented a caricature of the vigorous democratic culture that came with the formation of capitalism in Europe.[28] The result was, in Guha's powerful formulation, "dominance without hegemony," a structure which generated for India a much greater failure, that is, the "failure of the nation to come into its own."[29] Did Sundaram lose sight of these critical insights, related to the ongoing conditions of failure and crisis in the postcolonial nation-state, in his homage to the pioneering contributions of modern Bengal? Or stated differently, for our purposes, what prevents an engagement through site-specificity from affirming or resanctifying a given institutional site? How and where do we draw the line between a reverential remembering and a presumably more radical historical interpretation, and for whom?

Ultimately, such doubts and ambiguities are left unresolved, even as they are made more urgent in a final component of Sundaram's installation: the train tracks and eerie railway wagon that composed, according to the video, the "spine" of the piece. In figure 2.10, we see the great symbol of industrial progress—the Indian railway—take the form of a haunted and rusty old phantom. Here, the narrative of linear progress was disrupted; the tracks led to an unpleasant dead end and seemed challenged by the ominous rope above, evoking perhaps the knots and entanglements of the historical field, or worse, the fatal specter of a noose. More than anything else in the show, this disquieting picture of rails and derailment caused worry. It seemed to suggest, at best, a dead

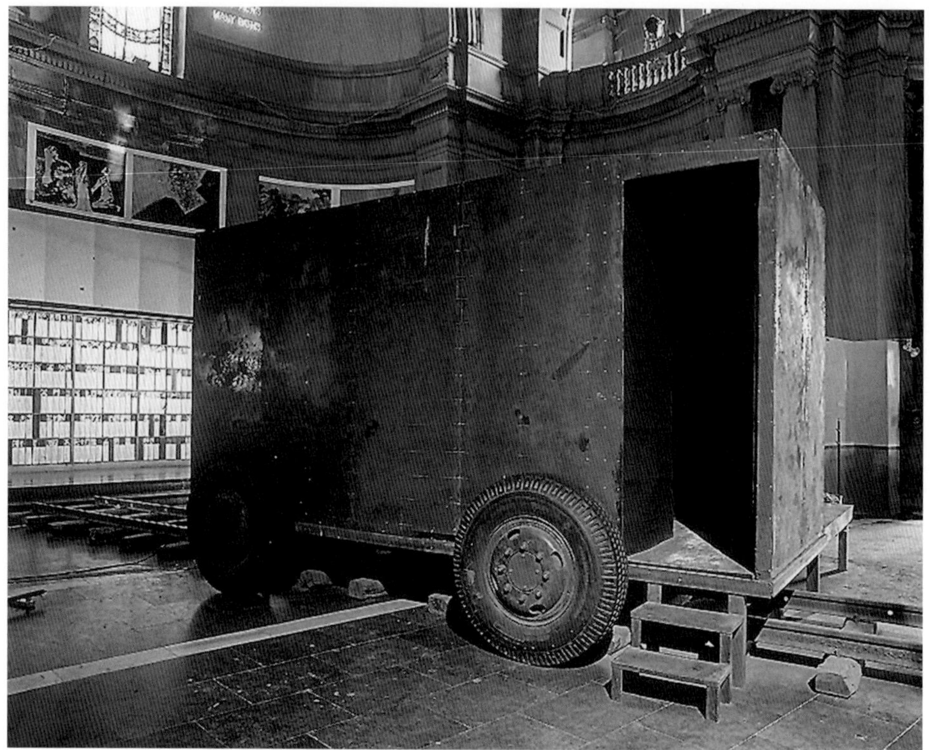

end, or at worse, a more calamitous result: the reference to Partition through the symbolism of the train and the layers of human suffering generated by this event became audible, immediate, and most palpable here. In this way, the artist forced us to confront the grimmest implications of India's "journey toward freedom"—namely, the ongoing instability of the social field produced by nationalism and the distance between the utopian visions of the intelligentsia and the much bleaker realities of the Indian populace who inhabit the so-called freight-car classes.

Contemporary Art and the Memorial Monument

By way of conclusion, I wish to consider Sundaram's project alongside a more widely discussed site-specific work, also commissioned in 1997–98—namely, the controversial installation at Berlin's Reichstag building by the New York–based German artist Hans Haacke. For this project, Haacke, a leading figure in the aesthetic movement that has come to be known as institutional critique, had installed a large rectangular cast in the courtyard of the Reichstag, the German Parliament building that had a democratic history before it was famously appropriated by Hitler's regime. Inside the box, he placed the words "DER BEVÖLKE-RUNG" (The Population) in neon letters. The box was then filled with earth brought by German MPs from their constituencies and allowed to overgrow, as seen in figure 2.11. The phrase referred to the bronze inscription "DEM DEUTSCHEN VOLKE" (To the German People) that was placed on the exterior of the building in 1916 (figure 2.12). This sign, as Haacke's work uncomfortably revealed, had been made by a Jewish family of craftsmen in Berlin whose members all perished under the Nazi regime. Haacke's project thus staged a dialogue with an existing monument—the Reichstag—and raised questions about the models of national unity represented by the building, with the garden replacing the notion of a "pure" German people with an evolving and organic population, the seeds, if you like, of a new collectivity.

The project also launched a vigorous discussion about the culture of memorial monuments in contemporary Germany (for instance, was this a Holocaust memorial?) and stimulated an inevitable comparison to Christo and Jeanne-Claude's 1995 wrapping of the Reichstag in polypropylene fabric, a more ambiguous spectacle, according to Andreas Huyssen, revealing a "Wagnerian blending" of history, myth, beautification, and packaging within its antimonumental stance.[30] Among other things, these debates in the German context foreground the relationship of architectural monuments, whether imperialist or fascist, to the historical violence they were built to serve. They also focus, for our purposes, some other pertinent questions: How might such monuments and memorial museums take part in not only remembering but also actively transforming the historical injustices of the modern past? And what can or should be the role of contemporary art in relation to these discourses of national public memory?

There are many differences between Haacke at the Reichstag and Sundaram at the Victoria Memorial, notwithstanding the textual/linguistic emphasis that is clearly central to both installations. For instance, the materials and strategies deployed by each artist could not seem further apart. Haacke's work was not a temporary installation but a permanent and organic structure that acquired its meaning through change over time. Moreover, the Reichstag is not a memorial museum

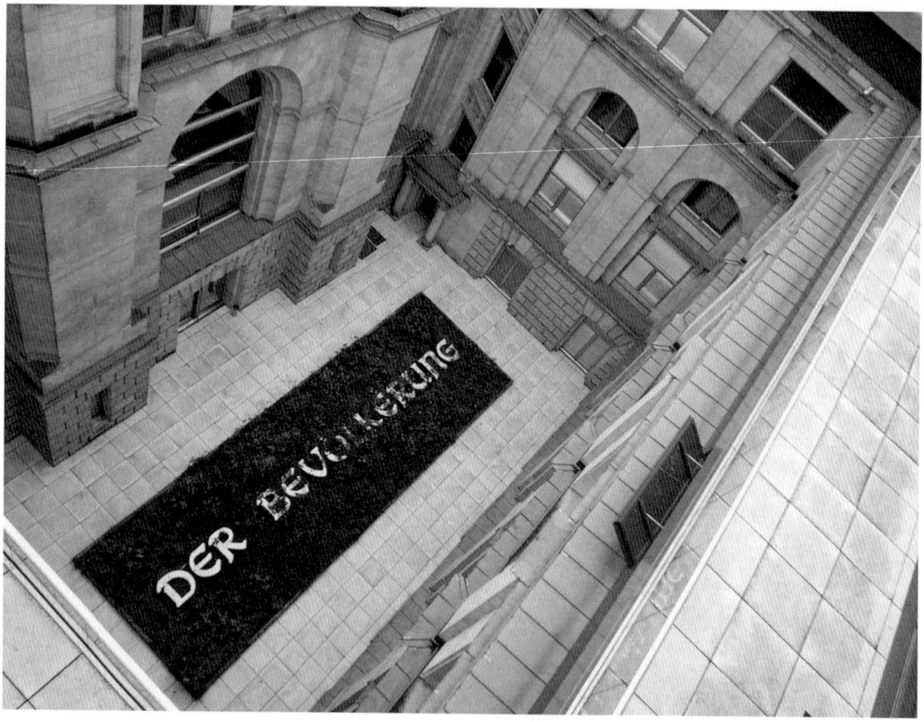

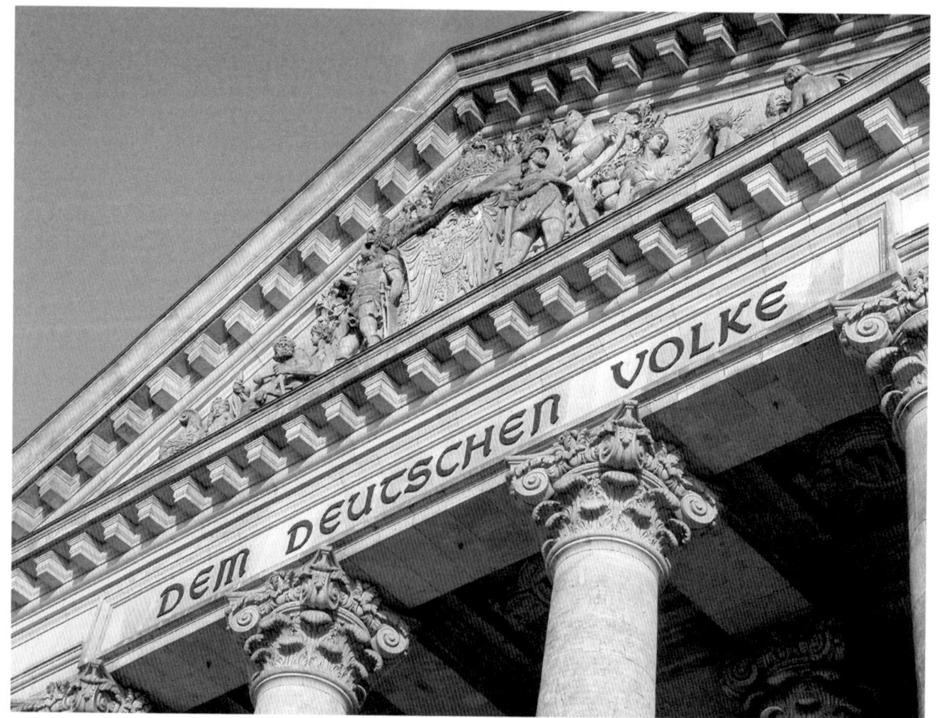
DER BEVÖLKERUNG
DEM DEUTSCHEN VOLKE

but rather an edifice constructed to house the German Parliament, although its identity, according to some critics, was permanently altered by the British architect Norman Foster, whose 1992–99 refurbishment project transformed the original structure into a museological object by literally placing it under glass. Interestingly, Foster's "Crystal Palace paradigm" was criticized for its unchecked continuity with Britain's imperialist museological past, which places the Reichstag post-renovation into an unexpected kinship with Curzon's building in Calcutta.[31] That each monument is distinguished by a magnificent dome serves as a further point of resemblance. As Haacke reflected later, "Many aspects of Foster's refurbished interior building I do not care for, but his dome is absolutely spectacular, a tourist attraction of the first order."[32]

In the end, these site-specific projects by Haacke and Sundaram, oriented as they are toward radically different societal structures and histories, with many points of difference and similarity, nevertheless converge upon a single, rather subversive thread: both present a powerful challenge to the rise of an "official" memorial culture that rests increasingly in the hands of the nation-state and its incessant drive toward the branding of identity and redemptive versions of the national past. The proliferation of the phenomenon of memorials, part of the "global rush to commemorate," has led to a boom in the business of memorial museums within the landscape of official national heritage.[33] As several writers have argued, historical consciousness at the beginning of the twenty-first century has increasingly taken museological form; everywhere, we seem to be placing monuments, museums, pillars, and memorials to commemorate the traumas of our twentieth century, a process that has led, paradoxically, to greater normalization, amnesia, and forms of forgetting and resulted in excess, saturation, even "memory fatigue."[34] The apparent globalization of the Holocaust paradigm seems to have reached its point of ideological overload in Daniel Libeskind's proposed master plan for the reconstruction of the World Trade Center site in downtown Manhattan. Libeskind, the architect of the acclaimed Jewish Museum in Berlin, was roundly criticized for his proposed "Freedom Towers": monumental, triumphant, sentimental, and grand. In short, memorials *have today become spectacles*, institutions fashioned for scripted experiences and manipulated into ever more curious shapes, which returns us full circle back to Curzon's foundational vision for the Victoria Memorial in 1901.

Sundaram's site-specific project helps interrupt this cycle of historical overdetermination and works against the ego-driven excesses of the builder by seizing in the most intimate fashion the forms, materials, and conditions of his site. In this way, History Project dramatizes the seminal role of contemporary art within the shape-shifting museological landscape of today, which appears increasingly susceptible to the "inflation of memory" and the memorial monument's triumphal return.[35] If the spectacular memorial culture inaugurated by Curzon's part-museum, part-memorial, part-monument configuration has indeed found a new lease on life, then the boundaries that once separated our understanding of these categories have also become more fluid, porous, and difficult to grasp. It is here, in this zone of ambiguity and uncertainty that runs counter to the hegemony of the branded vision, that the artist performs a discrepant negotiation with memory through the "recalcitrant materiality"[36] of physical forms. Sundaram's frames, photographs, vitrines, and file boxes, like the contents of the museum itself, are indeterminate and inconclusive, presenting—in Hal Foster's terms—"enigmatic prompts for future scenarios," and they ultimately raise more questions than answers for even the initiated viewer.[37] However, if the national appetite for self-aggrandizing gestures is matched increasingly by the skepticism of contemporary art, then, as James Young has suggested, it may well be that the future of memorialization lies in this place of perpetual irresolution. For, as Young has explained, "only an unfinished memorial process," in contrast to the finished monument or the stasis of a completed script, can ensure the life of memory itself.[38]

Let us return, then, to my earlier question: What is the role of contemporary art in relation to the discourse of memorials, museums, and monuments in South Asia? History Project gives us one possible answer to that question. Sundaram's project—polyphonic, dynamic, enigmatic, and antididactic—was a challenge to both the *ethics* and *aesthetics* of the memorial museum in its modern form. The piece refused to reify or enshrine the memory of India's history as a nation, to turn it into a spectacle or cliché, or to partake in the folly of "unlocking the past." It troubled the space of a settled institution and brought a familiar, if overlooked, public monument into significance and dissonance in an entirely new way. It presented the nation not as a stable foundation but as a precarious formation shaped through a history of ideas. It offered an image not just of a nation's triumph but also of its liabilities and future responsibilities. It was an experiment with the opening, rather than the foreclosing, of history, undertaken through acts of outreach and inclusion. If memorial culture in the modern era has been usurped by the needs of the nation-state, then the role of the artist is to enter this space in the forceful manner of the "advance guard," to find within its corners and arches the room for more creative expression, to shape a living landscape for memory itself, and to reinvest history with the project of the future.

3

THE WORLD, THE ART,
AND THE CRITIC

What's in a Name?

In his seminal investigation of the relationships between "the world, the text, and the critic," Edward Said pushed at the nerve cord of some of the most fundamental questions in the realm of intellectual discourse: What is theory? What is criticism? How does it function? When is it effective? And why? Such questions for Said were not well served by attaching qualifying labels to a given practice of criticism, like "Indian critic" or "postcolonial theorist," because identifications of this kind did little more than settle all too easily an often intricate field of thought procedures that acquired their shape over time. In some rare cases, Said observed, the critic's name by itself could function as a more meaningful marker of the kinds of formations at stake than a label of the latter sort. Thus, for Said, the names "Frye" or "Leavis" within the field of literature were enough to arouse passionate partisanship, to position a large swathe of ideas and assumptions, and to galvanize certain claims and premises while overriding others.[1]

To my mind, the name "Geeta Kapur" operates in something of this potent manner in the discursive arena of contemporary Indian art. It conjures a distinctive singularity of voice and sheer intellectual force within the field. It is the sign of an intense, often intimidating, register of discussion and is frequently interchangeable with theory itself. It can stimulate alliance with a set of concepts and values or provoke a strong-minded rejection of the same. It has the ability to cause "anxiety of influence," the condition of ambivalence identified by Harold Bloom that is part of the struggle between poets and their predecessors. One symptom of the phenomenon, according to Bloom, was the aspiring writer's "swerve away from the precursor" so as to "clear imaginative space for themselves."[2] This may help explain the conspicuous fact that Kapur's outsize contribution to modern and contemporary Indian art has yet to receive any proper consideration within the expanding discourses of the field.[3] For our purposes, the name "Geeta Kapur" thus provides a more productive point of entry into the sophisticated shape and substance of this Delhi-based critic's intellectual practice than any of the labels that have been attached to it thus far. Even the celebrated novelist Salman Rushdie, who fictionalized the Indian art world in his 1995 epic tale, *The Moor's Last Sigh*, seemed to recognize this when he used pseudonyms for many of the real life characters who appeared in the novel except for "the noted critic, Geeta Kapur."[4]

Described variously as "critic," "theorist," "curator," and "art historian," Kapur has fashioned a pluralistic practice that does not conform to a single vocational definition. At the core of her approach to art is a steadfast and enduring attachment to the various conditions — creative, intellectual, and institutional — of the working artist in India. Like a modern-day Giorgio Vasari, Kapur first positioned herself as witness to an unfolding tradition manifested in the "lives of artists" during the 1970s and 1980s in Delhi and Baroda, where she focused on chronicling individual practices, attending to biography, method, technique, and narrative. "I sought meaning in artists' studios," she has stated. "I tried to develop a practice of my own which would stand side-by-side with the artist's practice."[5] In 1981, she characterized this as a "partisanal" relationship, a term first privileged in her manifesto advocating the practices of figuration and narrative in a group of six painters (one of them, Vivan Sundaram) that would reappear in several later essays.[6] More recently, Kapur has defined her role as a "co-producer of meaning," emphasizing a shared sense of participation in the activities of creative work and an intellectual alliance with the imaginative effort of artists.[7] Curating, as conceived by Kapur, is another "form of narration," one that "deals with endings and beginnings" and contains possibilities for "scrambled sequences and contrary moves."[8] Together, her writing and curatorial acts expose what one scholar has called the "ingenious act of leger-demain"[9] that separates art history from art criticism, as if these existed as discrete domains rather than intertwined realities that are too often held apart in a false opposition. Indeed, Kapur does not seem overly invested in one side or the other of this particular balance sheet, occasionally referring to herself as a composite "historian-critic." Arguing instead for "agonistic relationships" more broadly within the field of art, and drawing upon the political theory of Chantal Mouffe, which insists on the democratic potential of contestation itself, Kapur's intellectual practice is best understood as a *parallactic* project, one that sustains multiple lines of sight without resolving their tensions and incommensurabilities.[10]

There has emerged a consensus in the past decade or so that art criticism today is in a perilous state. In these discussions, art criticism—destabilized by the increasingly chaotic forms of contemporary art and displaced by the indiscriminate modes of art writing connected to galleries, dealers, and collectors—exists in a state of worldwide crisis: it is exhausted, directionless, in a "mess," and suffering from a loss of authority and respect.[11] Yet this narrative of a global crisis of criticism has been drawn almost exclusively from the figure of the critic and the voice of art criticism as it has emerged from the artistic milieus of Europe and America. Geeta Kapur's five-decade-long practice of criticism, by contrast, has been based entirely within the Indian subcontinent *and* fashioned through a variety of contingent international contexts and influences. The result does not symbolize, however, a practice "other" to Western art criticism or a predetermined hybrid outcome of some sort. Nor does it represent a nativist project, which would imply the assertion of a native or organic relation to a place, a stance that Kapur, as I will show, rejects unequivocally. Rather, Kapur's is a project whose critical force comes precisely out of the tensions produced by such entanglements and the frisson of their dialectical negotiation. A highly synthetic intellectual constellation, Kapur's criticism is born out of an ongoing process of translation and interlocution and is therefore *itself* not easily attached to originary points or consecutive linear parts.[12]

Nonetheless, in the face of the shortened attention spans, reduced difficulty, and tendency toward celebration and congratulation that prevail in today's art world, emboldened by the instant "like" platforms of Facebook and Twitter, I turn to Kapur's intellectual practice as a calibrated instance of "strong criticism." Following art historian and critic Maurice Berger, strong criticism is not merely an authoritative criticism but one that is capable of engaging and influencing culture, even stimulating new forms of practice and expression, without forsaking beauty, provocation, or emotional connection. Strong criticism uses language and rhetoric to strive for the same levels of passion and beauty that are evident in the art it interprets. Strong criticism serves as a "dynamic, critical force" rather than mere art world boosterism or museum and gallery buzz. Strong criticism thus offers "the greatest hope" for the vitality and future of critical discourse today.[13]

In her recent effort to map art criticism in post-independence India, the Delhi-based writer and curator Vidya Shivadas analyzed five different English-language writers, not to recuperate "lone, heroic voices" but to "construct a field within which art writing takes place."[14] The first survey of its kind, Shivadas's study identified Kapur as an independent and "interventionist" critical voice who, more than any other single figure, brought theoretical understanding to contemporary art on the subcontinent and fashioned a practice that departed dramatically from older models of criticism based in connoisseurship and professional expertise. An independent scholar who has held occasional visiting positions, Kapur has been unaffiliated throughout her career and thus bears the profile of the autonomous critic or intellectual whose alliances have remained flexible and selective, standing at a distance from any single institution or the culture of institutions more broadly.

This is a model of fluid, politicized engagement between an intellectual and society, one that has been rigorously theorized in the Marxist and post-Marxist tradition, beginning with Marx and Engels's formulations in *The German Ideology*, continuing with Antonio Gramsci's concept of the "organic intellectual," and articulated with renewed urgency in the postwar period in Frantz Fanon's account of the "native intellectual."[15] I will return shortly to mark the special relevance of Fanon for grasping some of Kapur's intellectual orientations, in particular her commitment to the "national modern" and to a humanism born out of decolonization itself. For now, it is also worth noting that Kapur's criticism is informed by many intellectual frameworks beyond that of Marxist analyses, without being reducible to a single theoretical approach. As I will show, Kapur's writing keeps multiple and divergent critical perspectives in play, allowing them to intersect, even contradict at times, in order to fashion a terrain of leftist cultural analysis that self-consciously embraces the possibilities, poetics, and limits of language in relation to a paramount investment in the making of art.

And this leads to a number of questions: What is the precise nature—the content, form, and logic—of Kapur's "interventionist" contributions to contemporary Indian art and criticism? What procedures of thought and modes of writing support these strategies of intervention and mobilize its effects? What are the meaningful sources and sites of emergence for Kapur's self-styled intellectual practice? And what is an appropriate methodology to begin to capture a critical consciousness that actively resists ideological capture?

Against Civilizational Roots

Kapur's earliest piece of published writing was the MA thesis she completed in London in 1969 under the formative mentorship of the Marxist thinker, teacher, and painter Peter de Francia (1921–2012) at the Royal College of Art. De Francia was a "horizon-painter," according to the renowned English critic John Berger, with an exacting intelligence and an awareness of the broader world that brought a "largeness" of vision to the art scene in England in the previous century.[16] Kapur has stated that it was de Francia who first "steered her into Marxism, third-world ideology, and postcolonialism" and who enabled her to enter as a young student in her early twenties "more confidently into the discursive field."[17] Titled "In Quest of Identity: Art and Indigenism in Post-colonial Culture with Special Reference to Contemporary Indian Painting," the thesis was serialized in the spirited but short-lived magazine *Vrishchik* (Scorpion), edited by Gulammohammed Sheikh and Bhupen Khakhar in Baroda between 1969 and 1973, and has only recently begun to attract scholarly attention.[18]

The text is captivating not only because it marks the emergence of Kapur's critical voice, notably at home from the outset in the kind of experimental, artist-led initiative represented by *Vrishchik*; it also marks a prescient use of the term "postcolonial," well before the word was secured as an "ism" within Euro-American cultural studies. That Kapur would later challenge this institutionalization—expressing skepticism about the "rapid academicization" of the vocabulary during the 1990s and arguing for ways in which the realm of the visual could help "undo the overdetermined discourse of postcolonial theory"[19]—is one of several aspects of the thesis that give it an uncanny, almost reverberative, quality; it both reflects certain debates of the period, for instance, the discussions surrounding indigenism and internationalism in the third world during the 1960s and 1970s, at the same time that it anticipates and echoes Kapur's later investments and intellectual preoccupations. Kapur, for her part, has acknowledged the fragility of such lineages of critical writing in India, characterizing *Vrishchik* as a "little" magazine, one with "a short run but a long life,"[20] and described her own youthful effort in the thesis as part of "the earnest climb"[21] toward later themes, in particular the theme of the national modern that preoccupied the essays in her major book of 2000, *When Was Modernism.*

I suggest that Kapur's MA thesis represents a powerful "beginning," in the sense meant by Said: not a divine point of origin but rather "a first step in the intentional production of meaning" that establishes relationships of both continuity and departure to preexisting ideas and traditions.[22] For Said, a beginning authorizes subsequent texts and makes possible the "constant re-experiencing of beginning and beginning again"; the beginning's force is not to shore up authority or promote orthodoxy but "to stimulate self-conscious and situated activity."[23] From such a perspective, Kapur's initial moment of inquiry into the question of art in the culture of the former colony becomes something of a revelation. Drawing from Frantz Fanon's then recent formulations regarding decolonization and national culture, the thesis was a forceful argument *against* a romanticized model of organic belonging and the valorization of civilizational roots. The thesis also allows us to position, some five decades later, the meaningful coordinate that is Kapur's recent essay about the body of work produced by her deceased friend, the artist Nasreen Mohamedi (1937–90) — an essay whose very title, "Again a Difficult Task Begins," drawn from Mohamedi's personal notebook, speaks to the idea of iteration and reiteration as a critical process and a method of work. Although very different from the thesis, this essay both returns to and departs from Kapur's prior elegy to the artist written in the wake of Mohamedi's premature death.[24] As I suggest at the end of this chapter and in my epilogue concerned with Kapur's and Sundaram's "late style," these patterns of repetition and return — in Said's terms, of experiences of "beginning and beginning again" — are essential to the radical consciousness enacted in Kapur's writing over time and a means through which to productively approach the larger corpus of her work.

The MA thesis Kapur had formulated in London in 1968–69 set out not to solve the problem of cultural identity for India but to articulate the dilemmas of this ongoing "quest." Drawing inspiration from Fanon's call in *The Wretched of the Earth* for the intelligentsia of the former colonies to become "authentic and self-aware," the thesis drew from an eclectic array of thinkers—among them Octavio Paz, Jean Franco, Herbert Marcuse, Roland Barthes, Edward Carr, and John Berger—to call for a radical practice of "indigenism" based in a "sociologically angled viewpoint on contemporary art."[25] One of Kapur's main concerns was to "extend indigenism from a romantic pursuit" into "an instrument of criticism"; another was to replace the pervasive developmentalism of historical method with "self-directed questioning" and a reassessment of the past.[26]

Our young critic thus made a crucial distinction between indigenism and revivalism, whereby the latter stood for the indiscriminate turn to ancient or sacred symbols for instrumental or establishment ends. Revivalism's main offender, Kapur revealed in another issue of *Vrishchik*, was the recently appointed director of the National Gallery of Modern Art in Delhi, L. P. Sihare, whose reverence for modernism's Euro-American canon led to some controversial directions for the museum in the 1970s and 1980s.[27] For Kapur, Sihare's valorization of "Tantric abstraction," a contemporary painting movement in which esoteric Hindu and Buddhist imagery converged with trends in American postwar abstraction, amounted to an irresponsible revival of mystical symbols to sanctify Indian art in the international marketplace. Sihare, she complained, believes that a traditionally sacred symbol like the Hindu letter *om* can be "simply re-charged, like a battery," when it is fitted into a modern composition.[28]

If revivalism was a thoughtless and reactionary force, then indigenism, by contrast, involved "digging deep in the soil in which one is rooted in order to make it fertile again."[29] Although Kapur embraced the metaphor of roots in these early formulations, she did so to expose the false security of certain kinds of civilizational attachments and to trouble the idea of a complacent inheritance with tropes of stagnation, uprooting, and the necessity for more fertile ground. The argument was for a *discriminatory* relationship to cultural heritage and the past; the criteria for measurement was the extent to which the past could be reinvented to produce a critical relationship to the present and future. Accordingly, the contemporary artists that she turned to in the study— M.F. Husain, Bhupen Khakhar, and J. Swaminathan—were held up for their "conscious acknowledgement" of these dilemmas, rather than as "models or solutions" to what was, by definition, a continual quest. That Kapur would continue to return to the same artists in her writing over the next five decades, relentlessly reevaluating their innovations and impasses, affirming ingenuity and condemning complacency, seems to further confirm one essential truth about the thesis: that "there are no conclusions to such a study," just originality, uniqueness, ambiguity, and obsession.

Kapur's 1978 book, *Contemporary Indian Artists*, offered an expansion of her accounts of Husain, Khakhar, and Swaminathan and presented three additional chapters about painters in India "reckoning with reality"—namely, F.N. Souza, Ram Kumar, and Akbar Padamsee. This reckoning on the part of the artist involved an active struggle "with and against history," she stated, "the history that Indians will make out of the history that has been imposed upon them."[30] For Kapur, this process of recuperation was the opposite of a passive reception; it was a determined, creative, and energetic task that demanded intellectual vigilance. Her manifesto for the 1981 *Place for People* exhibition (an impassioned pitch for figuration in painting) captured the spirit of this effort; here Kapur dove deep into the ancient and medieval past to recuperate the human figure in the Indian imagination, "which has been smothered by romantic-expressionist sentiments."[31] The goal, she stated, was to recover "a *life-affirming classicism*," as if such a thing had previously only been a contradiction in terms.[32] Later in 1982, in her introduction to *Contemporary Indian Art*, a catalogue published on the occasion of the Festival of India exhibition in London, Kapur rejected the writer V.S. Naipaul's diagnoses of postcolonial India as a "wounded civilization." Although she considered him a "great writer," Kapur felt that Naipaul's thesis "was drawn from the idea of roots; a romantic idea" that led too easily to that of "disease, of a withering of the mind and will."[33] "Perhaps the thing to do," she countered, "is to stop the fuss and worry about the roots and to work overground for a bit."[34]

The rejection of a model of unbroken cultural roots and the determination to struggle aboveground at this moment anticipates some of the metaphors of labor and work that come to prevail in Kapur's theorization of modernism in her collected essays of 2000. There she famously declared that modernity, or in the case of art, modernism, "is my vocational concern and commitment. Even as it is hammered down as a vestige of the last century the stake in it has to be secured."[35] The subtle change in Kapur's vocabulary from "underground" to fully "overground," as it were, signals a move away from the lingering organicism of the thesis, which sought to pursue an authentic subjecthood even as it altered the terms of that quest, toward an increasingly antifoundationalist orientation based in the ongoing work of critical thought. It is an intellectual sensibility and relation to the past that gained theoretical force during the 1980s and 1990s through Kapur's expanded engagements with Marxist aesthetics and the emergent discourses of feminism and cultural studies.

In what follows, I examine the centrality of two key figures in particular within the Indian and British intelligentsia upon Kapur's formation during this period: the Indian painter, sculptor, and influential writer/teacher, K.G. Subramanyan, and the Welsh literary critic and Marxist theorist, Raymond Williams, respectively. The main site in which to trace this synergy, I suggest, is the *Journal of Arts and Ideas*, the lively periodical that Kapur and Sundaram helped launch in 1982, along with other leftist thinkers, activists, and artists in India, and which ran for almost twenty years. The journal's activities resulted in some thirty-three issues and signaled a substantive shift, as Kapur has stated, to "a sustained historical discourse on the conditions of art practice in the third world."[36] Today, the broad scope of topics and debates in this journal serve as a record of the intellectual energy directed toward the high-stakes terrain of culture in India during the economic and political transformations of the 1980s and 1990s. I turn now to the example of Kapur's essays concerned with the cinema of Bengali filmmaker Satyajit Ray, and the painting and sculpture of K.G. Subramanyan. These essays would later compose the core of *When Was Modernism* (2000), but many of their ideas were first published or subjected to rigorous discussion in the journal in the late 1980s and early 1990s. By comparing Kapur's critical engagements with the models of cultural inheritance represented by both Ray and Subramanyan, I point to some of the critic's own negotiations of inheritance at this juncture and reflect on some of the most emblematic essays of this period.

A Fraught Inheritance: The Nehruvian Imaginary

Kapur wrote two essays on the legendary cinema of Satyajit Ray (1921–92), an artist whose famed career drew unprecedented international acclaim and spawned a large literature during his lifetime, much of it hagiographic. Against this backdrop, one of her essays analyzed the treatment of myth and religion in Ray's films *Sant Tukaram* (1963) and *Devi* (1960); the second interrogated the "redemptive promise" of *Pather Panchali* (1955), the film that launched his career as a director.[37] In both texts, Kapur was concerned with Ray's status as India's "emblematic national artist in the decade after independence" and the limits and paradoxes of his progressive paradigm, defined by its lyrical beauty and secular humanism.[38] For Kapur, Ray came to most embody the challenge for cultural creativity in the euphoria of India's newfound liberation and the institutionalization of cultural policy that ensued under Jawaharlal Nehru, India's first prime minister.

Kapur's readings of Ray have been influential in the expanded interdisciplinary terrain of visual cultural studies in India, and especially in cinema studies, as Indian film scholar Moinak Biswas has acknowledged in his 2005 edited volume, *Apu and After: Re-visiting Ray's Cinema*.[39] In his introduction, Biswas described how Kapur's critique of Ray "opened up new modes of engagement with the films" for scholars of his generation, making it possible to be critical without necessarily being negative and to "go beyond aesthetic evaluation, to look at the historical convergence of the elements that form the aesthetic in question, to look into their cultural processing."[40] This kind of critical approach, he further observed, involves a "dispersal of the iconic work" and a subjecting of "the text to fragmentation and re-alignments, unpacking and re-assembling the elements" that lend unity to film.[41] Ultimately, Biswas argued that Kapur's interpretation challenged the "organic model of development" that underpins *Pather Panchali* and the broader bildungsroman of the Apu trilogy and made way for "the possibility of re-situating the films in their times, against a larger logic of inheritance."[42]

Kapur's essays on Satyajit Ray thus foreground the themes of reception, transmission, and inheritance in more ways than one, and they resonate with her earlier arguments against the complacency of "revivalism" and the problem of an unthinking connection to the past. In the first place, they offer highly nuanced formulations about how Ray, the midcentury artist poised against the aesthetic traditions of colonial Bengal—in Kapur's terms, the "aristocratic-folk paradigm"[43] of Tagore's Santiniketan—himself deals with the problem of cultural inheritance. For Kapur, the genius of Ray was the response he forged from within this historical situation, involving an expressed optimism in a common humanity. The problem with Ray was the limitations of this particular response, embedded in the ambiguous civilizational determinants of his films, and the latent links he sustained to "civilizational memory."[44] The simultaneously "evolving and devolving" framework of the Apu trilogy, Kapur argued, ultimately produced a "condition of hypostasis";[45] the "organic identity" of the rural boy as protagonist depicted in figures 3.1 through 3.3 was "posited against any kind of historical formation," and in the end the film "loses the future."[46]

If Kapur's account of *Devi* is somewhat more sympathetic, this is because Ray's anachronistic play with the period genre of popular mythological films could serve "the function of causing disjunction, of forcing upon us a double-take on our contemporary situation."[47] For Kapur, Ray's cinematic story about goddess worship in nineteenth-century rural Bengal was a "testimony against a dead order," and it remained something of a "protest against the empowering procedures of myth and religion."[48] Drawing on K.G. Subramanyan's concept of the "living tradition," defined as an active process of reinterpretation of the past that "must be perceived at the level of aesthetics proper," Kapur set out to understand in this essay how the "synchronic structure of a myth may be opened up" in the hands of an artist like Ray, how an "inherited iconography is transfigured and sometimes radicalized" and, just as crucially, how it is not.[49] Elsewhere she referred to the phenomenon of eclecticism, a hybridizing impulse based in "artistic nerve and wit" that could hypothetically lead to iconoclastic acts, a concept that Subramanyan had also elaborated in some detail.[50] In fact, many continuities with Subramanyan's thought become visible here: for example, the challenge of inheritance posed by a living tradition; the possibilities for eclecticism within the aesthetic field; the importance of ambiguity and the instability of signs (what Subramanyan called the "contingent multivalence" of art[51]); and the high degree of self-consciousness of interpretation itself—all these Subramanyan-esque values can be seen to inform Kapur's critical readings of Ray.

It is worth pausing for a moment on this scene of transmission—involving Geeta Kapur, K.G. Subramanyan, and Satyajit Ray—to observe the epochal reworking of modernism's past at a decisive moment in post-Nehruvian India. Subramanyan (born 1924) was after all a contemporary of Ray's and was, until his recent death in 2016, the most important remaining figure connected to the legacy of Santiniketan in Bengal.[52] He was born in Kerala only three years after the filmmaker

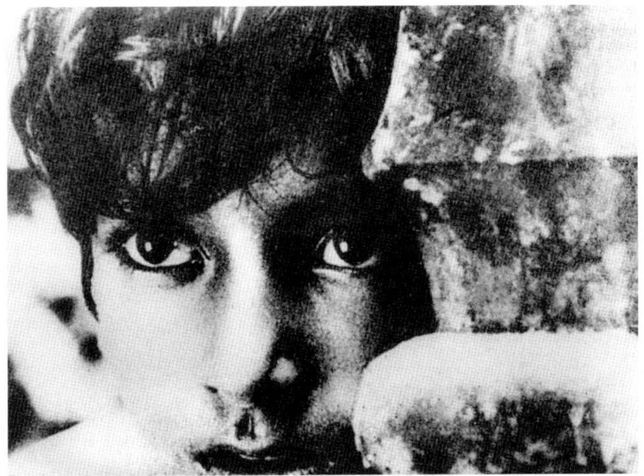

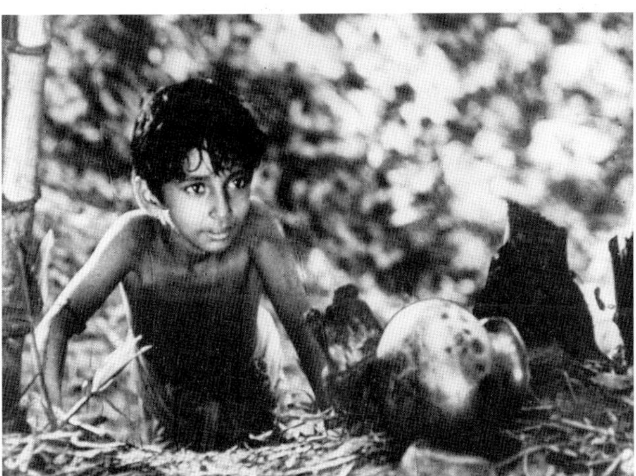

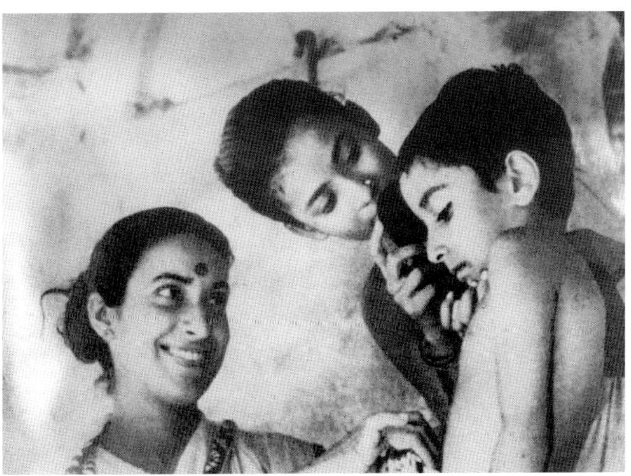

FIGURES 3.1–3.3 Apu, the young boy protagonist. *Pather Panchali*, 1955. Film stills from 115-minute black-and-white film. Directed by Satyajit Ray.

and came of age as a Gandhian student activist, imprisoned in the early 1940s for his participation in the Quit India movement. He arrived in Santiniketan in 1944, where he studied art under the tutelage of such modernist pioneers as Nandalal Bose, Benode Behari Mukherjee, and Ramkinkar Baij, before taking a position in 1951 at the newly established art school in Baroda. A transitional, dynamic, and modernizing figure, Subramanyan (his career and life story) belongs in some sense to a "long" twentieth century on the subcontinent, in contrast to the idea of a "short century" framework proposed for African modernism by Okwui Enwezor, intended to foreground the aesthetics of decolonization.[53]

Although K.G. Subramanyan predates Fanon's call in the 1960s to artists and intellectuals to become "authentic and self-aware," he stands as an exemplary embodiment in the Indian case of the consciousness Fanon assigned to the "native intellectual." For Fanon, the first line of difficulty and responsibility of the native intellectual was to reject the national culture born from "civilizational discourse," the unconditional affirmation of native culture in response to the dehumanizing effects of colonialism, a direction he called "a blind alley."[54] Instead, the goal of creative work was to articulate "a new reality in action" and to turn oneself into "an awakener of the people."[55]

Subramanyan's multifaceted career as an artist, writer, and educator of great consequence was similarly given to the search for a new national imaginary born out of the decolonizing projects of the postwar era. One of his abiding concerns was the problem of cultural inheritance for the modern artist in the absence of a stable, hereditary transfer of skill and ideas. His notion of the "living tradition," as something mutable that demanded revision and reassessment with each generation, was aimed against the "mechanical relay of thought and action"[56] and the production of stereotypes that passed from one generation to the next. Subramanyan argued instead for a constant reinterpretation of concepts and questions and a renewal of language (both visual and verbal) to respond to the needs of the time.

It is not surprising, then, to see Subramanyan's influence on Kapur in her critique of the ambiguous organic and civilizational devices in Ray's modernist-realist cinema. It is also interesting to observe Kapur's own negotiations of inheritance at this juncture, based in her open admiration of the creative work of both these illustrious midcentury predecessors. Kapur "forges her approach to these and other questions with care," observed her key interlocutor, collaborator, and co-curator, Ashish Rajadhyaksha, in the pages of the *Journal of Arts and Ideas* at the time.[57] For Rajadhyaksha, Kapur's subtle gestures of homage to her mentor, Subramanyan, revealed "a strategy in operation," one that also permitted her "retroactively to lay her own distance from some very tense confrontations."[58] Although Subramanyan came through the same "grand portals" of Bengal/Santiniketan as Ray, Kapur argued that the former's "irreverence," sharp wit, and sense of play enabled a continuous transformation of the cultural hierarchies at the heart of this tradition, to produce a modernism at odds with that of the filmmaker.[59] For Kapur, Subramanyan's formal experiments in painting, toy-making, mural-making, and sculpting from the 1950s to the 1980s (see figures 3.4, 3.5, and 3.6), drawn from a variety of sources—Santiniketan, Gandhi, Picasso, Dada, and pop—shows how the hierarchical chain of an aesthetic tradition "can be playfully interlinked and continually transformed."[60] His work puts modernism in the balance, she argued, and given how much of his work is based in parody, "he may also be putting in the balance his unease at adopting western modernism" at all.[61]

Subramanyan is thus the midcentury figure that best embodies the highly mediated, ambivalent, and paradoxical story of Indian modernism that takes shape in Kapur's 2000 book. It is telling that her essay on Subramanyan, "Mid-Century Ironies," self-described as "an interpretive prose-piece with a premium on lucidity," was the longest chapter of *When Was Modernism*.[62] In it, she emphasized the artist's "mastery" and "virtuosity," adopting a language of aesthetic accomplishment seldom present in Kapur. Hence the addition of a short epilogue confronting Subramanyan's more disturbing and misogynistic paintings of the 1990s, as she stated, "to give the sanguine story of the revered Subramanyan an edge."[63] Elsewhere, in the final essay of the book, "Dismantled Norms," Kapur appropriated Subramanyan's own vocabulary of "forms and norms"; the latter, for him, was the "route-map of the experience."[64] If Kapur's goal by the end of the volume was to "dismantle" these norms, to take even Subramanyan's route-map apart, I suggest it was less the iconoclastic act of dispersal involved in her critique of Ray and more a means of receiving, disrupting, and diversifying a truly indispensable intellectual debt.

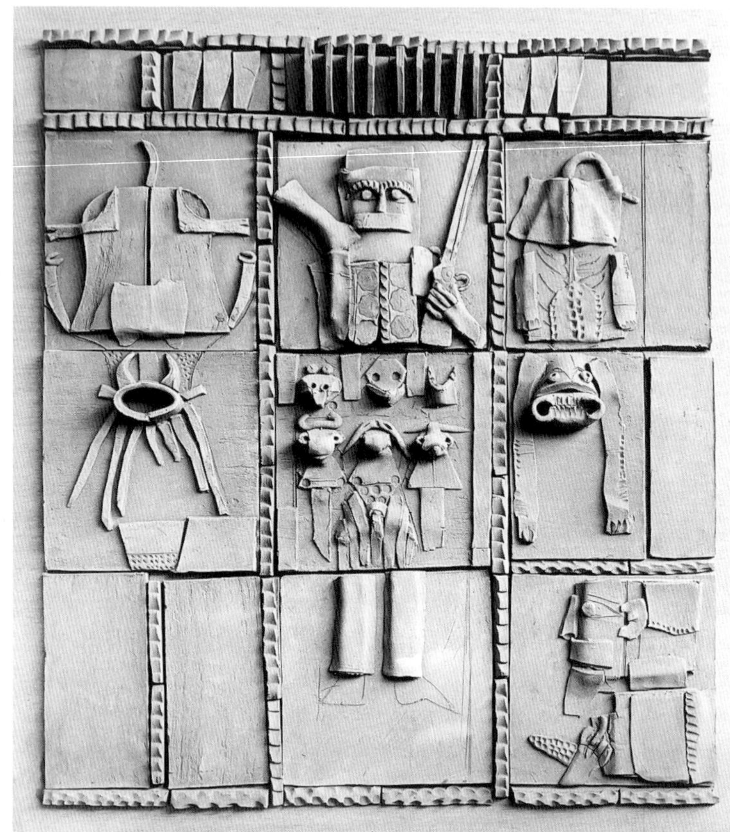

FIGURE 3.4
K.G. Subramanyan, *Hunter and Trophy*, 1970. Terra-cotta relief. Courtesy of Seagull Foundation for the Arts. © Uma Padmanabhan.

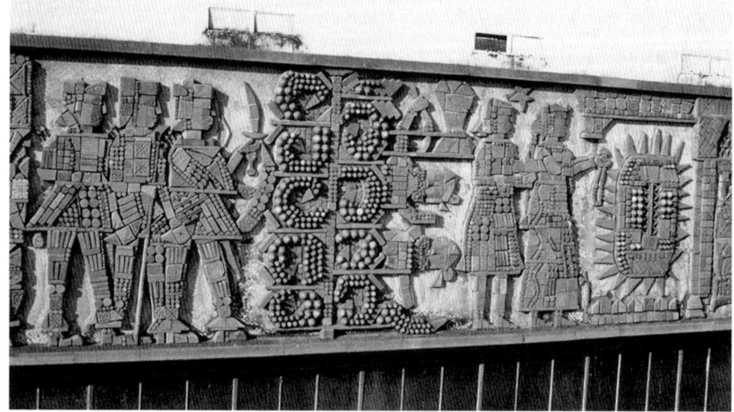

FIGURE 3.5
K.G. Subramanyan, *King of the Dark Chamber* (detail), 1963. Public mural in glazed terra-cotta, Rabindralaya, Lucknow. Courtesy of Asia Art Archive and photographer Jyoti Bhatt.

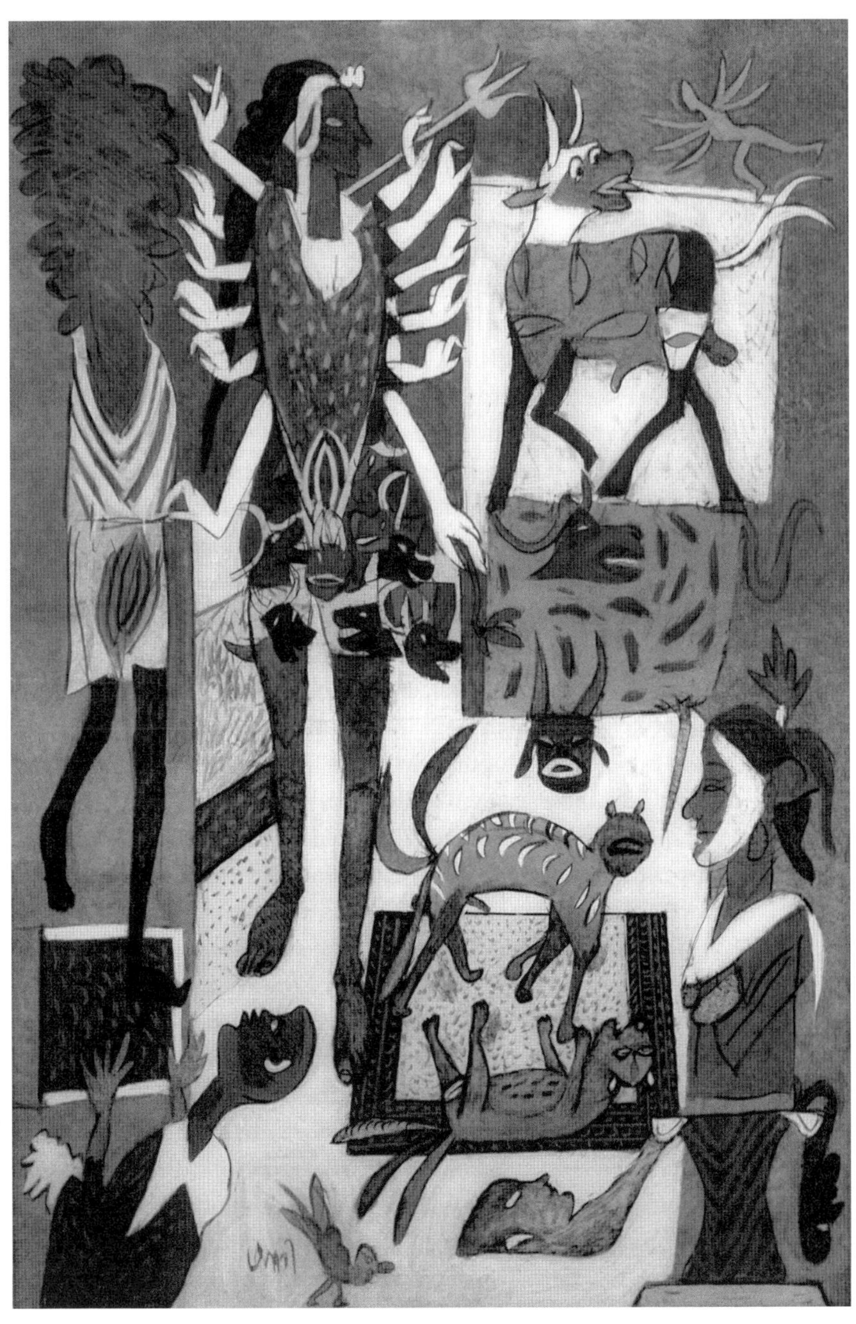

FIGURE 3.6 K.G. Subramanyan, *Ageless Combat I*, 1998. Reverse painting on acrylic. Courtesy of Seagull Foundation for the Arts. © Uma Padmanabhan.

Kapur and Method: Writing and Form

Is it possible to attribute to our critic a distinct "method" or "style"? On one hand, the very idea of a method, which presumes something coherent, linear, or systematic, is not easily connected to Kapur. On the other hand, her texts are extremely rigorous and display certain consistent procedures of thought and analysis that can acquire shape as purposeful patterns. Yet her writing can be difficult for students, who often struggle to decipher the density of her prose and her carefully calibrated, polemical flourishes. To my mind, Kapur's texts contain what Said called "a will to eccentricity," which he viewed as a "major project of contemporary critical discourse."[65] This is the phenomenon of writing *as displacing*, of texts as deviations and departures from the norm, whereby modes of expression—excess, exaggeration, and rupture—are put purposefully to the task of unsettling normative frames. The result is not an accumulative or additive project that anchors and legitimates, or that is readily available for quick consumption. Kapur's is not a user-friendly art history, in this sense, one that lends itself to programmatic functions or that can be easily integrated into dominant frameworks. Instead, Kapur's counter-methodology involves the staging of narrative *through* dissonance and disruption, which goes against the comfort of certainty and consensus and resists its own assimilation toward instrumentalist ends. It is a practice of writing that involves "unfitting itself," in Irit Rogoff's terms, which means it seeks to "unravel the very ground on which it stands."[66] For Rogoff, this is no less than the work of critical theory and a criteria that distinguishes the most radical forms of thought.

Kapur's reliance on the formal tool of the essay is instructive in this regard. Although she is the author of more than one book, few would deny that our critic is primarily an essayist. Her major work, *When Was Modernism*, is a compilation of "essays on contemporary cultural practice," and her 1978 book, *Contemporary Indian Artists*, consists of six chapters, each of them an essay about an individual artist. The essay, as Theodor Adorno reminded in his 1958 thesis "The Essay as Form," does not amount to something less than a book.[67] In fact, the perceived weaknesses of the essay format—that it is short, fragmentary, and partial—are actually its strengths. For Adorno, the essay was the form of writing that most resisted the atrophy of thought into sweeping statements and eternal truths: the essay *interprets* rather than unquestion-

ingly accepts; it dives into a matter where it needs to without pretending to be exhaustive; it is spirited, expressive, playful, "methodically
unmethodical."[68] The essay abandons, Adorno stated, "the main road
to the origins,"[69] and takes up instead other itineraries, different kinds
of knowledge journeys that are transacted not through a stable edifice
but through a "mosaic-like relation to other essays."[70] The essay is, in
short, the "critical form *par excellence*,"[71] more dynamic and intensely reflexive than the hermetic systems of deductive reasoning that Adorno
so detested in traditional philosophical thought.

Kapur's skeptical, investigative art history of the subcontinent has
been almost exclusively fashioned through the device of the essay, and
the form remains at the heart of her signature style. This contrasts
sharply with the case of another seminal intellectual figure in South
Asian art history, Partha Mitter. The latter, who received his doctorate
in London under the supervision of the Viennese art historian Ernst
Gombrich, shares with Kapur the distinction of pioneering new narratives for Indian modernism based in colonial and postcolonial methodologies, and these narratives proved to have broad comparative significance for the non-Western world. His four major books, valued for their
erudition and concise prose, represent the most comprehensive disciplinary account of the formation of ideas, institutions, and artists in
India over the past two centuries. The earliest of these, *Much Maligned
Monsters: A History of European Reactions to Indian Art* (1977), excavated the
colonial history of aesthetic perceptions of India for the first time in a
systemic manner and became a defining contribution to the nascent
field. Another, an introductory survey of Indian art from ancient to contemporary, sought a revisionist account of the canon; two other monographs concerned with modernism were conceptualized in chronological sequence, part of a projected trilogy, spanning "1850–1922" and
"1922–1947," as indicated by their titles.[72]

Mitter's contribution has been, in other words, "monumental," as
the preeminent historian Ranajit Guha has noted.[73] His turn to Europe's
intellectual traditions to fashion chronology, canon, and foundational
ground for modern Indian art history through the narrative form of sequential (or at least successive) book projects is no small achievement.
He has acknowledged, in particular, his indebtedness to the intellectual
paradigms associated with his former teacher, Gombrich, who helped
advance "the discipline of *Kunstwissenschaft*, the scientific study of art,"
a legacy that included such luminaries of central European thought as

Heinrich Wölfflin, Alois Riegl, and Erwin Panofsky.[74] It is meaningful that Mitter's association with Gombrich lasted some forty years, from 1965 until the latter's death in 2001. In a recent tribute to his mentor, Mitter explained how the conceptual framework for *Much Maligned Monsters* was shaped by Gombrich's "notion of schema and correction and the formation of stereotypes," and stated that Gombrich's "contribution to cultural theory" had been regrettably under-recognized.[75]

It is hard to imagine two more *dissimilar* approaches to the history of art—formally, methodologically, epistemologically—than those represented by Mitter and Kapur. Standing at odds with the philosophical tradition invested in the "scientific study of art," with its grand theories, universalizing arguments, and emphasis on artistic achievement in Europe in the tradition of Gombrich, Kapur's investments in history are instead tethered to the practices of contemporary art; her historiography has acquired its shape through the partial, inquisitive short form of the essay; her prose is characterized by disruption and repetition; her writing refuses linear chronology and announces its discomfort with the forms of closure that come with the consolidation of the canon. If Mitter's art history of modern India follows a coherent chronology and is presented through the rationality of a proposed sequence of books, then Kapur's by contrast is antichronological and delivered through the kaleidoscope of the essay's "mosaic-like" effects. Ajay Sinha, in his response to an essay by Mitter titled "Decentering Modernism," has also observed the enormous gulf that separates these two major intellectual figures. Drawing a contrast between Kapur's "historical materialist view" and Mitter's "idealist perspective," Sinha argued that Kapur's investments in feminism, her emphasis on the "plurality of beginnings," and her "performative acknowledgement of her own 'representational dilemmas'" (the phrase is from the title of one of her essays) provides a more critical and self-reflexive project for Indian modernism than Mitter's comparatively conservative provocation in the essay.[76]

Interestingly, the ambiguous legacy of Ernst Gombrich for the project of modernism in the postwar period has itself come under significant reassessment. The celebrated art historian's public lectures at the Slade School during the mid-1950s were attended by a range of international artists who sought a training in postwar London, such as K.G. Subramanyan, Anwar Shemza, and Ibrahim El-Salahi from India, Pakistan, and Sudan, respectively. For Subramanyan, for instance, Gombrich's *Story of Art* represented the most inclusive framework available at the time for approaching visual traditions outside the Western canon, and he included its insights in the introductory world art history course that he taught in Baroda from 1959 through the 1970s.[77] There, the story of art "became stories," in the words of artist Nilima Sheikh, as the Eurocentric narrative of Gombrich's wide-angled approach was subjected to an open-ended questioning by students, leading to more kaleidoscopic and polymorphic configurations.[78] However, Gombrich's dismissal of Islamic art as a merely "functional" aside in the story of art led to dilemmas of identity, even existential crises, for El-Salahi and Shemza—the latter in particular—as they struggled to negotiate their Muslim subjectivities in the unfolding frameworks of diaspora and the Cold War era, as Iftikhar Dadi has carefully shown.[79] At the very least, Gombrich's ideas have been received inconsistently and in a variety of conflicting ways, damaging for some subjectivities positioned precariously on the margins, while enabling for others, who pushed them in the direction of alternative results. For our purposes, it is also relevant to observe how a certain aspect of the inheritance from a previous generation, in this case, the foundationalist philosophical tradition represented by Gombrich, became interpolated in a variety of ways: at times dismissed and rejected, at other times reworked and plugged into new knowledge fields. I turn now to argue for the relevance of a very different intellectual figure in postwar Britain—the Welsh "New Left" literary critic Raymond Williams—for understanding Kapur's major contribution, *When Was Modernism*, published in 2000.

When Was Modernism: The Relay with Raymond

I prefer to approach *When Was Modernism* as a "worldly" text in the Saidian sense, not a lofty vehicle of timeless truths but a text whose meaning, potency, and importance emerge from the social and historical world in which it was embedded. That world was India in the late 1980s and 1990s, a period of massive upheaval in the country as liberalization and economic reforms led to a transformation of the social landscape, an escalation of religious conservativism, the rise of Hindu nationalism in politics, and an eruption of violence in the public sphere, often against women, minorities, and marginalized caste groups. These tumultuous developments brought the "idea of India" itself into new and urgent questioning as the values that ushered the young nation into existence—secularism, democracy, pluralism—seemed themselves to be at stake.[80] Kapur's book emerged in and through this environment and sought an approach, as she stated, that resisted at the end of the century "the temptation to succumb to a cathartic depoliticization of the narrative."[81] The goal, she explained, was to "make a sequential argument about the place of the *modern* in contemporary cultural practice in India and in the third world, to set up an ideological vantage point to view modernism along its multiple tracks."[82] Her substantive last section in particular, "Frames of Reference," attempted "theoretical exegeses" on the dizzying dialectics of contemporary visual art and thrust these essays into "mosaic-like" relations with other chapters concerned with individual artists, past and present.[83] "Throughout the book," Kapur explained further, "I try to tackle the contestatory nature of Indian modernity, pulling the concept away from its conservative version where it is seen as emerging from a respectable lineage that becomes by some ideological miracle the bearer of civilizational values."[84]

If the drive to "pull the concept away" from its conservative appropriations based in the discourses of civilizational belonging was consistent with themes in Kapur's earlier work, other aspects of the book appeared less familiar and generated more destabilizing effects. Indeed, the overall result was less a history of modernism in India than it was an archaeology of aesthetic modernity in South Asia. Resolutely antichronological and self-consciously antiteleological, Kapur's collection of essays offered "a theory of modernism at the stage of its exhaustion," to borrow Andreas Huyssen's characterization of the broader moment of theoretical transformation in cultural analysis at this time.[85] Huyssen was referring to the way in which theory, and French poststructuralism in particular, enabled a reading of modernism that differed substantially from those offered by earlier writers like Clement Greenberg, Franz Kafka, or even Theodor Adorno, "the modernism of the closed and finished work."[86] Suddenly, what became possible through the new landscape of theory was a story of modernism involving playful transgression; a story that could be undercut through the unlimited weaving of textuality; a modernism confident in its rejection of "the subject, of history, and of the subject of history"; a modernism whose lacks, absences, deferrals, and anachronisms could lead not to anxiety but to a transformative engagement with the aesthetic realm.[87] *When Was Modernism* both captured and reflected this radical spirit within thought practice itself. And the agility of the undertaking becomes most apparent, I suggest, by turning to the underexamined place of Raymond Williams in the text.

In many ways the figure of Williams was an unlikely beacon for the journey represented in Kapur's collection of essays. She never met the Welsh literary critic and founding father of cultural studies in Britain when she was in London in the late 1960s, pursuing her MA in criticism at the Royal College of Art. Nor did she include Williams's influential early works, *Culture and Society* (1958) and *The Long Revolution* (1961), in the frameworks of the thesis, in spite of a general sympathy toward the "New Left" discussions. This could perhaps be attributed to the still persistent separation between literature and literary criticism, on one hand, and other fields of cultural analysis on the other, a boundary that Williams's intellectual career would scrupulously and irreversibly dissolve. If there is agreement on this, the broader terrain of Williams's legacy remains a more ambiguous one, subjected to much debate during his lifetime and especially since his death in 1988. The Jamaican-born theorist Stuart Hall, for example, who arrived in Britain in the 1950s and cofounded with Williams the *New Left Review* before joining his Birmingham Centre for Contemporary Cultural Studies, stated that he was "the most formative intellectual influence on my life," while also noting that the issue of race was at the center of their most contentious disagreements.[88] Similarly, feminists have pointed to the total absence of women and gender in Williams's work, while acknowledging the inescapable value of his cultural materialist perspective for feminist critique.[89]

In relation to India, the literary scholar Gauri Viswanathan has argued that Williams's relation to colonial discourse, and his tendency to conflate "national" and "imperial" culture in particular, was particularly reprehensible.[90] For Viswanathan, Williams's relative silence about imperialism is "less a theoretical oversight or blindness than an internal restraint that has complex methodological and historical origins" and is symptomatic of the British Left's larger insensitivity toward imperial history.[91] Nonetheless, Williams's conception of the relationship between aesthetic artifact and historical formation as a horizon of both possibilities and limits, in his terms, as a nexus of the residual, the dominant, and the emergent, proved to be a significant framework for Kapur. Similarly, his privileging of the role of art in the latter half of his career and his tight vision of the relationship between the aesthetic and the social—"he literally taught many of us how to think about culture and politics together," according to a former student—established a critical orientation for Kapur's own narrativization of modernism within a colonial and postcolonial frame.[92] Still, she was drawn more to the subjectivist impulse of Williams's concept "structures of feeling," and the broad cultural materialist approach of his "base-superstructure" revision to Marxist theory, than to his later arguments about popular culture, mass media, and television. Although several of Kapur's essays will also address the uses of technology and the new digital landscape of what she calls "post-celluloid media," her attention to avant-garde appropriations in contemporary art stands at some distance from Williams's later preoccupation with television as an everyday mass-cultural form.

In hindsight, one could not have predicted Kapur's selection of the title of her book, *When Was Modernism*, which was the title of an essay by Raymond Williams of the same name, a move she described as "taking the cue" from Williams.[93] In a gesture of semantic relay, a passing of language and logic from one location to the next, Kapur began her title chapter with an epigraph of the final sentences of one of Williams's last public lectures at the University of Bristol in 1987. In it, Williams posed the question "When was modernism?" to initiate a historical and theoretical questioning of what he saw as a "highly selected version of the modern," one that functioned "to appropriate the whole of modernity."[94] He was referring to the dominant account that had been consolidated in the postwar era, a "selective appropriation" whose "open ideologizing permits the selection"—the kind of narrative, he warned, that "stops history dead."[95] The necessity of challenging the dominant account is thus the first of several important themes that animate and give critical force to Kapur's revisionist project.

The second is the problem of innovation stiffening into convention. For Williams the example was the historical moment at which the manifesto (for the surrealists, cubists, futurists, and constructivists) became the "badge of self-conscious and self-advertising schools."[96] The turning of freshness into fixity and conformity, like the hardening of arteries that once pumped young blood, was similarly crucial for Kapur, who argued strongly "against conformism," citing Walter Benjamin's call for every era to struggle anew against its overpowering effects.[97] Later, it informed her account of the trajectory of India's "irreversibly iconic" twentieth-century painter M.F. Husain, who, as she observed, "long ago buried that precious gift of doubt, uncertainty and flux that he grasped in [the painting] *Man* way back, at the very beginning of his artistic journey."[98] This concern with the pressure of convention and conformity is apparent, more broadly, in Kapur's ongoing reluctance to solidify a canon in the field of modern and contemporary South Asian art. Rejecting a more conventional or didactic narrative, Kapur instead presented that haunting rhetorical question "When was modernism in Indian art?" in a manner that repeated Williams's ambivalence about constructing new edifices with solid foundations. The "when," she reminded, if somewhat obliquely, "is a site of vexed doubling within colonial/postcolonial identity and the permanent ambivalences that it launches."[99]

A third theme is apparent in Williams's interest in the "restlessly mobile émigré or exile," a figure whose "endless border crossings" produced an experience of "visual and linguistic strangeness" that could not be seen or grasped in a unified way.[100] For Williams, "modernism thus defined *divides* politically and simply."[101] For Kapur, too, modernism existed as disjuncture, inequality, discrepancy, and difference, as Indian artists crisscrossing the mainstream resulting in both belonging and estrangement, at times productively, and in ways that could not be grasped through universal or systematic formulations. And finally, if Williams argued for a theory and historiography that connected meaningfully to the present and future, this was necessarily based in the recovery of an alternative tradition, to be found in the "neglected works in the wide margins of the century."[102] Kapur seized upon such a quest and expanded those margins to their widest possible global reach, undoubtedly farther than Williams, whose theorizing never left the Anglo-European context, could ever have imagined. Her book addressed, as she stated, the "hitherto unlogged initiatives"[103] that had yet to be articulated in a third world society such as India in the service of its utopian future. Thus, where Viswanathan had focused on the limits of Williams's imaginary in relation to India's colonial story, Kapur had enacted a productive relay with his post-Marxist vision for aesthetics, one that creatively marked the baton pass itself, to activate an alternative social and historical inquiry with far-reaching (and still unfolding) effects.

Indeterminacy, Revision, Navigation, and Return

Kapur's extensive output as a writer in the nearly two decades since the publication of *When Was Modernism* has taken many forms—scholarly essays in journals and anthologies, exhibition books and catalogue entries, contributions to art magazines, and personal interviews—which have appeared in a variety of locations and formats in India, Europe, Britain, and North America. It is a dynamic body of ongoing work that resists containment or summation, at times rejecting the terms and suppositions of its own inclusion and refusing predetermined (or overdetermined) results. More often than not, Kapur pushes back, for example, against the pressure to "represent" such categories as India, the third world, or the "global south" to uninformed metropolitan audiences in a way that inscribes dissension into critical discourse as a positive and constructive value. Since 2000, this corpus has included writing that emerges from or reflects upon curating; that engages with the careers of individual artists, past and present; and that offers broad theoretical responses to the conditions of intensification and acceleration for critical art practice in the twenty-first century.

In two widely cited essays from 2007 and 2009, for example, respectively titled "Secular Artist, Citizen Artist" and "A Cultural Conjuncture in India," Kapur constructed an intricate picture of the changing coordinates of citizenship, political economy, and democratic culture on the subcontinent and returned her readers to the perennial problem of art's relationship to these conditions. Drawing from earlier models of artistic radicalism in India from the 1930s and 1940s, like the Progressive Writers' Association (PWA) and the Indian Peoples' Theatre Association (IPTA), while critically evaluating more recent efforts, like the seminal engagements since 1989 of the antisectarian SAHMAT Collective and the explosion of radical forms of experimental documentary, video, and new media, Kapur has argued in these essays for critical discourse "to inscribe the artwork within the public sphere" to continue to activate both meaning and effect.[104]

These and other efforts continue to search for understandings of the subject, self, and society, along with their implications for the aesthetic, within the "expanding realms of indeterminacy" brought on by the age of neoliberal capital and the digital era.[105] It is telling that Kapur's vocabulary for this task has shifted away from metaphors of work and labor—and any residual effects of an organic model presented by the trope of a fertile ground—and toward a language of direction and navigation, in particular, toward the symbol of the oscillating compass.[106] In "A Cultural Conjuncture," for example, Kapur constructed a fictional compass to map a spherical diagram that pointed to priorities within the aesthetic field. Here, the critic's tool speaks to a redefinition of the critical task: a compass is an orientation device, one that requires a level hand but that is subject to forces of disequilibrium and that can shift with the smallest collision or turn. "My diagram proposes," Kapur stated with acute self-awareness, "in a cunning fit that serves, let me admit, my own purposes—that radical elements are now to be drawn from all round the circumference of the sphere: as much from within the 'classic' binaries of high and low, genre and avant-garde, as from the conceptual, the mediatic, the documentary, and the 'mythological.'"[107] Notably, Kapur's goal in adopting the device of the compass, an archaic tool used by mariners and explorers that seems increasingly threatened by the GPS systems of the digital age, is not to "fix" the direction of radical art but to find one's bearings and coordinates in the world—to "reiterate the significance of establishing, and then blurring, mediums and art historical categories."[108]

While these essays demonstrate a certain agility in their responses to relentless and ongoing change, Kapur's substantive essays on individual artists provide a more important lens through which to observe the full force of her critical consciousness at work. Although this may seem counterintuitive, it is partly because the latter texts in one way or another contend with the posthumous and increasingly global reception of major Indian cultural figures, including Bhupen Khakhar, M.F. Husain, Nasreen Mohamedi, and Mulk Raj Anand. As such, they reveal the nature of Kapur's responses to the expansion of the international discourse in which Indian art has been produced and received, and the changing frameworks of art historical knowledge itself. Her account of Mulk Raj Anand, for example, is determinedly anti-nostalgic, even as it traces the immense contribution of this icon of the Nehruvian era and vanguard member of the leftist intelligentsia across many branches of culture, including literature, architecture, painting, museology, photography, and the discourses of art.[109] Not surprisingly, Kapur's deep appreciation of Anand is met with a tinge of disappointment that in the end "he entirely gave himself over to the genre of the autobiographi-

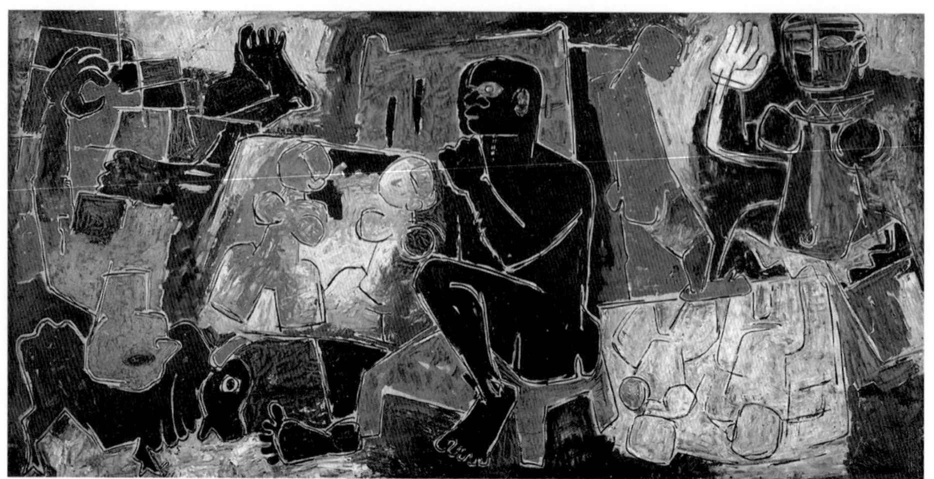

cal memoir, the memoir as a masquerade," in this case, a text of lesser intellectual demands and a "zone of vivid amnesia" in relation to Indian modernism.[110]

Kapur's numerous essays on the "irreversibly iconic" painter, M.F. Husain, which span a period of more than four decades, are similarly uncompromising.[111] In these texts that begin in the late 1960s and extend up to 2011, the year of the artist's death at the age of ninety-six, we witness the virtuosity of the critic as she repeatedly engages with the virtuosity of the painter, India's most iconic modern artist, whom she has justly described as both "patriarchal and picturesque."[112] For Kapur, Husain's cunning reworking of civilizational archetypes and buoyant sense of cultural plenitude most singularly embody "the originary drama of a people becoming a nation," evidenced in such unsurpassed paintings as *Man* (c. 1950) represented in figure 3.7, *Zameen* (1955), and *Between the Spider and the Lamp* (1956).[113] At the same time, the artist's increasingly loose brushwork and indiscriminate kaleidoscopic forms result in a fundamental "dispersal of his talent and energy" from the late 1950s on.[114] The great ambiguities and contradictions of Husain thus present the highest challenges of thought for the critic, and it is this figure that commands, more than any other artist, some of Kapur's most dialectical formulations: Husain is simultaneously ingenious, spontaneous, generous, and true, but also haphazard, inconsistent, and strangely detached; his forms are full of grace and agility, but also frequently stylized to the point of cliché; his talent comes with unself-conscious ease, but he is equally susceptible to haste and flamboyance; his good-willed populism and celebrity status are endearing, but his chronic capitulation to the commercial elite reveal the limits of indigenism as a productive endeavor.

Kapur's final 2011 essay on Husain, described by the editor of the volume in which it appeared as "wide-ranging and profoundly moving," displays a magisterial culmination of these dialectical operations sustained and intensified by four decades of engagement.[115] Here, Kapur privileges the motif of exile, the painful stage for Husain's final years in Dubai, Doha, and London, and expresses her sense of solidarity with the Muslim artist, the subject of relentless politicized attacks since the mid 1990s by Hindutva ideologues and India's growing right-wing middle class. The conditions surrounding Husain's exile, Kapur writes, are both "a personal tragedy and a national shame … he looms against the conscience of this nation with the grandeur of a Shakespearean ghost."[116] Revisiting the monumental mural-like painting, *Man* (1950), once again, Kapur this time proposes a boldly anachronist reading. The painting allegorizes, she observes intently, "a theme more epic than any of his other works dealing demonstrably with epics and myths, civilization and history. It offers from within the very paradigm of what I call modernist myths, the paradox of Husain's upturned life."[117] It is worth noting here that Kapur's reconsideration facilitated by the framework of exile does more than merely "update" the story; it provides the means by which the critic continues to actively engage with the underlying premises of a given cultural endeavor.

What defines the mastery of these essays is a certain logic of reassessment, revision, and reiteration and an awareness of the inexhaustibility of the subject matter itself. Like Monet's approach to the Rouen Cathedral, Kapur returns in these essays to the same subject again and again, not to claim the final word but to present a new view that has changed under altered conditions of atmosphere and light. "Again a Difficult Task Begins" is thus the resonant title of her last essay on Nasreen Mohamedi, which, along with her multiple texts on Husain and Khakhar (both included in her 1969 MA thesis, it is worth recalling), best embodies this reiterative mode. It is Kapur's fourth effort to interpret the work of this artist, her friend, whose tragic loss to a debilitating neuromuscular disease in 1990 set the tone for the first account, "Elegy for an Unclaimed Beloved" — undoubtedly Kapur's most heartfelt and empathetic piece of writing.

Twenty-five years later, Kapur undertook an expanded survey of Mohamedi's "liminally spiritual, plainly secular," highly concentrated, minimalist practice, in part by explicating the different methods of drawing—incision, inscription, encryption, *ecriture*—crucial to understanding both her life and her work.[118] Abiding by the artist's own delicately rendered horizontal lifts, visible in the example in figure 3.8, Kapur seeks a way in this text to "tilt Nasreen's philosophic inclinations towards transcendence" and to "alter the tragic register" of her own earlier writing, imbued as it was with the immediacy of loss. Elsewhere in the essay the critic's self-described "difficult task" involves rearticulating Mohamedi's "non-relationship" to the language of minimalist formalism in its North American milieu, while "looping" her into new questions raised by the emergent discourses of the global canon.[119]

Although art historian Emilia Terracciano has suggested that the slight differences that occur in Kapur's repeated literary interventions vis-à-vis Mohamedi invoke the "fraught challenge of completing her modernist project" and "disallows other possibilities," like the artist's nomadic status and her relation to the trauma of Partition, I argue—on the contrary—that there is no such investment in closure or act of completion at stake here. Rather, Kapur's elliptical returns and recursive loops are given to the expansion and proliferation of possibilities; these are critical inscriptions that favor multiplicity. They do not foreclose upon interpretation but instead open up a space of creativity and passion that, in fact, abides by the sense of transcendence and limitlessness of Mohamedi's own meticulous art practice. To my mind, this essay demonstrates something of the accomplishment that Roland Barthes described as a "will to bliss": that which goes beyond the experience of pleasure in a text, whereby language overflows in a way that "exceeds demand, transcends prattle," breaks through "the constraint of adjectives," and brings into crisis the author's relation to the intractable limits of language itself.[120]

(In)conclusion: Reading Geeta Kapur

Positioning the name Geeta Kapur as my point of departure, this chapter has aimed to articulate not merely the identity but the critical investments and distinctive modes of thought that have characterized our critic's hybrid practice of art history-theory-criticism over time.

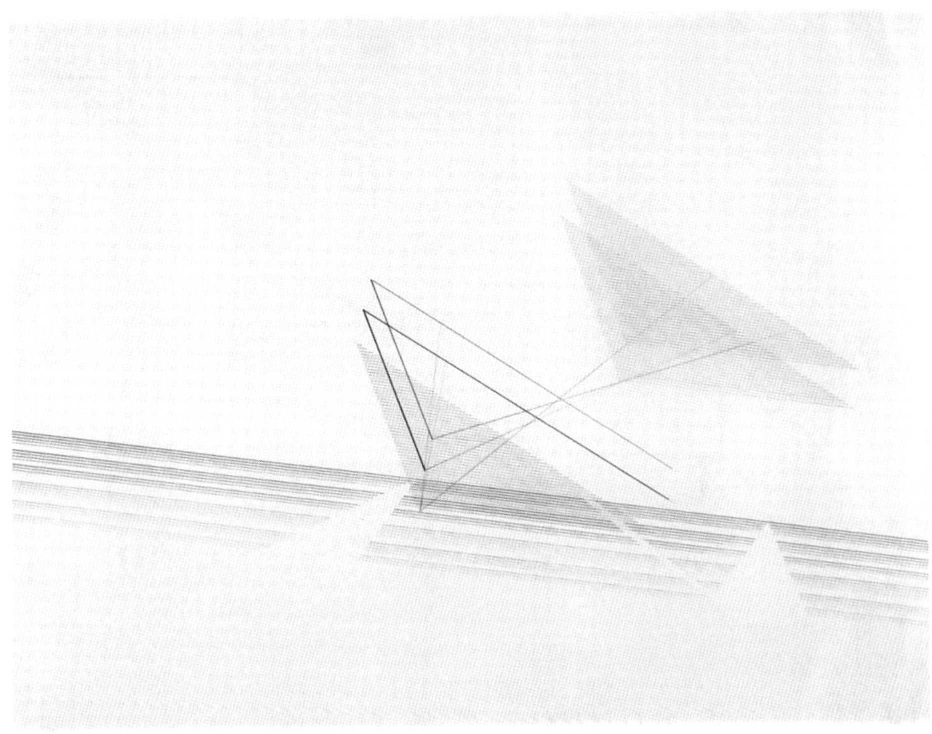

Her texts, which span an almost fifty-year period, themselves represent a vast field of entanglements and connections—between past, present, and future and between individuals, art, and ideas—that defy the logic of a chronological scheme or the certainty of an accumulation of concepts and facts. Instead, her essays, following Adorno's scrupulous observations on the essay as a critical form, take up countless itineraries that "interweave as in a carpet" and gain their texture and significance from the dense interrelational field they construct.[121] I have followed but a few of these "itineraries" by interpreting several exemplary texts, including Kapur's 1969 MA thesis, her research on contemporary Indian painters during the 1970s and early 1980s, her escalating theoretical contributions to the *Journal of Arts and Ideas* during the 1980s and 1990s (culminating in her book *When Was Modernism*), and the proliferating and multidimensional scholarship that has followed in the twenty-first century.

Kapur's uneven writing practice is characterized by that which Said once described as a "differentiated lucidity," a positive and productive aspect of critical discourse given to ambiguity, heterogeneity, and a multiplicity of views.[122] The result is an antifoundationalist practice, one that sustains tensions and incommensurabilities and produces complexity, uncertainty, and destabilizing effects. By "antifoundational," I am not suggesting that Kapur's art history of the twentieth century somehow lacks solidity or attention to detail or that it has no basis in historical fact. On the contrary, Kapur's writing stakes itself resolutely on the terra firma of grounded realities and empirical inequalities and *against* the metahistorical deployment of universal abstractions, at the same time as it actively interrogates the underlying assumptions of a given aesthetic act. This type of perpetual upturning of presuppositions, with its heightened awareness of the limits of thought and suspicion of established conventions of all kinds, is a mainstay of the tradition of "critique," not to be confused with the finding of faults or, in Foucault's terms, the "little polemical activities" of passing judgment on a thing.[123] By critique I mean a more generalized practice that often stands at odds with the orthodoxies of academic disciplines and that apprehends the ways in which categories are constructed and how the field of knowledge itself is realized and produced. There is a broad consensus that *this* kind of thought practice, this critical labor of thought upon itself, is being steadily effaced in our current era of conservativism and neoliberalism, its utility and legitimacy under threat from all sides. "What we need now," as feminist historian Joan Scott has argued, is "a reassertion of the value of critique, a defense of its scholarly integrity, and an articulation of its philosophical presuppositions."[124] One of my own investments in attending closely to the relations between the world, the art, and the critic involves this challenge to rise in defense of critique.

I have also argued that a consistent feature of Kapur's intellectual work is the manner in which it struggles against the transmission of cultural practices and ideas as a stable or uninterrupted process over time. The question of the reception of culture, as Kapur stated early in her MA thesis of 1969, involves an active *quest* for identity, which is the opposite of the notion of a *bequest* that underlies passive or root-based models of inheritance. Kapur's essays recalling such key figures as Satyajit Ray, K.G. Subramanyan, and Raymond Williams belie a critical negotiation with these dilemmas of transmission and inheritance in the cultural realm, both past and present. They confront, for instance, the Nehruvian inheritance of a secular, democratic vision for India, even as they discreetly rework the intellectual legacy of a British post-Marxist tradition for the subcontinent, as witnessed by the author's "relay with Raymond." Moreover, Kapur's negotiation with her (almost exclusively male) predecessors does not involve claiming herself heir to a continuous, coherent lineage of thought. It involves, rather, subjecting the processes by which the past is inherited by her protagonists *and herself* to systematic and ongoing critique.

As such, these essays refuse the premise of an unbroken or primordial relation to the past and serve to undermine notions of origin and arrival. Accordingly, language that valorizes the "birth" of modernism or the "triumph" of modernism is rejected in favor of a rhetorical strategy ("when was modernism?") that disallows the fixing of beginnings and endings. It is no surprise, then, to realize that the question format that Kapur borrowed from Williams to serve as the title of her book is itself an important conceptual device in the venerable practice of critique. Adopted by many major thinkers of the twentieth century, the question-as-title, according to Judith Butler, not only poses the problem, it also "enacts a certain mode of questioning which will prove central to the activity of critique itself."[125] Kapur's essays consistently reveal, to put it differently, both a critical interrogation of a given predicament of culture and an original mode of working through that predicament within a continually changing historical situation. The difficulty—or rather, fragility, as I stated in the introduction to this book—of this radical intellectual work is that it leads not to a place of arrival or conclusion but to an unfinished, even limitless, process that can be at any point started and restarted again.

This returns me ultimately to the force and strength of Kapur's inimitable prose, the singularity of the critic's relationship to language, and the manner in which critique itself exists as a performative practice of the self. There is no doubt that the reiterative quality of Kapur's elliptical writing—the loopy forms of repetition, relay, reversal, and return that work against teleology and linear chronology—can sometimes be disorienting to follow, but that is, of course, partly the point. On occasion, her writing has been misunderstood as merely duplicative; it has also been seen as overbearing or authoritative or, paradoxically, as impenetrable and opaque. But these are somewhat predictable reactions to a practice that is profoundly centrifugal in the end. By this, I mean that the critic's thought perpetually exerts an outward force. Her texts, following Foucault, "initiate discourse": they effect the dispersion and proliferation of meaning and produce possibilities for the formation of other texts.[126] They also bear the combustive energy of Adorno's radical vision of the essay, what the philosopher described as the form's "childlike freedom" to "catch fire, without scruple, on what others have already done."[127] Adorno's pyrotechnic vocabulary recalls Kapur's own metaphors of combustion in relation to the impulses of art. "What combusts will transform," she has stated, expressing her preference for language that effects transformation and change.[128] Kapur is drawn to acts of combustion and moments of rupture—a break, a jolt, a kind of mortality in which something new might take hold—because they can stimulate crucial shifts in consciousness and "fuel new forces in the future."[129] But to heed this instrumentally or adopt it as a formula would be to necessarily fail. In the end these are creative, imaginative acts. Forces of explosion and implosion; emergence, struggle, and perpetual becoming; the endless urgency of the here and now—we are propelled back to an earlier question: What kind of inheritance is this?

URBAN ECONOMIES

Let's begin with an essential question: Why turn garbage into art? What kind of mischievous operation is this? What assumptions underlie such an artistic strategy? What are its social, material, and conceptual effects? Several objections could be made at the outset regarding, for instance, the negation of the abject and the problem of aestheticization. Bringing garbage into the sanitized space of an art exhibition typically involves extinguishing its visceral sensory impact. From this perspective, the transformation of trash's most repellent features—odor, filth, flies, grime—into artificial, lyrical, or glossy digital forms amounts to an elaborate gesture of sterilization. What kind of processing plant does the gallery space become? Doesn't the materiality of actual garbage contain something beyond that which is recuperable? And isn't garbage therefore fundamentally incongruent with the realm of aesthetics, making all such attempts seem rather frivolous in the face of the "real" environmental and societal crises related to the endless mountains of human waste we produce and deposit on the planet each day?

Countless artists from the Euro-American avant-garde—Marcel Duchamp, Joseph Cornell, Kurt Schwitters, Robert Rauschenberg, and Armand Arman, to name a few—embraced precisely these ambiguities and difficulties when they made the wager in favor of trash, devising truly ingenious ways to confront the degradations of value attached to all that culture has expelled or discarded. Indeed, the project of making art out of trash has a very long pedigree within the aesthetic projects of modernity and postmodernity. Duchamp's *Fountain* of 1917 is the well-established point of departure, a work that, in spite of its iconic status, remains axiomatic today. This is because the porcelain urinal that Duchamp signed as "R. Mutt" and submitted to the first exhibition of the Society of Independent Artists in New York (only to be rejected by the committee) functions, in the words of Octavio Paz, as a question mark suspended permanently over the notion of artistic creation itself: its "meaning" rests fully in the puzzlement it creates.[1] Following Duchamp's provocation, artists throughout the twentieth and twenty-first centuries have intervened in the structure of meaning-making either randomly or systematically by reintroducing objects and materials discarded from the cycles of production and use and asserting their worth in indeterminate ways. For the artist, the aestheticization of waste is therefore "an economic move, an attempt to invert value, to recuperate the negative,"[2] and to disturb the implicit or hidden judgments in our culturally defined systems of discrimination and value. No wonder, then, that the redrawing of the ledger line between rubbish and art is a tactic that has been passionately pursued in every realm of aesthetic practice throughout the modern era, including literature, cinema, performance, music, and theater.[3]

In his 2005–8 project, *Trash*, which used actual garbage from the megacity of Delhi as the basis for large-scale multimedia assemblages, Vivan Sundaram joined this long tradition of investment in the discarded form, while departing from its now-classic antecedents in a number of significant ways. For this project, comprising installation, video, and digital prints, the artist filled his studio with a sprawling cityscape made of debris gathered from the streets of Delhi with the assistance of a group of local "waste-picker" boys.[4] Alternately playful, buoyant, disorienting, and dystopic, *Trash* seized the medium of waste to question notions of value and obsolescence within the conditions of consumer capitalism and to foreground the systems of reuse and recycling that are particular to a society such as India. In chapter 1, I examined Sundaram's sensitivity to entropic forces—erosion, decay, dilapidation, ruination—in such projects as his 1991 series in engine oil and charcoal and his installation at the Kochi-Muziris Biennale, *Black Gold* (2012), suggesting that the artist's attention to such processes does not also imply acquiescence or resignation. In chapter 2, I turned to

Sundaram's *History Project* (1998), which probed the themes of nation-hood, collective memory, and subaltern belonging, and showed how strategies of installation and site-specificity helped to subvert, at least temporarily, the authoritative edifice of the memorial monument.

In this chapter, I will show how the multiple dimensions of Sundaram's *Trash* do not only amplify and intensify some of these earlier concepts and strategies: for instance, the materiality of debris, the aerial perspective, the role of memory, and the theme of alterity. The project also lays the gauntlet for a new ethical confrontation staged at the meeting between human subjectivity and societal waste. This is the locus of reckoning implicit in the title of sociologist Zygmunt Bauman's book *Wasted Lives*. The phrase does not refer to those who have "wasted their lives" through a lack of industry or willingness to work but signals instead a different moral alliance with the portion of humanity in the new millennium who have become casualties of economic progress. For Bauman, such people are the "surplus humanity" who most bear the consequences of globalization and who, deprived of adequate means of sustenance, are left with the daunting task of their own survival.[5]

As I suggest in the pages that follow, the vibrant digital photographs of *Trash*, which play with false perspectives and modernist tropes, evoke the notion of the "kinetic city" as it constantly modifies and reinvents itself in response to these extreme conditions.[6] As well, Sundaram's provisional collaboration with the waste-pickers, involving an alliance with these marginalized boys and their local advocacy groups, under-scores the social distance that separates the bourgeois artist from the labor of the menial worker. The social disparities of class and caste implicit in this association are further probed and complicated through the sculptural installation 12 *Bed Ward* (2005) and the single-projection video titled *The Brief Ascension of Marian Hussain* (2005). These two additional components of *Trash* are also free-standing installations, and they draw attention to the physical spaces of the informal economy and the built environment of the urban poor without resolving the contradictions that inevitably arise from the tension between stability and impermanence. Like Bauman, Sundaram's investment in the vocabulary of waste to evoke the subjecthood of "wasted lives" should not be miscon-strued as sentimental or fatalistic, or worse, as an irresponsible form of aesthetic appropriation. On the contrary, waste emerges dialectically—through tropes of dwelling, sleep, isolation, and work in both the video and the sculptural installation as a most intimate, inventive, and productive category, "the midwife of all creation" in Bauman's terms, one that opens onto both material and existential conditions and an indispensable feature from which to imagine alternative economies of societal consumption, expulsion, production, and design.[7]

Some viewers might see a parallel between Sundaram's *Trash* and recent works by contemporary Chinese artists that present the perversities and altered realities of an Asian landscape morphed by globalization.[8] Others might place it alongside some of the exuberant works of bricolage emerging from the dynamic contradictions and so-called informal economies of cities in Africa and Latin America.[9] Still others might connect it to the work of Mierle Laderman Ukeles in the United States, whose performances among janitors and sanitation workers in New York City in the late 1970s exposed the social prejudices around garbage and the marginality of its labor forms.[10] My analysis, by contrast, further situates the project within a growing discussion around the city in South Asia as the locus for numerous urgent concerns regarding citizenship, democracy, politics, and the state.

Departing from an earlier era of intellectual interest in the nexus of the Indian village, exemplified by the rise of post-independence "village studies" in the field of social anthropology and, later, the preoccupation with the peasantry within the framework of subaltern studies, the current "urban turn" in South Asia invokes a broad spectrum of knowledge practices.[11] What its participants and interlocutors share is an overriding concern with the extreme social disparities of the post-industrial city resulting from economic liberalization. Sundaram's approach to the city in *Trash* can be situated within these interdisciplinary discussions among scholars, activists, architects, and urban practitioners about the megacity and its staggering complexities. Further, several strategies in the project relating to form, media, and aesthetic process *actively* intervene in the different heterogeneous discourses of the city and facilitate a self-questioning of knowledge frameworks across the spheres of planning, architecture, housing, and urban theory, to name a few of the relevant arenas of inquiry. In other words, contemporary art itself functions here as a practice of urban history and analysis and emerges as a vital form of discourse about the city and the built environment. Moreover, the "vertical collaboration" between the bourgeois artist and the waste-picker boys expresses the ethical band political necessity that Arjun Appadurai has called "deep democracy," involving new kinds of alliances between intellectuals and the poor, as well as a "democratization of research" and thought.[12] *Trash* thus expands upon the impetus to forge an interface between artists and the urban matrix from the radical position of the "subterrain of the city,"[13] a parallel formulation conceived by Kapur at the time, both an urgent zone of democracy in crises and a powerful space of collective imagining with immense interpretive resources.

Post-Landscapes

My own relationship to Sundaram's *Trash* began in 2005 with a visit to the artist's studio located in the former village of Aya Nagar, now part of the outskirts of Delhi en route to Gurgaon, a locality that has been mutated in the past two decades by outsourcing, call centers, mega-malls, and a real estate boom for the Delhi middle class. The journey to Aya Nagar from the affluent, gated suburbs of south Delhi, according to Chaitanya Sambrani in his contribution to the *Trash* exhibition catalogue, "is like a constantly unfolding time capsule of the city's engagements with modernity."[14] Delhi today is an exemplary megacity, a place where the dreams of urban planners meet the chaotic excesses of relentless municipal development, and where the uncertainties of citizenship caused by migration and overcrowding call up the massive displacement of people resulting from the Partition of the subcontinent in 1947. As the writer Rana das Gupta has argued, the traumatic past of Partition continues to haunt the physical and psychic spaces of the city and is inseparable from the "eruption" of capitalist excess that has transformed urban experience there in the wake of the neoliberal reforms of the 1990s.[15] Similarly, the proliferation of low-cost media and technology, which spread like wildfire through Delhi's urban fabric during the same period, produced a largely illicit culture of mediatized experience built through systems of waste, piracy, recycling, and appropriation. This "wild zone of piracy" or "pirate modernity," in Ravi Sundaram's terms, signals both innovation and survival on the part of the urban poor and a new era of uncertainty for the city itself.[16] Crucially, it is not merely Vivan Sundaram's studio in Aya Nagar but more fully his life and art practice over the past five decades that bears an umbilical connection to this place. The frenzied urban expansionism of Delhi; the palimpsest of its modern and premodern past; its unreconciled legacies of Partition; its dazzling culture of resilience; its human casualties and sheer brutalities: as I will argue, these are the elements of urban experience that get thematized, indeed *theorized*, in the multiple components of *Trash*.

At the artist's studio in 2005, I had been invited to observe—along with some hundred others at an open-studio event—a vast indoor built environment composed entirely of garbage that had been locally collected with the assistance of the waste-picker boys. The assemblage was an immense urban landscape, or rather a "post-landscape," in cultural theorist W.J.T. Mitchell's terms, signaling less a genre than a medium of exchange, not a product but a cultural process, something more of a verb than a noun.[17] Sundaram's recombined garbage city consisted of a multitude of materials, relationships, forms, and scenes, visible in figure 4.1. There were towers of tin cans taped together, high-rises of recycled metal and cardboard, freeway flyovers of discarded synthetics, fields of undulating deflated plastic bags, and dense communities of junked plastic utensils. Dozens of playful vignettes could be detected at the micro level, for instance, a football match of toothpaste-tube players being cheered on by a group of onlooking recyclables. At the macro level, the impression was that of ordered chaos, with separate but distinct zones of patterned materials.

And yet, the scale most crucial to Sundaram's trashscape was arguably the unit of the neighborhood. This is where order, structure, and identity resided and where mounds of otherwise meaningless debris acquired a particular character or look. If the neighborhood is the locus of "place-making,"[18] the activity of inhabiting and transforming a place through mundane interactions with others on a daily basis, then Sundaram's emphasis on the neighborhood, as something that is patterned through reiterative practice, presents us with a kind of morphology, a portrait of *how* the city is produced. Sundaram's depiction of the urban order, as we shall see in his large-format digital print, *Master Plan* (figure 4.6), is therefore the opposite of high modernism's planned social vision. Those great utopian schemes privileged the future at the expense of the past like "large altars dedicated to progress," as James Scott has argued in his far-reaching critique of modernist planning's imperialist ethos.[19] What Sundaram presents instead is a kind of micro-sociology from below, a dynamic arena of mixed-use disorder, an "informal" economy to the formal master plan. How the artist prioritizes this dialectic between formality and informality using the aesthetic strategy of

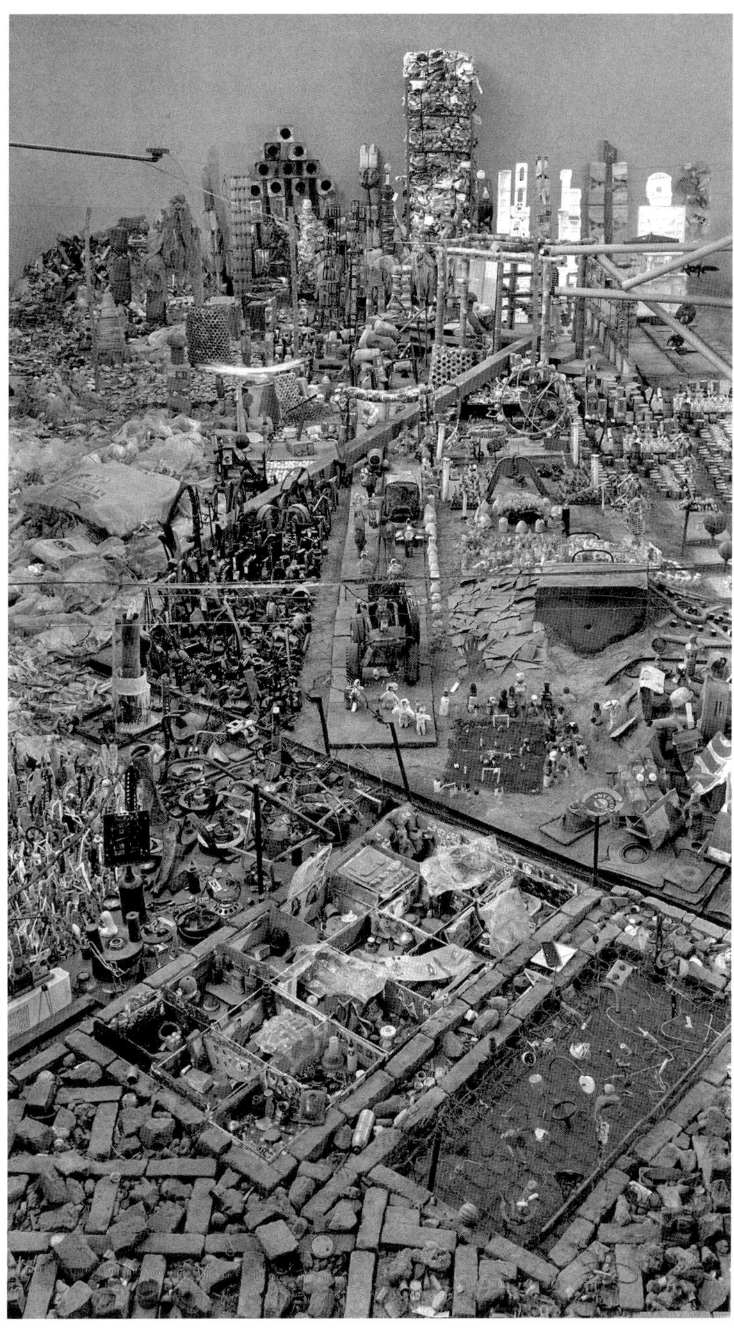

FIGURE 4.1 Vivan Sundaram, *Prospect*, 2005–8, digital print. Courtesy of the artist.

the overhead view, and in relation to both the past and the present, are issues to which I will shortly return.

Significantly, this rubbish-scape studio installation from 2005 was not intended for posterity. It served instead as an ephemeral stage-set from which the final product, including two videos, the sculptural installation called *12 Bed Ward*, and a series of digital photographs, was derived. One week after the open-studio event, Sundaram destroyed the entire constructed landscape and documented the destruction in a fourteen-minute, single-channel video, titled *Turning* (2008). In the video, the camera gradually zooms in and out of many intimate spaces and details, which are increasingly subjected to disturbance by wind and other forces, recalling the unnerving moments before a terrible storm. As the flight of a toy plane and bird become more and more frantic, the viewer senses the impending carnage. Incorporating citations of verse from the thirteenth-century Sufi poet Jalaluddin Rumi, the video focuses on destruction as a distinctly un-spectacular fate, something that occurs through precarious and wobbly forms of disconnection and collapse. The whole idea, Sundaram stated, was to highlight that "in poor countries, huge amounts of population live with an immense sense of instability; from moment to moment, they do not know when they will be destroyed, when their houses will be demolished."[20]

Turning thus captures the reality of "place-breaking" alongside the processes of urban "place-making" by enacting gestures of erasure and displacement that are common features of city life. The discipline of planning has many words for this, according to urban theorist John Friedmann—"people removal, squatter eradication, slum clearance, gentrification, rehousing, redevelopment—some terms more benign, others more brutal, but in the end, the results are the same."[21] This is the immense human cost of the demolition of place, large and small, as both physical dwellings and patterns of human relationships are destroyed in the name of capitalist development. If garbage represents here the teleological endpoint of a merciless consumer society—that which is devoured and discarded, leaving others precarious and unstable—then Sundaram's ambitious salvage operation, his recovery of an entire urban economy from its debris, also points to the proliferating forms of human ingenuity and the systems of survival and creativity that have been forged in response to our late-capitalist era.[22]

Inside-Outside Urban Experience

The anthropologist Mary Douglas was one of the first to observe in her classic study, *Purity and Danger*, that if garbage is, by definition, that which is thrown "out," then the very existence of garbage implies some hidden understandings about the boundaries between inside and outside.[23] In a similar way, Sundaram's interest in garbage as a medium is to highlight the boundaries and barriers, both physical and cultural, that separate insiders from outsiders and demarcate spaces like the slum or the ghetto from the gated communities or freeway flyovers designed to avoid them, not just in India but in most cities today. "I suggest that the urban middle and upper classes, rather than turn away from the garbage they generate," the artist has said, "must face the reality of the urbanscape and the people outside of their gated colonies."[24]

These ideas about living inside and outside the spaces of a city like Delhi were also embodied in the peculiar title and punctuation points of Sundaram's exhibition when it opened at the Lalit Kala Academy in Delhi in 2005: *living.it.out.in.delhi*. His large-format digital prints bearing the word "barricade" in their titles portray these divisions explicitly (see figures 4.2, 4.3, and 4.4). In this series, the barrier is marked against other elements of the landscape, for instance, *Barricade (with mattress)*, *Barricade (with red beam)*, and *Barricade (with props)*. Playing with false perspectives, sharp angles, and close-up views, these landscape pictures of dark gorges, crowded horizons, and disorderly yet delineated fields result in a kind of hyperreal frontier, as far from a "natural" terrain as possible. They present instead the deeply unnatural quality of such boundaries, revealing their reprehensible artificiality and exclusionary acts.

They also call up the long history of investment in such barriers by nineteenth-century urban planners like Baron Haussmann in Paris, or the modern concern with their social consequences by his famous interlocutor Walter Benjamin. Indeed, Sundaram's work forces the latter's account of the modern city, with its emphasis on the *display* of images and commodities, and its impact on the viewing subject into confrontation with a new set of extreme conditions. The shift in focus is not merely from the Benjaminian preoccupation with the activities of consumption to the domain of disposal and waste; it is also from the site of the first-world city to the urban realities of the so-called third world, or from the experience of the nineteenth century to the unfold-

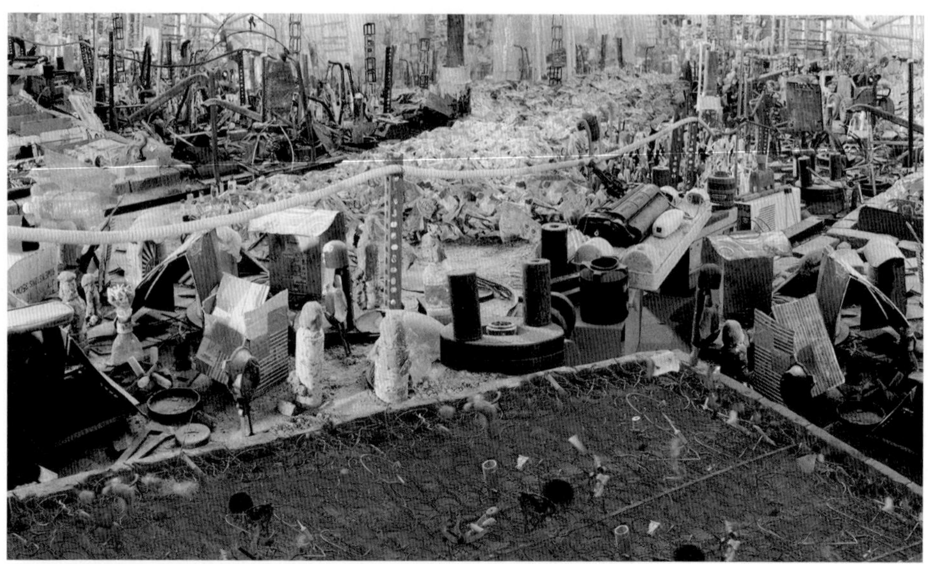

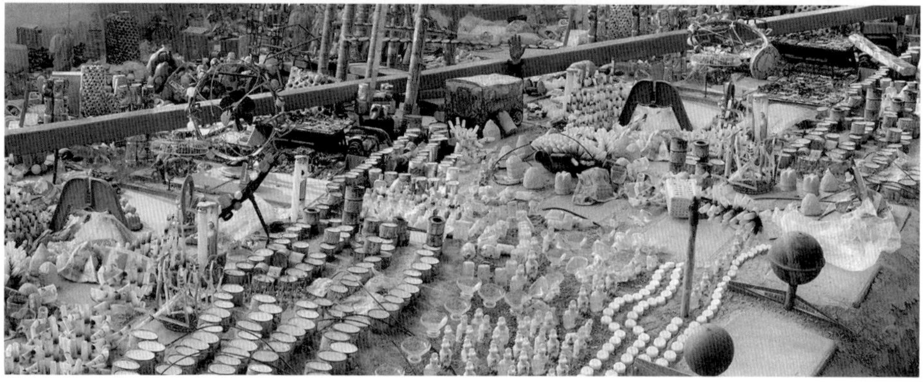

ing crises of the twenty-first. In other words, it is the classic ideal of the city as the embodiment of civil society and the production of "high" cultural values and good taste that Sundaram's overwrought garbage city—his unwieldy trashopolis—seems to relegate to the waste heap once and for all.[25]

What, then, is the theory of urbanization being offered here instead? Tania Roy has argued that Sundaram's project "moves across genres" of landscape art, surveillance, the archaeological survey, and the archive to construct "a supplement to the dominant representational practices involving the megacity."[26] Sambrani has similarly suggested that the artist puts forth "an alternative ecology, an other system of ordering that foils the dreams of undiminished progress."[27] Their acute percep-

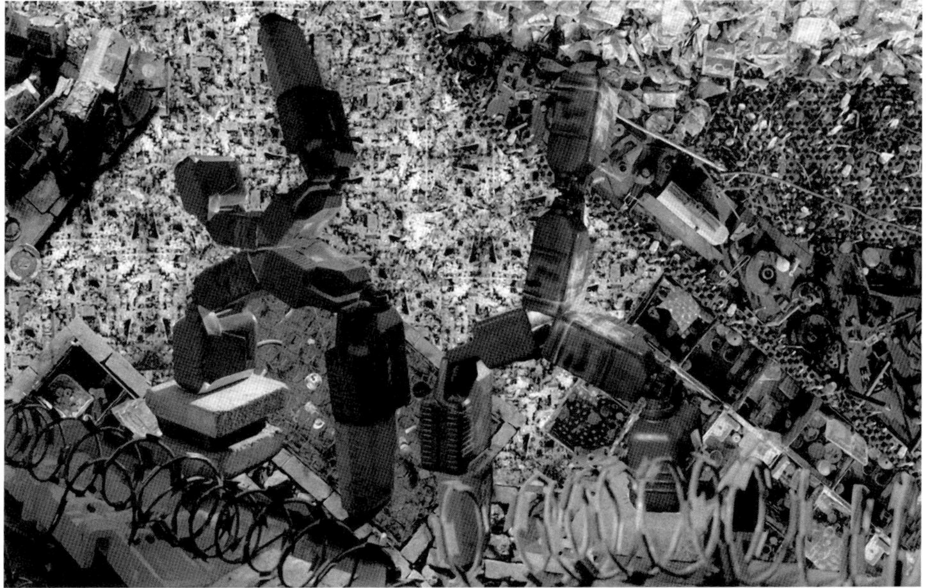

tions point to the nature of the urban thesis that lies at the center of *Trash*, and foreground the problem of representing "the urban" as a discrete and bounded form of human settlement. The relentlessness and increasing ubiquity of our urban condition has made it almost impossible to pin down, as the urban theorist Neil Brenner has noted, presenting a radical challenge to the knowledge practices that strive to contend with urbanization's ever more amorphous forms.[28] For Brenner, urban theory lacks a proper "cognitive map," a theoretical and cartographic orientation that can decipher the emergent realities and potentialities of cities in the midst of the "deep phenomenological dislocation" of our times.[29] Sundaram's images mark this sense of dislocation through their often playful rendering of coordinates across dystopic space *and* time. In the digital print *Fly* (2008) shown in figure 4.5, for example, a superhero soars over the landscape through a cloudless sky, recalling the bypasses and elevated flyovers which sanction speed and agility for some and debilitating stillness and immobility for others. The picture points, in this sense, toward the phenomenon described elsewhere as *chronopolitics*—namely, the presence of new kinds of relationships between haves and have-nots based in extreme forms of temporal displacement and the crisis of radically unsynchronized space.[30]

Mike Davis's influential portrait of a "slum ecology" and the con-

FIGURE 4.4 Vivan Sundaram, *Barricade (with Props)*, 2008, digital print. Courtesy of the artist.

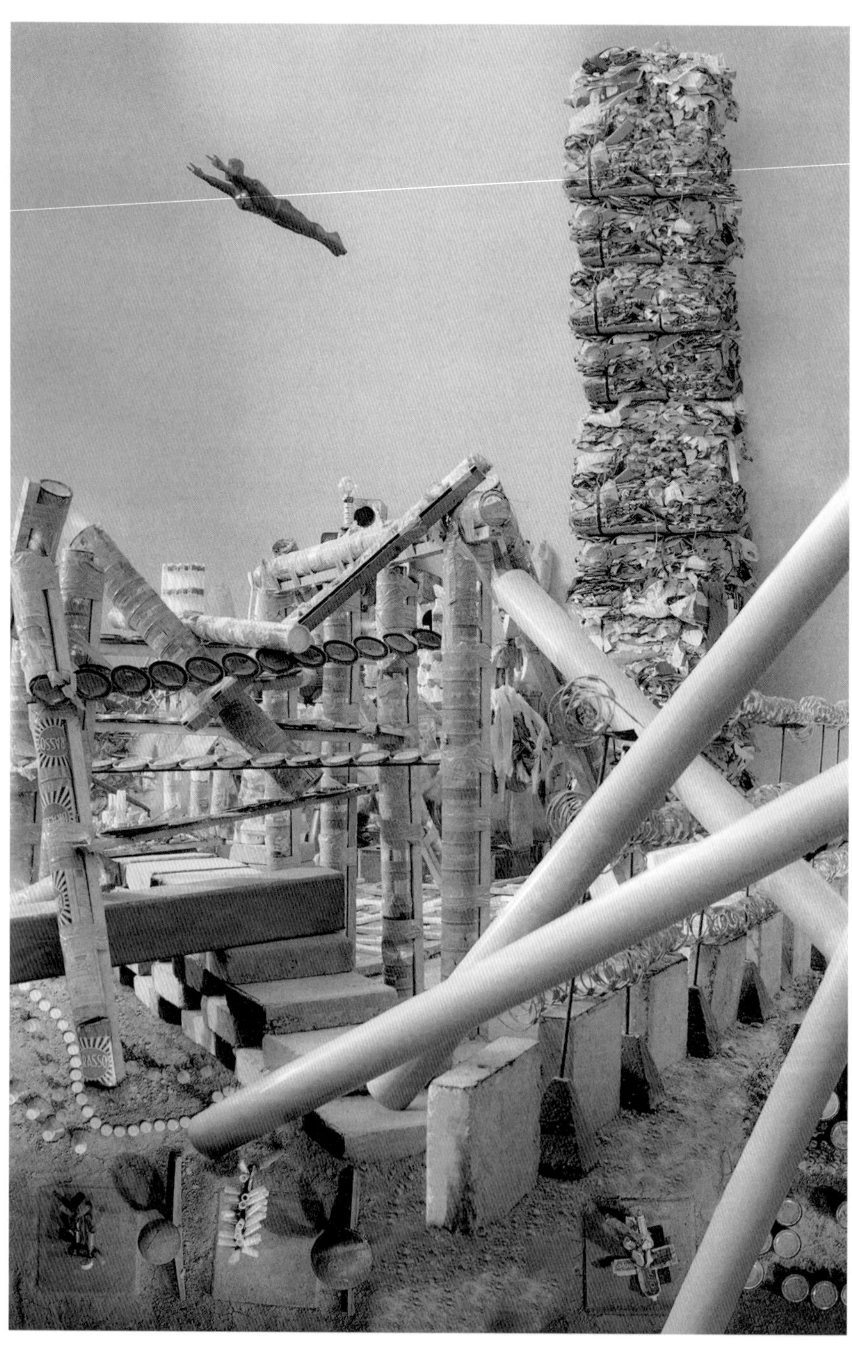

FIGURE 4.5 Vivan Sundaram, *Fly*, 2008, digital print. Courtesy of the artist.

ditions of planetary crises characterized by "super-urbanization" represents another possible vocabulary for some of the processes we see in Sundaram's art.[31] For Davis, "super-urbanization" is defined by population growth *regardless of* economic growth, overcrowding, unprecedented levels of urban poverty, and life-threatening destruction to the environment. Davis's account of how the world's mega-slums have spread and hardened like some new tectonic plates into the earth's existing geology of mountains, rivers, highlands, and valleys to constitute "our planet of slums" is indeed a powerful portrait of urban underdevelopment at the planetary level. And yet, his map of human vulnerability embedded in such material conditions, which overwhelmingly belong to the global south, has proven insufficient for grasping the dynamism of systems of reinvention and repair and the specific forms agency and subjectivity connected to such processes. Sundaram's images, by contrast—as I have suggested—expose the dialectics of inside and outside, boundaries and neighborhoods, accumulation and implosion, that suffuse such landscapes with resilience and contradiction while giving them the appearance of structure and coherence. In other words, the very notion of a discrete and bounded urban form is revealed *through art* to be an ideological effect. Moreover, by adopting multiple visual scales and perspectives, and a historically situated optic of the local—as I elaborate in the next section concerned with a single image, *Master Plan*—Sundaram presents an account of modernist space that, although constructed from above, has been equally subjected to radical reinvention from within.

Master Plan

The theme of urban squalor and filth that is uncomfortably equated with the idea of the slum has, in fact, had a long history in representations of the subcontinent extending back to the middle of the nineteenth century, the heyday of British imperial rule in India. The Victorians responded to the ever-present dirt, disorder, and chaos of the place as if it were a nightmare, against which the clean, orderly world of the European was established. And yet, this classic imperial trope—of the colony as the embodiment of filth—is not a perception that we can fairly think of as "Western." As Dipesh Chakrabarty has shown, the reflex of disgust at India's squalor is equally present in Indian writers,

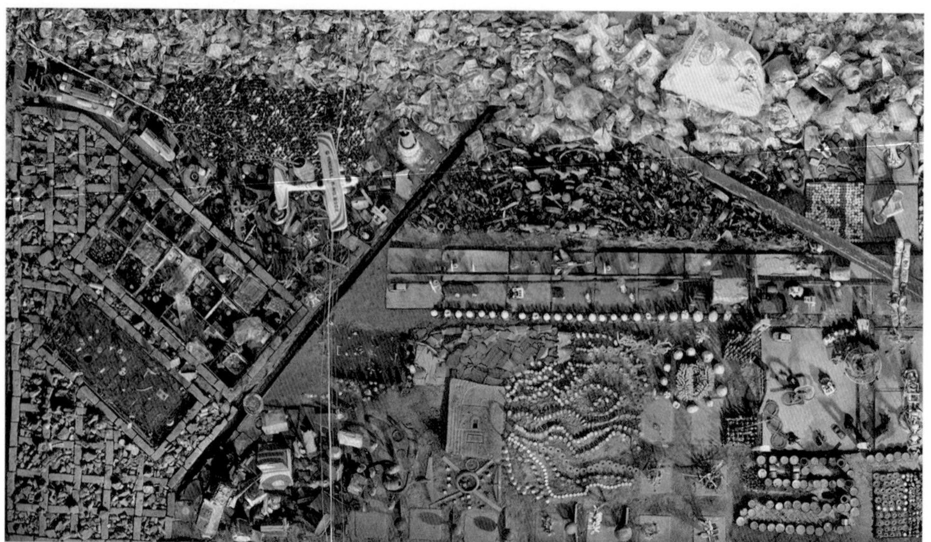

from those in exile like V.S. Naipaul or Nirad Chaudhuri to nationalist leaders like Mahatma Gandhi.[32] "I feel feverish when I think of slums," Jawaharlal Nehru, India's first prime minister, was reported to say, revealing his impatience with the challenges of overcrowding, hygiene, and sanitation in India's cities.[33] Nehru's slum anxiety was widespread among the English-educated Indian intelligentsia and political elite, who occasionally linked the problem of filth to the failures of domestic servants or—in the case of Gandhi—to the absence of a civic consciousness on the part of the Indian masses. The perception of the country as filthy was therefore, in Chakrabarty's terms, part of the "language of modernity," reflected in both imperialist and nationalist projects of social reform directed at that societal body in India variously seen as dirty, ignorant, "backward," or non-modern.[34]

The nationalist vision of planned development that would serve to "clean up" such unruly space—often with a heroic ruthlessness that sought to wipe the slate clean—is the theme of Sundaram's huge digital print, rather inadequately portrayed in figure 4.6, a majestic composition titled *Master Plan* (2005–8). The trope of the master plan, with its aerial view inviting surveillance and control, was, of course, the preferred model of celebrated urban planners like Haussmann in Paris, whose utopian aspirations had profound implications for the urban environment. Sundaram's image recalls the classic episode of this in the Indian case: Nehru's commission to Le Corbusier in 1951 to build the new capital city of Chandigarh in Punjab, the northern Indian state still reeling from the bloody violence and refugee crisis of Partition a few years earlier.

Nehru wanted a modern city, a future-looking landscape, as he stated, "unfettered by the traditions of the past, a symbol of the nation's faith in the future."[35] "You can rely on us at 35 Rue de Sèvres to produce the solution to the problem," was Le Corbusier's famous response. "Your capital can be constructed here."[36] Inspired in part by Lutyens's imperial plan for New Delhi, but also by the architect's iconic United Nations building in New York, completed a few months earlier, Le Corbusier's "master plan" for Chandigarh was a vast landscape project that was ultimately, in his words, a "question of optics," involving "harmonious dimensions" achieved through the town-planning principle that he called "sectors," defined as the unit or "container of family life."[37] Although much more can be said about this legendary encounter, for our purposes, if Le Corbusier defined his mission as defining a "truly modern Indian architecture," then India in turn gave Le Corbusier the largest project of his career.[38]

But Sundaram's master-garbage-plan evokes another, less well-known story within this story: that of Nek Chand, a humble villager from Punjab whose family was uprooted by the trauma of Partition and who eventually found work through a refugee settlement program in construction for the new city of Chandigarh. As a low-level bureaucrat in the Department of Public Works, Nek Chand's duties from 1955 on included supervising the city dump, which put him in touch with much of the debris from the twenty-six villages that were demolished to make room for Le Corbusier's landmark project. Nek Chand began using this debris—broken pots, metal scrap, oil drums, cracked bottles, bulbs, electrical fittings, chinaware, and twisted pipes—which he had stored in a secret clearing in the woods, not far from Le Corbusier's High Court building, to create a small kingdom of primordial sculptures. What began with things like monkeys made from cement poured over bicycle handlebars expanded over the years to include gardens and theaters of broken crockery, walls of clay pots and discarded electrical outlets, and vibrant armies of humans and animals made from the colorful glass bangles worn by Indian women (see figures 4.7 and 4.8). In figure 4.9, Sundaram's image *Barricade (with Coils)*, with its unusual arm-like forms, recalls the iconic figures Chand made with such bracelets. Here, the "barricade," made of stacking coils and helixed loops, seems

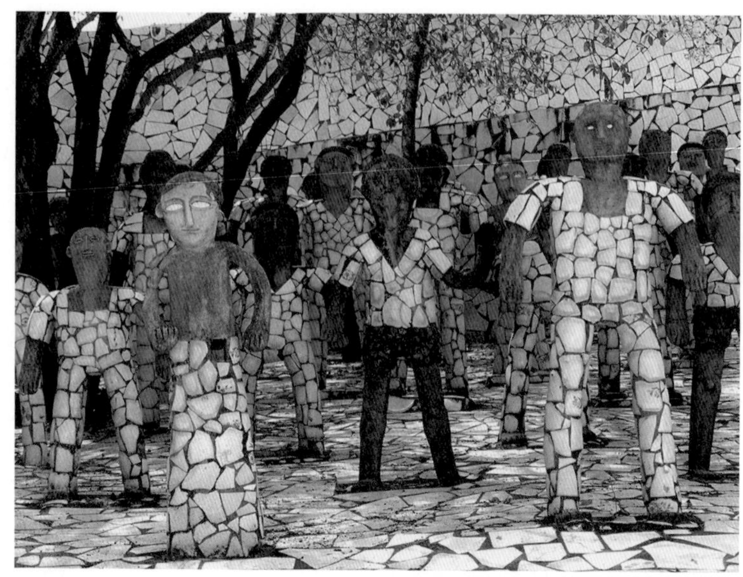

FIGURE 4.7 View of Nek Chand Rock Garden, Chandigarh. Courtesy of Adam Jones, PhD/Global Photo Archive/ Flickr.

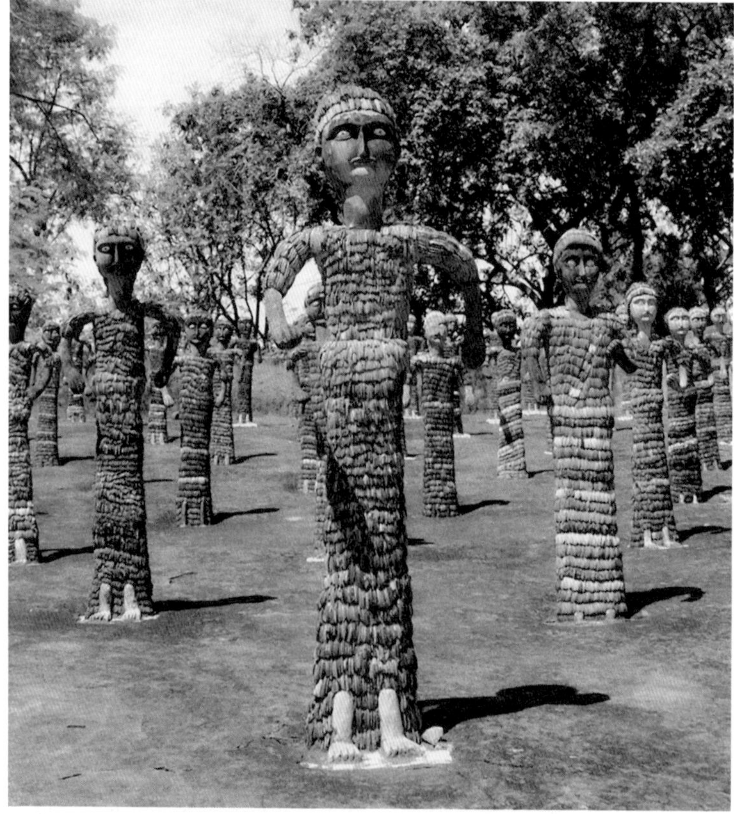

FIGURE 4.8 Sculptural figures made with glass bangles, Nek Chand Rock Garden, Chandigarh. Courtesy of Anja van der Vorst/ curlytraveller.com.

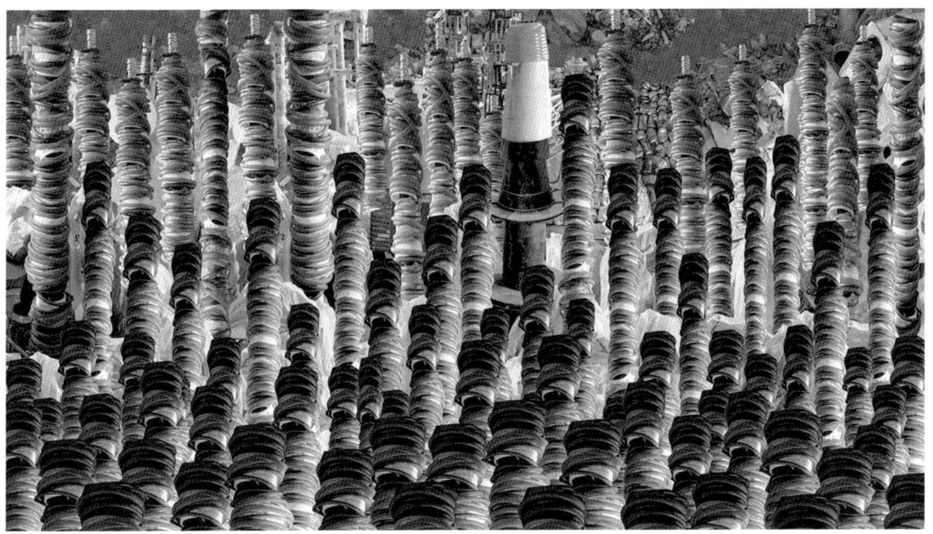

FIGURE 4.9
Vivan Sundaram, *Barricade (with Coils)*, 2008, digital print. Courtesy of the artist.

less a barrier than a flexible threshold, as the precedent of India's greatest sculptor-recycler, not to mention the militancy of the "outsider artist," appears to be acknowledged in an unstated homage.

Scholars who have studied Nek Chand, often through the lens of folk or outsider art, have also noted the rather poignant fact that his project was a self-stated attempt to re-create the ancestral village he had lost through Partition.[39] The response Nek Chand received when he revealed, after fifteen years, his secret sculpture garden to the chief architect of Chandigarh in 1969, four years after Le Corbusier's death, was perhaps even more heart-wrenching. The architect M. N. Sharma was overwhelmed by what he saw but also terrified. "His fantasy world," Sharma recalled, "was on Government land," next to Le Corbusier's great landmark buildings: it was not part of the master plan, and thus unauthorized and illegal. "I did not have the heart to go by the rules and I advised him to continue his work in secret," Sharma wrote later.[40] Nek Chand did precisely this, and it was not until the 1980s that his covert and obsessive salvage operation received public recognition and official sanction.

What is known today as Nek Chand's "Rock Garden" is thus simultaneously many things: a mini fantasy world within Le Corbusier's kingdom built over decades out of its rubble and debris; a clandestine archaeology of the past against the wishes of Nehru's modernist vision, who wanted Chandigarh to be a complete break from the past; an extraordinary aesthetic achievement in its own right, usurping some of the fame of Le Corbusier's host city; and a poetic violation of the *master plan*, through a tenacious, lifetime practice of recycling and the stubborn materiality of debris. There is no reason to expect that Le Corbusier, who was in James Scott's terms, "visually offended by disarray and confusion" and driven to distraction by "the physical environment that centuries of urban living had created,"[41] would have allowed the project to exist had he somehow lived to see Chandigarh's future. What Sundaram's image thus evokes are these two incommensurable relationships to the environment, the utopian authority of the master plan, on the one hand, and the lived economies of reuse and self-invention, on the other—two utterly discrepant histories of the modern which nevertheless coexist, and always have, in the cities of South Asia and, more broadly, in the resilient human geographies of the postcolonial world.

Notable in size and scale, Sundaram's *Master Plan* also possesses the uncanny ability to summon the past while pointing simultaneously toward the present and future. In particular, the wrecked circuit boards and broken gadgetry that become visible in the details of the print call up more recent technological narratives of the city and the specific forms of urbanization that have resulted from the digital era. In Delhi, for example, as Ravi Sundaram has shown, the emergence of cellular networks and digital media in the metropolis during the late 1980s led to a complete transformation of the fabric of the city, dispelling the hopes of rational planning once and for all. What emerged was a vast spectrum of "minor practices" on the ground that either bypassed the normative legal structures envisioned by government and corporate elites or ignored them altogether. The result—a "volatile mix of urban expansion, random violence, media explosions, and accelerating consumption"—was a "wild zone" of piracy, according to the author, which turned the city into a predatory and high-speed arena of "kinetic shock experiences," creating new kinds of crises for its inhabitants.[42]

Meanwhile, Delhi's latest Master Plan 2021, the third in the history of the city, following those of 1962 and 2001, was recently unveiled with much fanfare by the government—and met with equal criticism by the public and media. The plan, authored by the Delhi Development Authority (DDA), the civic authority of the country's capital, envisions a "global metropolis and a world-class city, where all the people would be engaged in productive work with a better quality of life," for the projected population of 23 million in the city by 2021. The plan advocates "solutions" to numerous problems that currently plague greater Delhi—traffic chaos, power shortages, water scarcity, and insufficient housing—by privileging business, industry, and transportation, the presumably rational sphere of the formal sector, with little attention to the implacable reality (or historical existence) of the informal economy. For Delhi activists, the plan's argument that commercialization and privatization can resolve the city's problems is nothing but an ideological ruse; they argue that its neoliberal logic places the principle of planned development and its top-down perspective into radical question yet again.

Delhi's millennial master plan departs from its Nehruvian predecessors in its embrace of the idea of the "world-class city," both a vague signifier and powerful ideological device that somehow clarifies what does and doesn't belong. Thus, freeway flyovers and shopping malls are projected as world-class; slums and squatter settlements are not. The discourse of the world-class city culminated in Delhi's fraught experience of hosting the Commonwealth Games in 2010, which saw an acceleration of changes in the name of clean-up and beautification. As the urban geographer Asher Ghertner has argued, Delhi's new planning regime is thus based more than ever before on a politics of the gaze that often prioritizes the criteria of visual presentation over issues of access and social inequality: what matters most is the appearance of being "world-class" defined in visual terms.[43]

World-classness is thus an aesthetic project and a mass dream that, alas, belongs to many, even those whose needs are excluded from its aspirational vision. "Who participates in the aesthetic imagination of the future," Ghertner writes, "and how the capacity to participate in such politics is cultivated among those historically excluded are perhaps the key political questions confronting India's increasingly urban future."[44] The practices of art, fueled by passionate engagement and creative experimentation, can intervene in important ways in the new regimes of visual culture that Ghertner has described. Seizing indirect address, encoded propositions, and subtle signs of dissent, artists can point toward more democratic options within the hierarchical field of the city's visual culture. In Sundaram's case, the paradigm of salvage further provides the basis for real and symbolic moments of inclusion, pointing to the need for broader participation in the discourses of the city and an expansion of the expressive practices related to citizenship and political solidarity.

Subalterity and the Operations of Salvage

The failures and fallacies of the modernist imagination and the unful-
filled social promises of the postcolonial nation-state provide an important subtext for the digital photographs in *Trash*. But how does this
relate to the recycling operation that filled the artist's studio with debris? How should we evaluate, in particular, the pronounced gestures
of social outreach and collaboration that were a constitutive feature of
Sundaram's "salvage paradigm"? As noted earlier, the artist had collected the garbage at ground level with the assistance of a group of
low-caste waste-picker boys. Sundaram had met the boys through the
Delhi-based NGO Chintan, which promotes the human rights of the
waste-pickers, often women and children from *dalit* (or untouchable)
castes or slum-dwellers who are outside the protection of any sort but
who labor within a massive informal economy. Waste-pickers are the
most marginal figures in India's unique *kabadi* economy, a home-grown
system of grassroots recycling that is acclaimed for its efficiency at
the societal level but based in archaic systems of caste exploitation,
whereby entire segments of society, viewed as ritually polluted, are required to perform the task of waste collection by hand. In an interview,
Sundaram described the structure of his collaboration in some detail:

> For over a year, I had been attending meetings every other Sunday
> with Chintan (the NGO). I'd sit in for two to three hours and listen
> to their problems and established some relationship. Once I got this
> idea, I asked the *kabadiwallahs* for 100 kilos of this and that—three
> tempos [small pick-up trucks] arrived at my studio, during the mon-
> soon, it was filthy. We had to fumigate the material (thousands of
> flies died!), lock the studio, let the fumes settle and come back the
> next day. Waste pickers are constantly picking through things, and
> that's what we did next. We sorted through it all, laid everything out
> in different areas, and then made a six-inch mud base and started
> building our city.[45]

The inclusion of the waste-pickers in the project through the intermedi-
ary work of Chintan calls attention to the daunting nature of collecting
garbage by hand; it also serves to highlight several crucial urban processes connected to the "informal economy." The informal sector is the
uneven geography, famously fluid and infinitely variable yet always precarious and threatened by annihilation, that structures the very fabric of

urban life. In the discourses of urban planning, informality is plagued by the problem of representation: for example, how does one specify this zone of informality when it is by definition invisible, subterranean, and yet absolutely essential to the ways our cities function today? And who is left inside and outside of citizenship itself within the hierarchies that structure these unsanctioned spaces? As Ananya Roy has argued, the question of urban informality is thus *always* a politics of representation, bound up in the transnational historical discourses of first and third world development and the epistemologies and problematic legacies of social science paradigms for poverty, inequality, and subalterity more broadly.[46] Policy discourse today, she adds, is "rife with tales of self-sufficient squatter settlements," "thriving women's cooperatives," and instances of "heroic entrepreneurship."[47] Thus, as the pendulum has swung from idioms of crisis toward a more utopian celebration of grassroots movements, there is a greater need for a reexamination of language, representational tropes, and theoretical models across the disciplines.

These issues and dilemmas are deftly confronted in two final components of *Trash*: a two-minute-and-twenty-second looped video projection, *The Brief Ascension of Marian Hussain* (2005), and a freestanding installation, titled 12 *Bed Ward* (2005). Both directly address the plight of the waste-picker and navigate the often strict separation between artistic practice and the discourses of policy. Not only are Delhi's waste-pickers today degraded by social stigma and abject working conditions, but their livelihoods are increasingly threatened by the privatization of municipal waste management, a situation that places the new "formal" economy in direct conflict with the "informal" economy.[48] This damaging collision is a prime example of the phenomenon identified as "eviscerating urbanism," a set of processes transforming Indian cities like Delhi, Bombay, and Bangalore into congested, overwhelmed landscapes or "hazardscapes," whose victims are the immense numbers of urban poor that are effectively rendered superfluous.[49]

In a still from the video in figure 4.10, the viewer perceives one of the waste-pickers, Marian Hussain, sleeping peacefully amid a small mountain of garbage, being ignored by numerous passers-by. Initially, one fears that the figure is a corpse because it is hard to imagine how such a mound of trash could produce the conditions to sustain human life. And yet, the figure is protected by sleep, both a public act and a technique of necessity for exhausted, homeless, or indigent bodies.

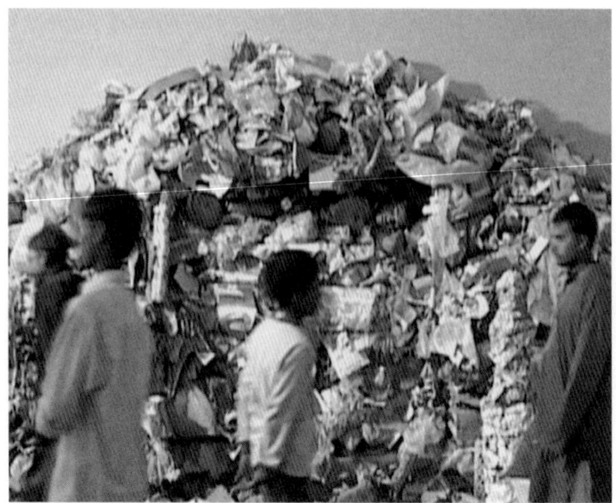

FIGURE 4.10
Vivan Sundaram,
The Brief Ascension
of Marian Hussain,
2005, video still.
Courtesy of the
artist.

For the very poor, as Appadurai has argued, public sleeping is actually "the sole form of secure being," providing respite, however temporary, from harassment, hunger, or eviction.[50] This encounter with the liminality and vulnerability of the sleeping figure recalls a series of nocturnal photographs by a younger Delhi-based artist, Dhruv Malhotra, aptly titled *Sleepers* (2008–present).[51] Malhotra's long exposures of the city at night present anonymous rickshaw drivers, migrant laborers, and other tired protagonists in different crumpled postures of sleep—on overpasses, sidewalks, benches, and public lawns. Like Sundaram, the photographer's eye in this series is on the relation between the sleeping figure and the urban landscape in which he or she slumbers, in a way that draws out the isolation and vulnerability that define such tenuous relationships to the city.

As the young protagonist in Sundaram's video slowly awakes from this ambiguous state of passive (in)security, he proceeds to stretch into a ballet-like extension from his perch atop the garbage heap (see figures 4.11 to 4.13). The video thus moves, as Sambrani has described, "from the material to the ethereal, from squalid earthliness to a transcendental (future) realm that remains to be (fully) defined."[52] If the looped footage of Marian Hussain's ascension offers painful, hopeful, and even elegant escape, the creaky mechanical sound of the audio is a reminder that such an existential transcendence is also fraught and inevitably "brief." Although beautiful, the boy's flight does not lead to a permanent resolution or offer the means of (neo)liberal redemption. To be sure, there is no slum-dog-turned-millionaire deception or false

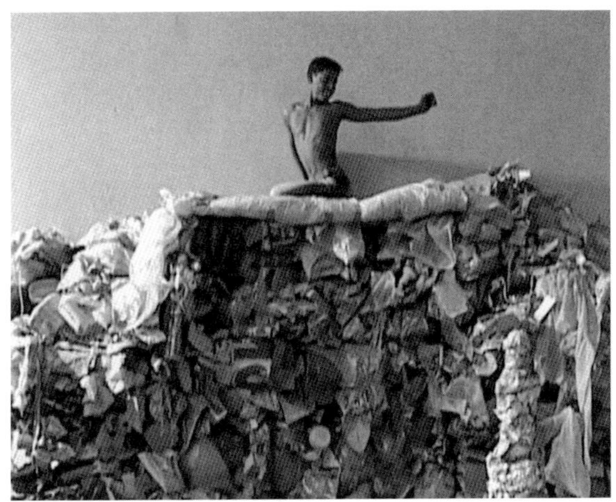

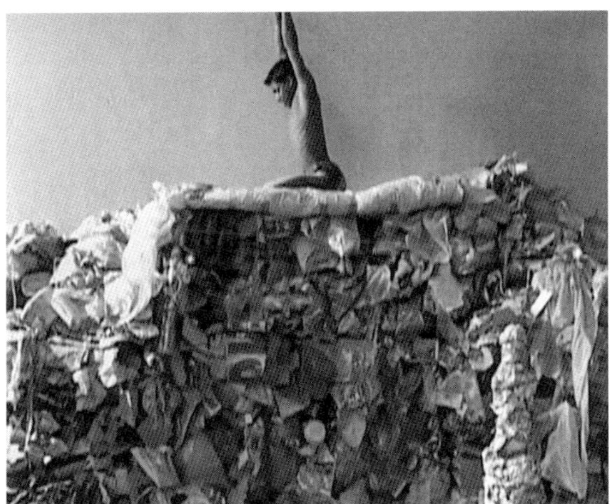

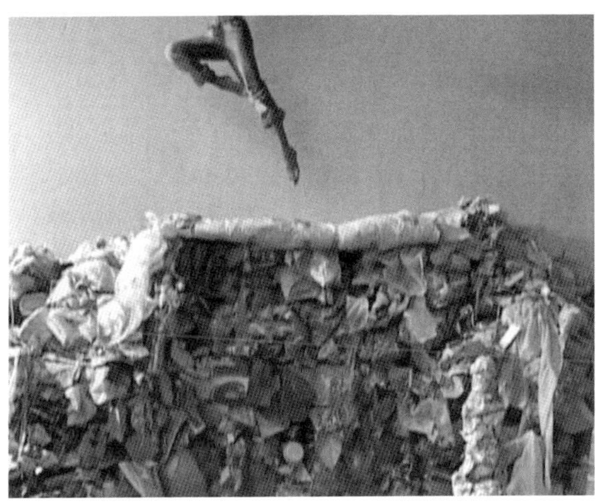

FIGURE 4.11–4.13
Vivan Sundaram,
*The Brief Ascension
of Marian Hussain,*
2005, sequence of
three video stills.
Courtesy of the
artist.

resolution offered here. Instead, garbage becomes a meaningful site for the archiving of trauma or pain and a potent means for rediscovery or transformation. Drawn into the service of beauty, it becomes a way to reorganize a past that has been marginalized or buried and to "reassemble the pangs of history in an oddly resilient form."[53]

In the Canadian photographer Jeff Wall's painstaking construction of the subterranean dwelling of Ralph Ellison's *Invisible Man*, the marginality of the black man is, in part, transacted through the excess of junk that surrounds him. The same is true for the heap of trash that both shelters and threatens Marian Hussain, the boy with the Muslim name. Part fallout shelter, part survivalist pod, part bunker against an unlivable world, this highly ambiguous architectural form evokes the broad spectrum of insecure housing practices—slums, pavement dwellings, squatter settlements—that is the built environment of the urban poor. It also points to the link in Indian cities between the politics of space and ethnic fear, a "macabre conjuncture," in Appadurai's terms, that has turned Muslims into the targets of sectarian conflict and discrimination, resulting in their systematic exclusion from housing or the outright destruction of their dwellings and neighborhoods.[54] The dwelling at the center of the video thus symbolizes the challenge of "spectral housing," a constellation that refers to the dynamics of "shortage, speculation, crowding and public improvisation" that shapes the new swollen realities of cities on the subcontinent today.[55] For Appadurai, writing about Bombay in particular, spectral housing marks the space somewhere in between the fantasies of urban planning, on one hand, and "bodies that are their own housing," on the other.[56] Marian Hussain's dwelling is properly "spectral" in this sense. It represents the accumulation of such forces of excess and lack, which are amassed, quite literally, into a pile of trash. Moreover, the creative encounter between artist and subject transforms that structure into a space of improvisation and, with the regenerative force of a compost heap, makes possible new lines of inquiry and alternative approaches to alterity itself.

In this project, Sundaram thus forces a confrontation with radical forms of social difference and the politics of representation of the informal economy, while negotiating the impasse within policy discussions that Roy has referred to as the "seduction of the squatter."[57] This is the gaze that looks toward the space of the squatter with fear, contempt, and disgust, at one end, or a desire for subjectivity that runs the risk of romanticization, at the other. Roy thus asks, how do we "gaze" at structures like the squatter shack, the favela hut, or the shanty-town shed? Similarly, how should we view the figure of the waste-picker, Marian Hussain, whose subjecthood is linked to the sphere of detritus in the most literal and existential of ways? And how should we assess the work of the bourgeois artist as he embraces this difficult, indeed overdetermined, field?

Gayatri Spivak's signature, but often misunderstood, essay, "Can the Subaltern Speak?," first published in 1985, remains a prescient point of entry into these dilemmas, as a recent book-length reconsideration of her intervention suggests.[58] Spivak's account of the ethically charged double meaning of representation itself—the difference, in her terms, between "speaking for" as in politics and "re-presentation" as in philosophy or art, in short, between a "proxy and a portrait"—surely remains one of the most rigorous intellectual engagements with the mechanisms of "othering," drawn as it was from a powerful synthesis of feminist, post-Marxist, and poststructuralist threads.[59] By explicating the discontinuities between subjectivity and agency and the "globe-girdling" relays of appropriation and reinscription, Spivak insisted on a theory of the limits of representation and the radical challenge of irreducible alterity. "All speaking, even seemingly the most immediate, entails a distanced decipherment by another, which is at best, an interception. That is what speaking is," she argued.[60]

For Spivak, the point was not to resolve the aporia, which continues to challenge the basis for equality and common ground, but to approach the problem of asymmetry through acts of imagining, to "somehow attempt to supplement the gap."[61] "Imagining" here is not the same as escape; it is rather an intellectual faculty that engages with difference and bespeaks a certain social responsibility.[62] Here, then, is a way to grasp the contribution of the "semionaut" artist within the fraught arena of representation's double bind: he seizes the creative challenge of representation and refuses to shy from the epistemological impasse it presents. *The Brief Ascension of Marian Hussain* is more than merely a "sweet escape fantasy," as the critic Holland Cotter somewhat hastily declared.[63] The video does not cancel the fact of waste's harmful materiality, its hazardous toxicity, or its role in producing sickness and death. Instead, the project sustains the contradiction between waste as a productive and creative category on the one hand, and its injurious and degenerative capacities on the other. Similarly, there is no attempt to make "the subaltern speak" but rather a will to mark the space of that subjectivity, as Spivak stated, "with something other than silence or nonexistence."[64] In the end, the infinite difficulty and irresolvability of such tensions belong to the dialectical space of the city itself—a site of continuous hope and despair, shelter and brutality, refuge and trauma, alternating between dreams and nightmares. For Marian Hussain, the air-born protagonist of the video, there is no guarantee of a soft landing here. The same can be said for the viewer in search of the security of a (false) resolution: instead, within the forces of inequality lies the possibility of a modest awakening and the urgent necessity of not forsaking the subject-position of the radically other.

The Immortal Soles of *12 Bed Ward*

A final component of *Trash*, the isolated installation titled *12 Bed Ward*, departs formally from the video and digital photographs and imbues Sundaram's engagements with garbage with a different kind of affective force. It was the British sculptor Tony Cragg, similarly known for his experimentation with discarded forms, who observed with a certain dissatisfaction that "thousands and thousands of materials are called trash."[65] We are reminded that a full accounting of Delhi's waste would require detailed consideration of its multitude of forms—sewage, industrial waste, electronic waste, biomedical waste, construction debris, abattoir remains, and so on. In *12 Bed Ward*, Sundaram approaches this problem, presented by garbage's almost infinite forms, on the one hand, and its high degree of particularity, on the other, by moving away from the umbrella signifier of his title and toward a more focused and specific contemplation.

In this stark installation (see figure 4.14), the viewer enters a dimly lit room and encounters twelve steel single-bed frames, their sleeping surface made of "reincarnated soles."[66] These are the worn rubber soles of Delhi's sneakers, sandals, shoes, and *chappals* (or slippers), which are painstakingly recovered by waste-pickers and separated from the discarded shoe, because of their value within the *kabari* economy. The row of uninviting beds, the starkness of the overhead bulbs, the menacing presence of an overseer's chair—as Sambrani has suggested, these elements link *12 Bed Ward* to the sculptural installations of Mona Hatoum, whose similarly threatening domestic forms evoke violence, conflict,

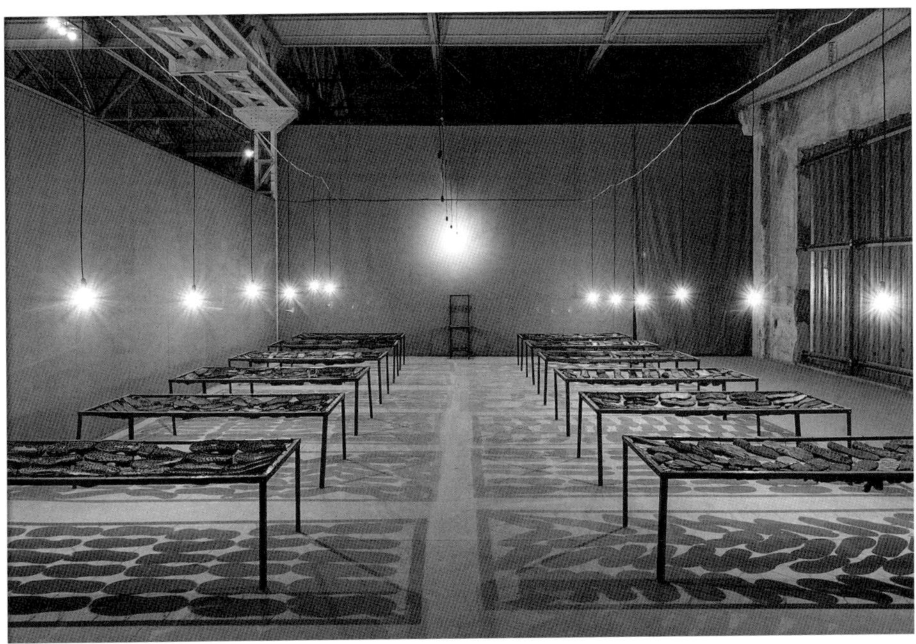

FIGURE 4.14 Vivan Sundaram, *12 Bed Ward*, 2005, installation with steel bed frames, old shoes, string, wire, and lightbulbs in a darkened room. Courtesy of the artist.

and state authority, with specific reference to the Palestinian experience.[67] At once calling to mind a hospital ward, an interrogation room, a refugee camp, and a police precinct, 12 *Bed Ward* is a "paradigmatic space of abjection," in Sambrani's terms, a room that threatens of social persecution and conjures, in the broadest sense, the humanitarian crises wrought by our political modernity.[68]

At another level, however, the spectral presence of the rubber shoe soles is a harsh reminder of the specific subterranean circuits and invisible value chain that determine the so-called informal economy and implicate the lives of waste-pickers like Marian Hussain. The room is equally reminiscent, for example, of a *kabari* shop in Delhi, the cornerstone of the system of informal recycling where "raw" waste is purchased, sorted, reprocessed, and resold. The urban geographer Vinay Gidwani, who has studied such unwelcome spaces, describes the latter as "a dingy, poorly lit, one-room establishment tucked away in a bylane in a slum, an old city neighborhood, the corner of a colony, or in one of Delhi's numerous urban villages."[69] Increasingly threatened by the corporatization of waste collection, such *kabari* shops are now doubly displaced, often located in nondescript spaces on the outer margins of the city. Visiting one such place, called Mundka, in west Delhi, one of Asia's largest recycling markets, Gidwani describes a grim Dickensian world where the shoes are burned in hot ovens and open vats with "belching acrid grey fumes."[70] "As the soles heat up," he explains, "along with the adhesive that binds them to the body of the footwear, plumes of noxious grey smoke waft into the air. The smoke catches the back of the throat," making it impossible to breathe without coughing.[71] For the people, mostly young women, who have no choice but to seek work in these appalling conditions, the resemblance with the gas chamber is all too real, as a number of these questionable spaces, including Mundka itself, have been destroyed by fire and acts of arson in recent years.

Thus, while 12 *Bed Ward* summons the generalized experience of modernity's political and human cost, the specificity of the found object—here, the tragic status of the reincarnated "sole" visible in figure 4.15—signals the grim realities and material spaces that facilitate the afterlife of Delhi's trash. It is a well-known fact, as Gidwani states, that without these intricate circuits and physical places, largely invisible to most city dwellers, a city like Delhi "would soon choke under the weight of its waste."[72] The artist's installation, through its logic of selection, inclusion, and material support, offers a radical disruption of this value chain, one that lays bare recycling's own contradictions and makes visible its most suffocating effects. In other words, by turning to the immortality of the "sole," a superb homonym for garbage's cycles of life and death, Sundaram invites us into a compassionate alliance with the material and existential reality of the waste-picker and to *feel*, as it were, the marginality of this sole/soul.

The Endgame of Garbage

With *Trash* Vivan Sundaram undoubtedly joins a long history of modern artists who have critically challenged, subverted, and appropriated the codes surrounding the status and reception of objects within consumer capitalism, from the "ready-mades" offered by the dadaists and surrealists in prewar Europe to the pop-art silk-screens of Andy Warhol in New York, evoking especially those artists who link such strategies to environmental or ecological concerns.[73] But I have suggested that what Sundaram brings to the question of garbage is not only a critique of the excesses of contemporary capitalism, or an environmental sensibility about reuse and recycling, however important these may be. What is

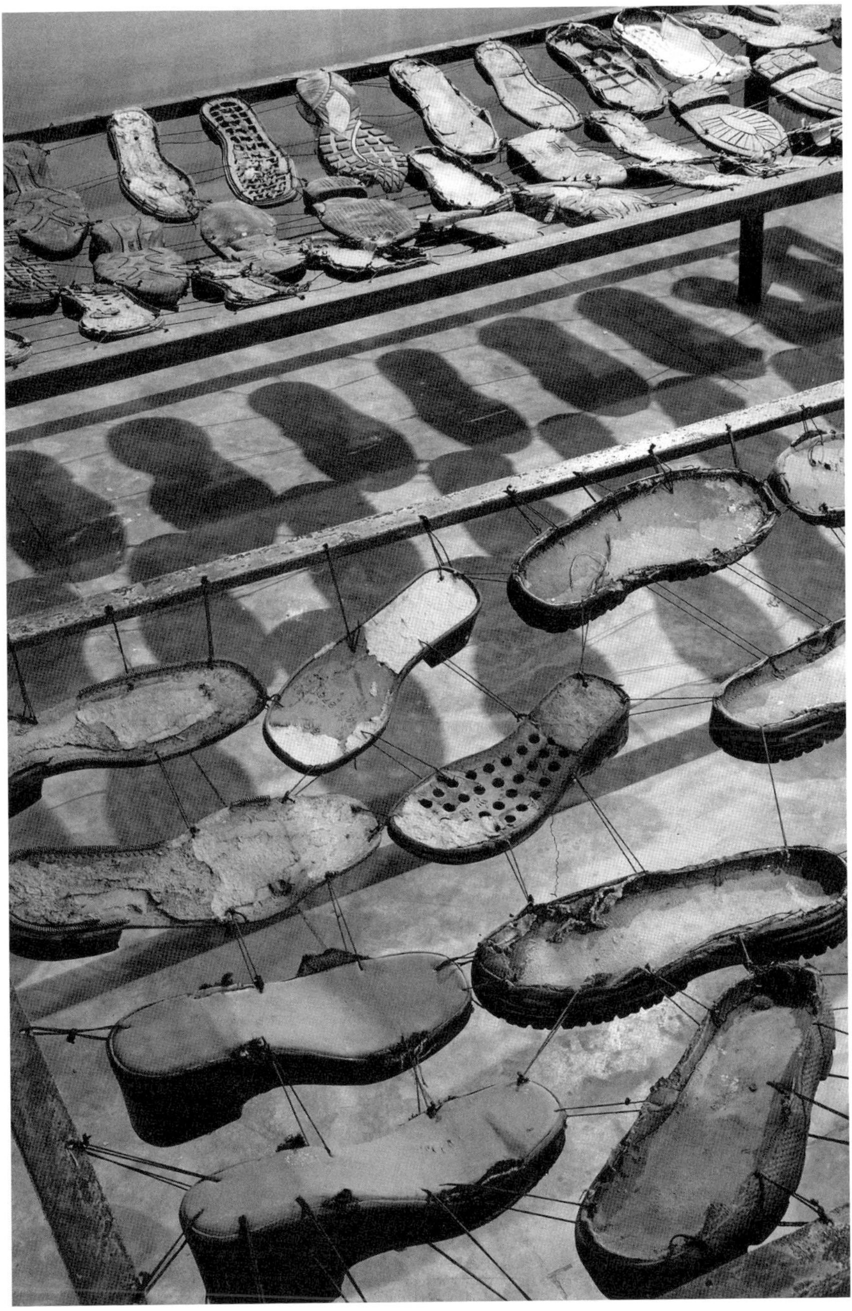

FIGURE 1.15 Vivan Sundaram, 12 *Bed Ward*, 2005, detail of installation. Courtesy of the artist.

also at stake in this work is a social and ethical consciousness emerging in part from the distinctive constructions of the human environment that the hierarchies of caste in India have produced, entangled as they are with issues of class. Here, the modernist history that has equated garbage and filth with poverty and "backwardness" gets exposed as a paradigm rooted in the colonial past but equally present in the conceit of postcolonial modernizers like Nehru and Le Corbusier, who sought to produce a new consciousness for Indians through a rigorous reordering of civic space, in architectural terms, through a "master plan."

The capacity of Indians to frustrate these colonial and nationalist calls to discipline public space is, of course, legendary—embodied in the extraordinary subterfuge of a figure like Nek Chand, whose violation of Le Corbusier's "master plan," through assemblages of Chandigarh's debris, constitutes one of the most poetic responses to the master of modernism—a story that would border on the mythical if it weren't for the fact that the feisty Nek Chand, until his recent death at the age of ninety, continued to supervise the expansion of the Rock Garden throughout his life, in between public battles with Indian bureaucrats bent on claiming his work as "national heritage." I have also suggested that the poetics and politics of a counternarrative like Nek Chand's, and the methodological challenges of bringing it into visibility, are at the heart of the urban problem of formality and informality and the representational dilemmas of the subaltern in South Asia. It may be that I have piled too many issues onto Sundaram's already large assemblage of garbage; but when it comes to the interlinked problems of modernity, globalization, and urbanization in the postcolonial societies of the global south, we are dealing unquestionably with a large, odorous heap.

I conclude with a final point concerning the nature of Sundaram's "salvage paradigm," a term that historically positions—among other things—the hierarchical discourses of the other. It is well known that in the history of anthropology, the desire to preserve and collect vanishing cultures by an earlier generation had damaging, if not deadly, consequences. That impulse to salvage what the forces of modernization destroyed at the beginning of the previous century (namely, an "authentic" cultural other) was linked to misguided benevolence, imperial gestures, and fatal acts of possession. Anthropology's salvage paradigm was so thoroughly connected to death, evoking the dusty, suffocating basements of ethnographic collections and the museum as a mausoleum, that—as Virginia Dominguez argued by the 1980s—"salvage" symbolized "a set of intellectual, aesthetic, and institutional practices that we seek to bury rather than preserve."[74] "Beyond the Salvage Paradigm" was thus the subtitle of an important discussion among scholars engaged in a rethinking of the identity of anthropology in the new geopolitical arrangements of the late twentieth century.[75]

Some three decades later, Sundaram's *Trash* presents a model of aesthetic practice that does indeed go "beyond" the residual traces of this ideological complex. Although salvage here remains bound up in the hierarchies of representation, it also signals a set of alternative practices in the arts—linked not to death but to the forces of life—involving collection, recycling, creativity, and renewal as part of an investment in the *production* of culture. These gestures of salvage are no longer static and wholly appropriative acts but rather akin to techniques of composting, an active process by which detritus and waste are gathered to create the conditions for future change. For Sundaram, salvage in response to the challenge of waste involves listening, archiving, storytelling, and play, alongside collection, collaboration, and connection to place. Trash makes history, labor, and trauma visible through its radical retake on the discarded form. Paradoxically toxic and yet as vital as oxygen itself, this material in the hands of the artist provides the basis for our collective survival.

LATE STYLES

> Perhaps I will do little more today than
> turn, and return, around these turns,
> around the "by-turn" and the "re-turn."
> —JACQUES DERRIDA, *Rogues*

One of the challenges of writing "alongside" contemporary art is that it is, by definition, a moving target. Its dynamic, shape-shifting, and unpredictable activities refuse to stand still for the observer for very long. As an active and inventive practice, it tends *not* to adhere complacently to the contours of a scholarly paradigm or to be pinned to a particular intellectual schema. Moreover, it is difficult to discern the shape and parameter of a thing from inside its dynamic unfolding. These are some of the problems that surface when connecting our protagonists' ongoing activities in the sphere of contemporary art to the phenomenon known as "late style," an idea that positions human creativity as it manifests itself in the late stages of a life. It is pure hubris, of course, to bestow late style onto living artists and writers because late or final works only gain their status as such in relation to the (unknowable) threshold that is the end. At its best, late style animates the poetics of mortality and forces a confrontation with finitude and temporality. At its worst, it invokes clichés about final chapters and golden sunsets and sets the stage for geriatric decline. And yet, late style is a concept wedded to the problem of beginnings and endings, to art, artifice, and the processes of culture, and to the question of inheritance, however insecure. I thus turn in this epilogue to the banner of late style not to fix my subjects to a final chapter, as it were, but to reflect on the status of creative expression in and through the processes of life and to draw attention to angles of vision, narrative trajectories, and imaginative exits in relation to the current text.

Significantly, in 2010, Kapur and Sundaram began working with researchers at the Hong Kong–based Asia Art Archive to digitize their entire personal archive for posterity. As the first archiving project related to contemporary art in India, this was a pivotal undertaking for the nonprofit art organization. The same could be said for the artist and the critic who, in the process of consolidating two separate bodies of work into a singular presentation, were forced to confront the dilemmas of their own transformation into an archive. In practical terms, this entailed the conversion into electronic form of a vast corpus of artworks and writing, as well as materials collected over some five decades—photographs, exhibition catalogues, newspaper clippings, and hundreds of artist slides—related to the emerging art world of post-independence India. Like others from the post-1960s generation, our protagonists appeared to have accumulated a great deal during their lives, even as they were perpetually engaged in boundary-crossing and experimental activities that seemed largely ephemeral or without value at the time, itself a sign of a certain faith in art's mission.[1] Bearing the evocative title *Another Life*, suggesting past lives and potential rebirths, the archive is now available online, and it represents a singular gift (for us ahead) of a dense corpus of ideas and practices that has already proven to be a crucial resource for this book.[2] However, this digital bequest also raises issues surrounding transmission, legacy, and assimilation and reopens the themes of transference and inheritance introduced at the beginning of my study. On the one hand, an archive appears to shore up legacy; it collects, orders, and facilitates a transfer according to a logic of inclusion and exclusion. On the other hand, the unfinished nature of archived information creates generative possibilities; it can galvanize new questions and dissonant links and becomes a locus for the active production of knowledge.

These dilemmas were among those discussed at a symposium, *The Subject of Archives*, hosted by the Asia Art Archive at Jawaharlal Nehru University in Delhi in February 2011. The event was occasioned by the launch of Kapur and Sundaram's digital personal archive, and it brought together artists, curators, students, and scholars to reflect on the complexities of archiving today, particularly with regard to India, where colonialism led to a fundamental reorganization of knowledge in the archive. The event also recognized the paradox that the act of preserving a legacy can hasten its assimilation or congealment into fixed narratives, even as it provides the opportunity to interrogate the processes by which narratives are constructed. Far from settling the question of inheritance, then, my subjects' latest projects tend to strain against the archive's "Pompeiian logic" (i.e., the approach to life as if in stone) and reveal a more difficult, ambivalent set of sensibilities that are alert to the dilemmas of memorialization and consecration—leading not to a simple conclusion but, on the contrary, to the impossibility of a resolution along these lines. By using the occasion of archival construction for self-reflection and critique, and by embracing the physical shift from the material to the digital, both artist and critic appear here to be deflecting the memorializing functions of the archive even as they seize the methods of documentation and dissemination that a new era of technology affords. In other words, this digital bequest is highly attuned to the never-ending transformations to the production and reception of knowledge and the inexhaustible processes of the cultural arena—indeed, it comes to us with these strings attached—and it is in keeping with the affiliative resolve discussed in my introduction to this book.

The truth is that both Kapur and Sundaram, who are now in their late seventies and who have clearly adjusted to the physical effects of aging on the body, appear to be more agile than ever, producing new forms of art and writing that are uncompromising in volume, scale, and ambition, and with an intensity of engagement and degree of productivity that begs easy description. Some of these projects—like Sundaram's 2011–12 exhibition-cum-performance titled *Gagawaka: Making Strange*, and his follow-up series of sculptural objects from 2013, *Postmortem*, or Kapur's exhibition titled *Subject of Death*, the first of five exhibitions she curated in 2013 and 2014—explicitly foreground questions of mortality and engage with themes of illness, sexuality, aging, and the body.

And yet, other projects contain less obvious expressions of the finitude of life, sustaining instead more elusive, recursive, and elliptical gestures that refuse and frustrate notions of arrival and the teleology of the end-game that mortality throws up. These projects are, to my mind, especially luminescent and speak to the more fraught sense of temporality—and preoccupation with the future of the past—that has long characterized their different bodies of work. Such projects display at once an awareness of the clock running down and a certain recalcitrance where chronology is concerned, leading to anachronistic gestures and out-of-sequence story lines. They speak to the instability of the forces of history and memory in order to resist any easy assimilation into history's memorializing forces. Thus, each new activity brings less an accumulation and more a *distillation* of long-standing principles and aesthetic concerns. In what follows, I turn briefly to some of this recent activity and discern several intertwined aesthetic strategies at work—for instance, anachronism, ellipsis, exacerbation, and return—that mark a highly cultivated process of self-reflexive critique and a will to enter the archive self-consciously through energized engagement and noncompliant acts. However, if we are to understand the force and ambition of these projects as signaling a "late style," then it is necessary to begin by examining some of the uncertainties within that concept itself.

Late Style as a Preexisting Condition

It is useful to recall that the discourse of late style emerged crucially through the discipline of art history, where it was central to questions of periodization and to "style studies" within the formation of the field. It was the German art historian and archaeologist Johann Joachim Winckelmann (1717–68), and his cohort in the late eighteenth century, who first inaugurated the three-period approach to style (early, middle, late) as a developmental sequence, which they projected onto the ancient Greeks.[3] In Winckelmann's neoclassical formulation, involving rise, culmination, and Hellenic decline, the late phase signaled exhaustion, corruption, degeneration, and decay. During the course of the nineteenth century, lateness changed, confusingly, from a symptom of demise to a symbol of transcendence and was extended from history to individual biography. Late works, for example, in Goethe's analysis represented the pinnacle of aesthetic achievement: they pointed to perfection, arrival, and the realization of the sublime. Adorno's goal was precisely to discredit such a teleological, periodizing historiography of aesthetics, part of the intellectual and cultural zeitgeist that he loathed and that—in Edward Said's words—"all his writing struggled mightily to insult."[4] Said's posthumously published book, *On Late Style* (2006), an unfinished and partial set of reflections on the theme, has revitalized discussions of lateness once again and helped to reactivate this dense and paradoxical history of ideas to serve the needs of the twenty-first century.

Said's approach to late style marks it as a contingent and mostly unsentimental affair; it is always embedded in a particular time and place and not a universal or transhistorical value that is somehow untethered to societal conditions. For him, following Adorno, late style characterizes the mature phase of a creative career, but not as harmony, serenity, and resolution, nor as a process of aging and wisening as in the ripening of a fruit. It signals, rather, an outpouring of almost youthful energy in the advanced stages of life that points "against the grain" of the current social order, toward difficulty, contradiction, and irreconciliation. Late style is therefore, in Said's terms, a "vulnerable maturity," one that is "hell-bent on remaining untimely and contrarian"[5] but that is nevertheless distinguished by a lifetime of technical preparation and a "desire to go the whole way towards extravagance."[6]

A reaction against the normalizing forces of history, the condition is further complicated by the self-conscious awareness on the part of the artist or intellectual of the discourse of late style itself. Thus, for Said, Adorno "is lateness itself," and—as Stathis Gourgouris has observed—Said's own ideas about lateness were conceived entirely through the disruptive experience of his own personal battle with leukemia, to which he succumbed in 2003.[7] In other words, "to come late into the discourse of lateness," as another pair of authors have stated, is to "enter into quite a different relationship to it," involving radical self-awareness, willful investment, and forms of disruption and exacerbation.[8] Although very different in formal terms, this quality of vigorous and self-conscious confrontation characterizes a number of recent projects by our artist and our critic. In each new undertaking—be it a performance, installation, exhibition, or manifesto, to cite some of the examples that I will now proceed to examine—we can observe a range of provocative aesthetic strategies that sustain the sense of intractability and tension and that point determinedly "against the grain."

Reckoning, Irresolution, and Conundrum:
Gagawaka, *Postmortem*, and *Aesthetic Bind*

Sundaram's 2011–12 exhibition-cum-performance, titled *Gagawaka: Making Strange*, represents a prescient point of entry into these concerns. Undertaken after the artist experienced a period of illness and hospitalization, the series is formally an extension of the 2005–8 multimedia project *Trash*, discussed in the previous chapter. Made from repurposed and recycled materials — for instance, truck tires, paper cups, kitchen scrubbers, and women's handbags — these wearable sculptural garments were incorporated into a virtuoso performance involving fashion designers, runway models, brand names, and a catwalk. Writer and curator, Deepak Ananth, has described this departure from *Trash* as the artist's "plunge, upwards, as it were":[9] that is, out of the detritus and degradation of the slum, and into the sphere of the infamous culture industry; out of the dystopic streets of the city, and into the giddy spaces of media, fashion, the runway, and the brand. The name, *Gagawaka*, a fictional brand inspired by pop cultural references to Lady Gaga and the 2010 FIFA World Cup song "Waka Waka" by Shakira, is itself a playful provocation along these lines. Here Sundaram appears to be adapting the Brechtian strategy of "making strange" to the new regimes of spectacle and runaway brand consumerism that have come to define neoliberal India, while foregrounding the seemingly irresolvable problem of the art world's inextricable entanglements within them. And yet, the preoccupation with medical materials in Sundaram's line of haute couture — surgical masks, X-ray film, cervical support bandages, pill wrappers — points conspicuously toward the less glamorous universe of illness, medicine, and the fragility of the human body.

Two years later Sundaram brought these more disquieting elements to the fore in a subsequent series, titled *Postmortem (after Gagawaka)* (2013), comprising large and small mannequins, tailor's dummies, anatomical models, and wooden props. Using surrealist (or postsurrealist) devices to present the human body on a darker stage, *Postmortem* was an experiment in dissection, one that seized techniques of dismemberment and distortion to splay open the body's internal framework and to probe its physical and psychic parts. Simultaneously playful, erotic, violent, even foolish, these highly constructed "organic" constructions, as seen in figures Epi.3 and Epi.4, behaved like a bad-mannered set of

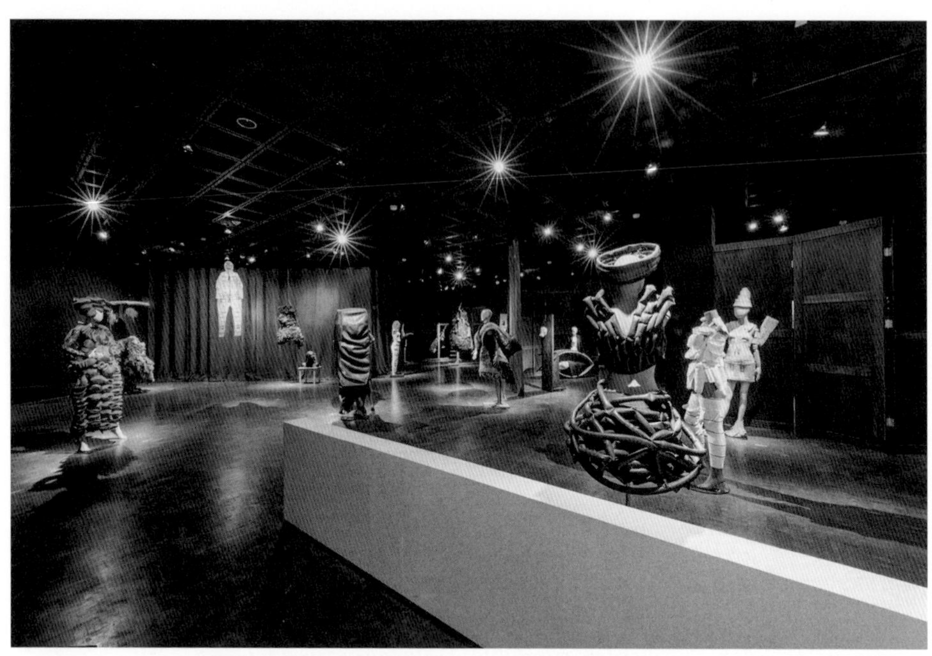

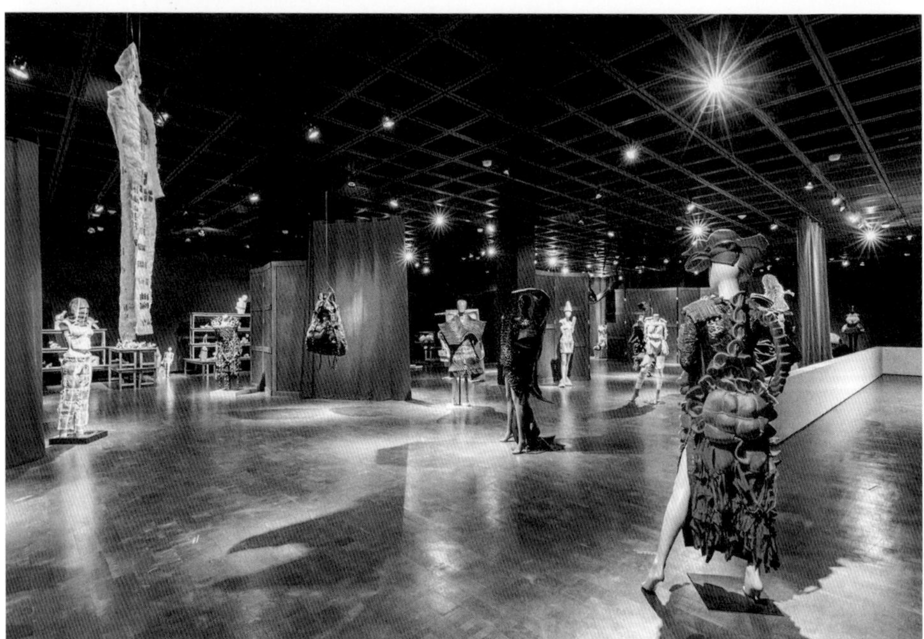

biological specimens, disrespecting nature's most basic forms and creating havoc with the body's utilitarian parts.

In *Postmortem*, we encounter hands reaching out from buttocks; spleens and penises protruding in odd places; fists punching through strange surfaces; bones breaking free of their oppressive skeletal systems. Elsewhere, in figure Epi.4, a shell of skin is cut back to reveal the fantastic instrument that is the human spine. Several of *Postmortem*'s forms seem almost prenatal, as if they are awaiting human life; others are more like mutant specimens, as if altered by the most reckless of gestations. Here, as the garments recede ever so slowly, fashion's upbeat tempo is calibrated against the more gradual processes of aging and mortality; plyboard benches from the runway show become coffins, closets, and curiosity cabinets; and we are reminded of the futility of instant transformation like body-building or plastic surgery, at best only temporary age-defying acts. No wonder that these wooden benches, part of the physical structure of *Gagawaka*'s stage performance in Delhi, become so crucial to the expanded autopsy examination that is Sundaram's *Postmortem*. The artist has repurposed his own work here to construct a different kind of stage set: namely, a theater of extreme nakedness where the physical experiences of pain and pleasure, and the trauma of existence itself, become exposed (see figure Epi.5).

Although a postmortem is an autopsy, an examination of something after its death, Sundaram's *Postmortem* did not unequivocally put the spectacle of fashion embodied in *Gagawaka* to death. On the contrary, as co-curator Miwon Kwon and I asserted in an exhibition (see figures Epi.1 and Epi.2) that brought these two bodies of work together for the first time, *Gagawaka* "plus" *Postmortem* signals a new equation and proposition that is more than merely the sum of its parts.[10] This is because the interaction between Sundaram's audacious line of haute couture and the experiment in dissection that haunts it called *Postmortem* does not permit a settled relationship between "fashion," on the one hand, and "the body," on the other, as if these were discrete entities that could somehow exist apart from one another. On the contrary, the sculptural garments of *Gagawaka* are brought to life in vibrant and altogether different ways, animated by their intimate encounters with *Postmortem*'s peculiar anatomical forms. Similarly, the mannequins and material traces of *Gagawaka*'s fashions live on in *Postmortem* and allow us to see the former's fashions as participants in the latter's dissection and de-

FIGURE EPI.1
(opposite, top)
*Making Strange:
Gagawaka +
Postmortem*, 2015,
installation view,
Fowler Museum at
UCLA. Photograph
by Joshua White/
JWPictures.com.
Courtesy of Fowler
Museum at UCLA.

FIGURE EPI.2
(opposite, bottom)
*Making Strange:
Gagawaka + Post-
mortem*, 2015,
installation view,
Fowler Museum at
UCLA. Photograph
by Joshua White/
JWPictures.com.
Courtesy of Fowler
Museum at UCLA.

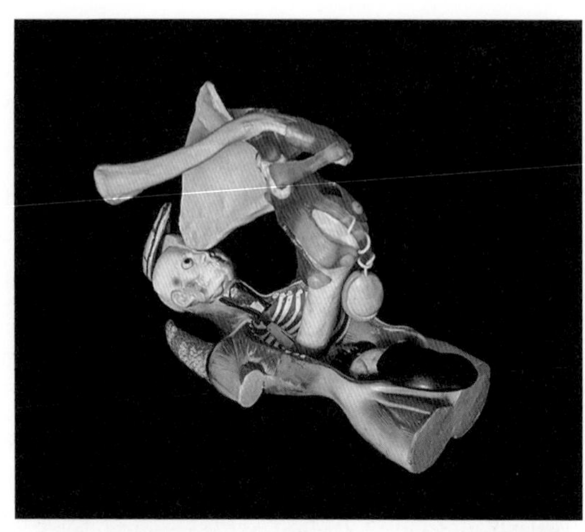

FIGURE EPI.3 *Postmortem* sculptural object, 2013, fiberglass body organs, anatomical samples. Photograph by Idris Ahmed. Courtesy of the artist and Vadehra Art Gallery, New Delhi.

FIGURE EPI.4 *Making Strange: Gagawaka + Postmortem*, 2015, installation view, Fowler Museum at UCLA. Photograph by Joshua White/ JWPictures.com. Courtesy of Fowler Museum at UCLA.

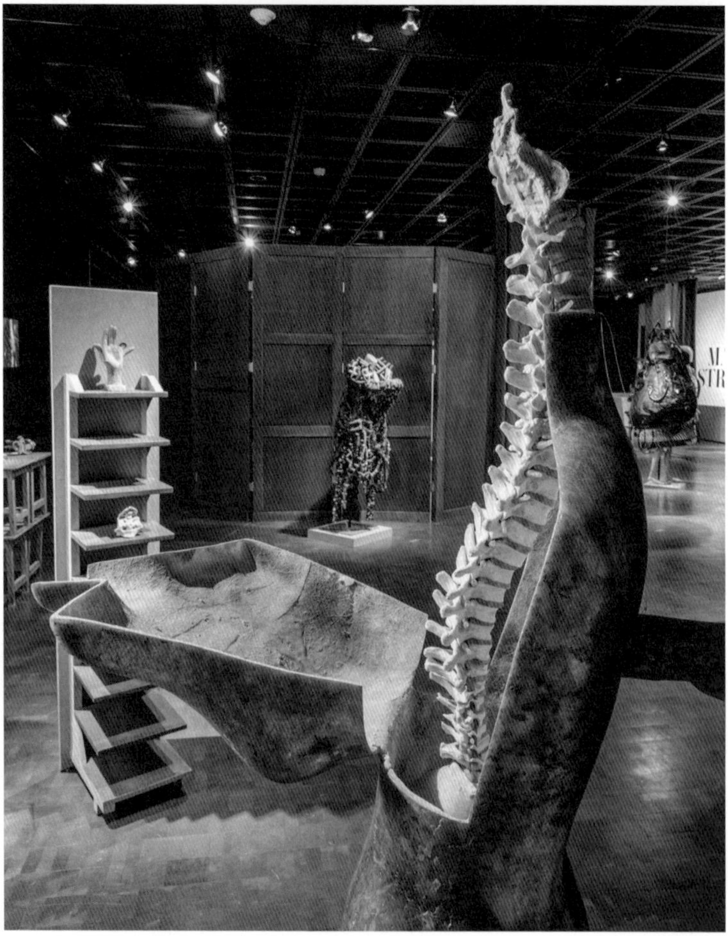

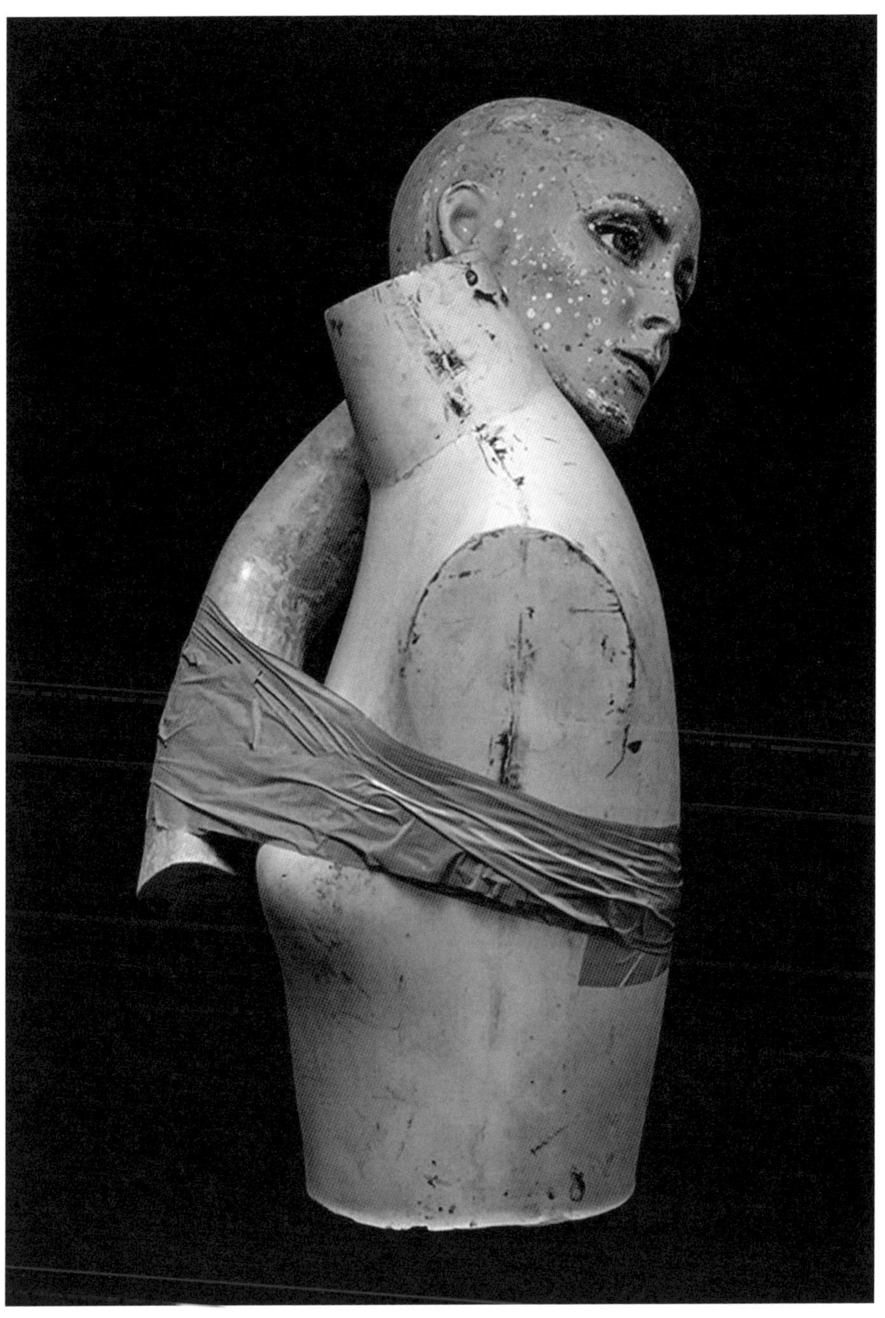

FIGURE EPI.5 *Postmortem* sculpture, 2013, fiberglass mannequin, tape. Photograph by Idris Ahmed. Courtesy of the artist and Vadehra Art Gallery, New Delhi.

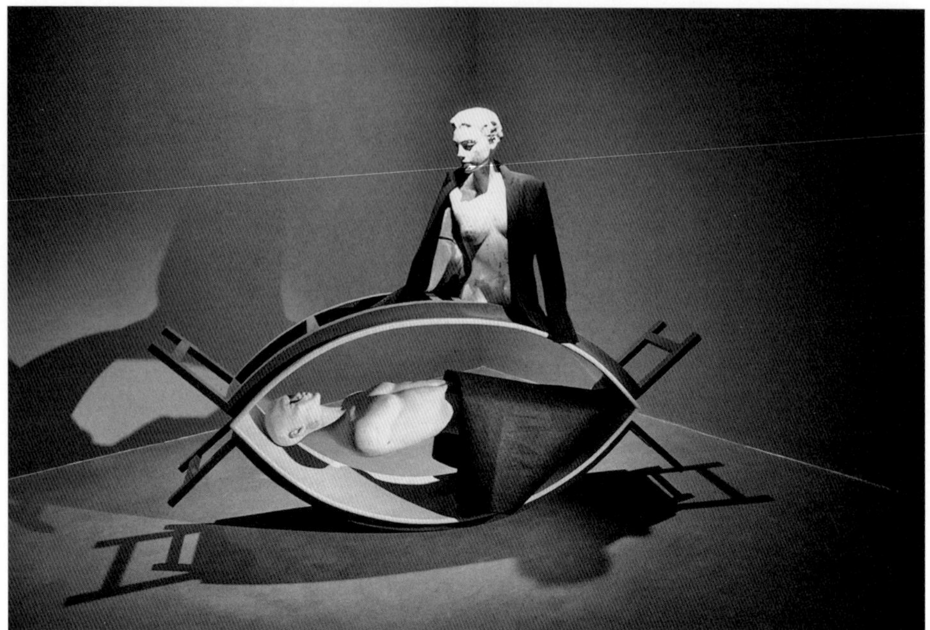

construction, so the dynamic relation of "haunting" goes in both directions (see figure Epi.6). In other words, the connection between them
is relational or dialectical, implying a fluid chain of synthetic associations. Alternately affirming and undermining each other, these projects
bear the same paradoxical spirit of reckoning-without-reconciliation
that was a crucial feature of "lateness" for Adorno and Said.

A similarly ambitious project, a series of five exhibitions curated by
Kapur at the gallery Chemould Prescott Road in Bombay, ran parallel to
these activities by Sundaram and brought some of *Postmortem*'s sculptural
forms into its quite different fold. The occasion for Kapur's series, titled
Aesthetic Bind, was the fiftieth anniversary of this historic gallery space,
one of the oldest of such venues in the subcontinent, which famously
nurtured the first wave of modern artists in post-independence India at
a time when modernism itself could not be taken for granted. Working
with Chemould director Shireen Gandhy, whose parents founded the
Bombay institution, to mount the exhibitions in relatively quick succession during an eight-month period from September 2013 to April 2014,
Kapur presented over 56 contemporary artists from South Asia and a
total of 119 works. By reinventing the walls, colors, lighting, and mood

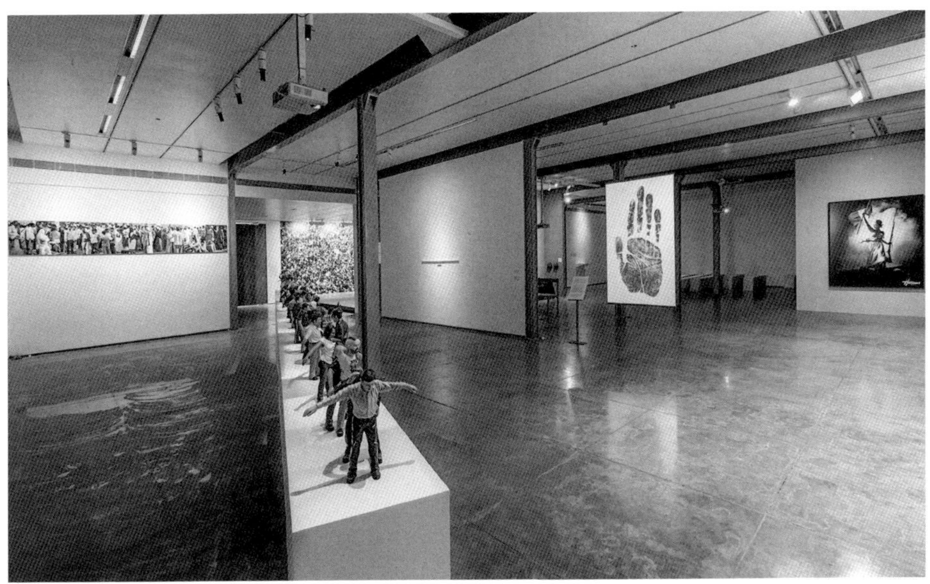

of the gallery space anew each time, Kapur prioritized the phenomenological encounter with art and the relay of meanings produced by objects in space. She also composed precise curatorial statements for each
show that were expanded into an exhibition book.[11]

Significantly, the project reflected a number of investments expressed in Kapur's writing over the past two decades, for example, her
enduring commitment to curating as a critical act, her alignment with
the problematics of region and nation, and her assertion of the concept
of the "citizen artist," which appeared in the title of show number two
(see figure Epi.7). It also galvanized new ideas and gestures, in particular, more metaphysical orientations and a greater emphasis on the
realm of the imaginary. And yet, the evocative title *Aesthetic Bind*—one
can be bound to the aesthetic, or "in a bind," philosophically speaking—pointed less to a place of authority or mastery than to a persistent
sense of difficulty, dilemma, constraint, and conundrum. The project
was thus both a major showcase of contemporary art on the subcontinent and a profound attempt by Kapur to elaborate and revisit the conditions of her own acts of writing, thinking, and curating through the
course of her five-decade career.[12]

In the same way that *Postmortem* brought mortality to the fore, *Aesthetic Bind* addressed death in the boldest of terms. Within the logic of

FIGURE EPI.7
Citizen Artist: Forms of Address, installation view, exhibition curated by Geeta Kapur, 2013. Photograph by Anil Rane. Courtesy of Chemould Prescott Road and the artists.

five non-hierarchically organized events, each one following the next without climax or suspense, the advent of death causes a definitive rupture in the sequence. Such was the force of the first exhibition, *Subject of Death*, which explored how art—and painting in particular, since the exhibition consisted mostly of painting (it did not concede, in other words, to *that* death)—had the capacity to "immortalize absence," to become, in Kapur's subtle formulation, "a preemptive move against nothingness." It did so by remembering the death of Bhupen Khakhar, the enormously influential and openly gay painter whose work and life gave rise to many creative projects, some of which I explicated in this book's introduction. "Because death came so rapidly to Bhupen," Kapur explained, "he addressed it every which way—with rage, with pleas for compassion, with unconcealed terror."[13] Khakhar's intense, even ferocious, works from this period were thus placed at the center of an ensemble that included a variety of acts of mourning, homage, and slow surrender to mortality, by a range of junior and senior artists from India. Moreover, as I argued at the outset, the act of positioning (in Kapur's terms) "Saint Bhupen hanging resplendent in his gallery and among friends" also provided a self-reflexive response to discourses of philosophy, criticism, and queer sexuality, not to mention memorialization itself, from within the formats available to the curator and critic.

The second show, titled *Citizen Artist: Forms of Address*, elaborated Kapur's theory of the socially engaged artist, a line of thinking that has been central to her vision of a contestatory citizenship and her conceptualization, since the 1990s, of the core suppositions surrounding an Indian avant-garde. This show differed dramatically from the first in its formal selections, incorporating multichannel video, sound, and performance projects by younger artists and collectives like Raqs Media Collective, CAMP, Tushar Joag, Gigi Scaria, Rashid Rana, Jitish Kallat, Shilpa Gupta, and Inder Salim, along with photographic works by Ram Rahman, Gauri Gill, and Pushpamala N. An altogether different proposition was explored in the third show, *Phantomata*. Here, Kapur pointed to the realm of the imaginary, the elusive and multisensory space of phantasm, dreams, memories, and thoughts, where consciousness and the Lacanian symbolic meet the immateriality of the projected image. *Phantomata* was a show concerned with light, lenses, receptive surfaces, and forms of printing that impress or leave traces upon these surfaces; it featured haunting video works by Sonia Khurana, Ranbir Kaleka, Nikhil Chopra, and Raqs Media Collective, alongside the anachronistic

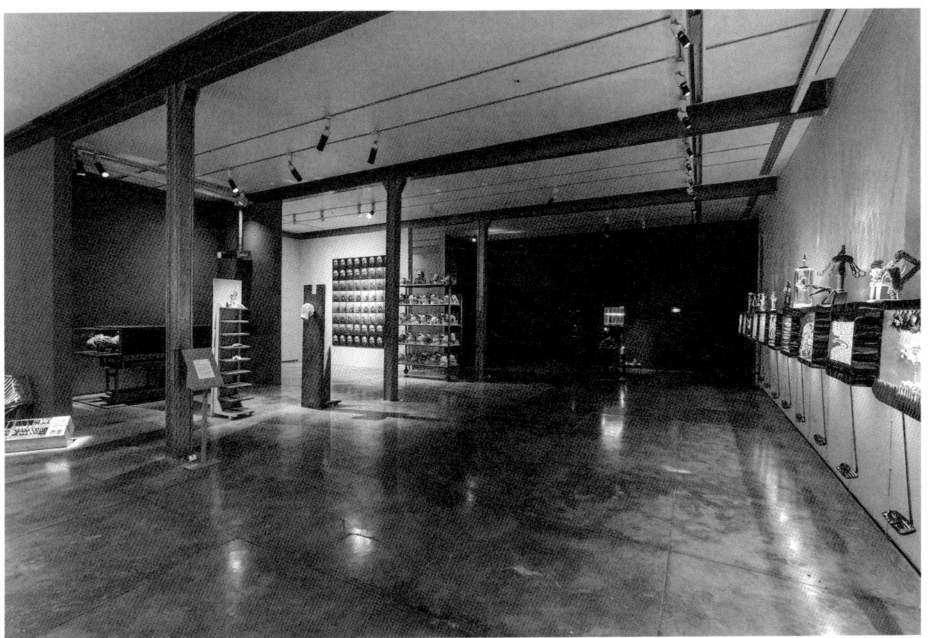

technological devices of Susanta Mandal, Sudarshan Shetty, and L.N. Tallur.

Figure Epi.8 presents a view of the fourth show, *Cabinet Closet Wunder-kammer*, which was entirely different yet again. It seized upon Adorno's insight that the mausoleum and museum, as structures that enshrine both mortality and material decay, have much in common. Here, Kapur returned once more to death's imposition by placing the pleasures of the *Wunderkammer* into a dialogue with the claustrophobia of the crypt: from the installations-cum-vitrines produced by Atul Dodiya, Shakuntala Kulkarni, and Mithu Sen to the light-box dioramas of Anant Joshi and Archana Hande, the suffocating casts of Yardena Kurulkar, and the coffined mannequins of Sundaram's *Postmortem*. Conveying something beyond the merely macabre, these strange coffins and embryonic vitrines became more like toolboxes containing resources for the future, uncannily pregnant with the forces of life. If the fifth and final show, titled *Floating World*, promised relief from these morbid depths through more buoyant metaphors, such effects were also undercut by Kapur's preference for art with a gravitational pull. In the uneasy *mappa mundi* of Gulammohammed Sheikh, the high-voltage, wired cartography of Reena Kallat, the incendiary matchstick chandeliers of the late Hema

Upadhyay, and the sublime Yamuna River full of filth in the photographs of Atul Bhalla, we are left with a hazardous, threatening, and polluted world, both vulnerable and yet distinctly sublime in the end.

What distinguishes *Aesthetic Bind* as a late cultural endeavor is not merely the curator's orchestral command of grand motifs and finely tuned parts sustained over the course of five different performances. Nor is it the level of difficulty of the genre's sequence and scores or the gravitas of its limitless themes: democracy, politics, dreaming, and death. If shows one and four counter the definitive nature of death *with* the vital creativity of life, then show number five places art alongside civic challenges in a way that sustains the contradictions that are present throughout. It is this pervasive sense of uncertainty and indeterminacy that most characterizes the lateness of Kapur's curatorial vision, embodied in the essential ambiguity of the title and the lack of a final solution to "the bind."[14] Moreover, the mode of recourse to earlier concepts and ideas in these exhibitions and the insistent return to specific artists and works of art enmeshed in intimacy, friendship, and love point to the reiterative process that is crucial to Kapur's radical consciousness and method of work, as I argued in chapter 3. If these acts of redoubling, reassessment, and return at times create echo chambers and discordant effects, they are also principled devices that favor multiplicity and the proliferation of discourse in the realm of aesthetics. In the next section, I turn to the philosophical concept of ellipsis to link the activities of the curator back to those of the artist and to further trace the forms that lateness takes in the individual art and writing of Sundaram and Kapur.

Ellipsis, Anachronism, Exacerbation, and Return

The notion of ellipsis, evoking patterns of repetition but a lack of circularity, provides a powerful lens through which to understand the ethos and spirit of these late projects. In the first place, ellipsis obscures origins and endings: it enacts instead, as Jacques Derrida argued in the final essay of his landmark book, *Writing and Difference* (1967), not only practices of displacement and doubling but also sublimation, suspension, moments of pause, and in-conclusion.[15] The state of ellipsis is precisely that of "not being circular, not moving around and toward a center, but coming endlessly to the limit."[16] If traditional knowledge was symbolized by the closure of the book, then for Derrida ellipsis was the philosophical mode most connected to the openness and creativity of the text. In his own elliptical reading of Derrida's brief five-page thesis, his friend, the philosopher Jean-Luc Nancy, described this essay as both a non-ending and an opening that nonetheless carried "the entire orbit of his thought."[17] What takes place through ellipsis, according to Nancy, was a mode of discerning, an apprehension of "a fine penetrating insight," and this was Derrida's preferred way of knowing.[18] Moreover, for Nancy, ellipsis made it possible, indeed pleasurable, to approach the work of a friend—to confront the problems of proximity and intimacy—because ellipsis enables a break in circularity and allows for elements to be introduced in writing that are alternately discontinuous, aphoristic, intimate, and discrete.

The exchange serves to highlight a number of themes that recur in my subjects' late works: namely, themes of repetition, friendship, reinscription, and return, and a doubling-down on the wager against origins and ends. Finally, as Derrida himself elaborated in a 2002 lecture, in its incompleteness—its failure to achieve the fullness, unity, and singularity of the circle—ellipsis shared a relationship with democracy itself: "Democracy perhaps has an essential affinity with this turn or trope that we call the ellipsis," he wrote.[19] I suggest that it is precisely this vision of democracy to come, forged against the notion of a teleological horizon, that seems to animate more urgently than ever Sundaram's enduring engagement with the politics of memory and Kapur's steadfast and seemingly anachronistic investment in the concept of the avant-garde.

The role of memory within the heightened political tensions of Indian democracy, for example, were explored in Sundaram's large, room-sized installation *Memorial* (1993–2014). Conceived around a single photograph—a news photo of the body of a corpse, a forgotten victim of the communal riots that wracked Bombay in 1992 and 1993—*Memorial* comprised a built environment of diverse sculptural forms that invited acts of mourning and scopic self-reflection. Referencing histories of minimalism and arte povera, the room included arches, plinths, gateways, thresholds, and vitrines, all conversing with the photograph in one way or another, in delicate gestures of entombment, erasure, assault, and consecration. Significantly, Sundaram completed *Memorial* in 1993 in response to the Bombay riots that followed the attack on the Babri Masjid; but he reconstructed the installation in 2014 for an exhibition at the Kiran Nadar Museum of Art in Delhi, and again in 2018 at the Haus der Kunst in Munich. It is notable that the restaging of *Memorial* after more than two decades did not depend upon the exactness of either of these reinstallations. On the contrary, the recent ensembles, although similar to the first, included subtle modifications and new sculptural elements in the room. Here, the elliptical gestures of repetition and difference served to reanimate the work for a politics of the present: just as the past cannot be wrested back from time, the new iteration cannot replicate the first. Instead, the goal is to reactivate art's meanings and forms in relation to the violence of the current conjuncture and to produce a new meditation on memory itself—on what it means to appear, disappear, and reappear over time.[20]

409 Ramkinkars was the title of Sundaram's next major project but one year later: a sculptural installation and immersive theater performance with live actors concerned loosely with the work of the legendary Bengali modernist Ramkinkar Baij (1906–80). Baij was a unique figure in twentieth-century Indian art: a painter, sculptor, and (less well-known) theater artist, he was connected to the esteemed institution of Santiniketan for most of his life. However, Baij's own humble background, along with his flexible experiments with form and genre and his decisive orientation toward peasants and workers, points to an ambivalent relation to this high intellectual context and imbued his work with a radical sensibility. Drawing inspiration from Baij, and deploying his earlier hermeneutic method of the "retake," Sundaram's return to this modernist pioneer took the form of an ambitious collaboration that involved two years of preparation with Anuradha Kapur, theater practitioner and former director of the National School of Drama, and three additional theater specialists and scholars.[21] The result was a two-and-a-half-hour theatrical experiment, held at the IGNCA (Indira Gandhi National Centre for the Arts) in Delhi, comprising approximately ten nightly performances in the spring of 2015.

This complex, multilingual, and nonlinear show was "conceptualised on a grand and bold scale" by Sundaram, according to one reviewer, involving elaborate tableaus, props, and sound and lighting, both inside and outside of the gallery space, culminating in a one-hour open-air performance.[22] The project derived its title from the four hundred pieces of sculpture produced by Sundaram (plus the nine letters in Ramkinkar's name), which included re-creations of such iconic works by Baij as *Santhal Family* (1938) and *Mill Call* (1956), depicting tribal and

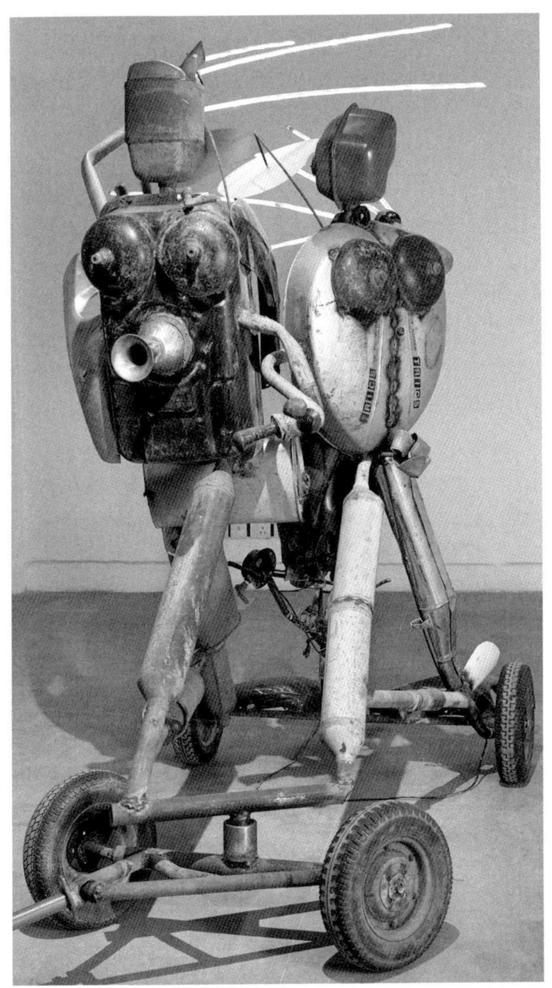

worker figures, respectively. Sundaram's version of the latter, *Mill Recall* (depicted in figure Epi.9) was a mobile industrial stage prop on wheels made from old manufacturing, scooter, and motor car parts, deliberately *unlike* Baij's immovable, open-air sculpture.[23] At the center of the project was a small army of terra-cotta figures (figure Epi.10), which Sundaram titled *The One and the Many*, an installation that pointed both in form and title to the tensions and transpositions between the individual and the collective, a recurrent theme in Baij's work.

The art historian Parul Dave Mukherji has noted the many layers of complexity in this project, in which Sundaram's sculptural assemblages explicitly reference and reinterpret Baij's work, without any pretense

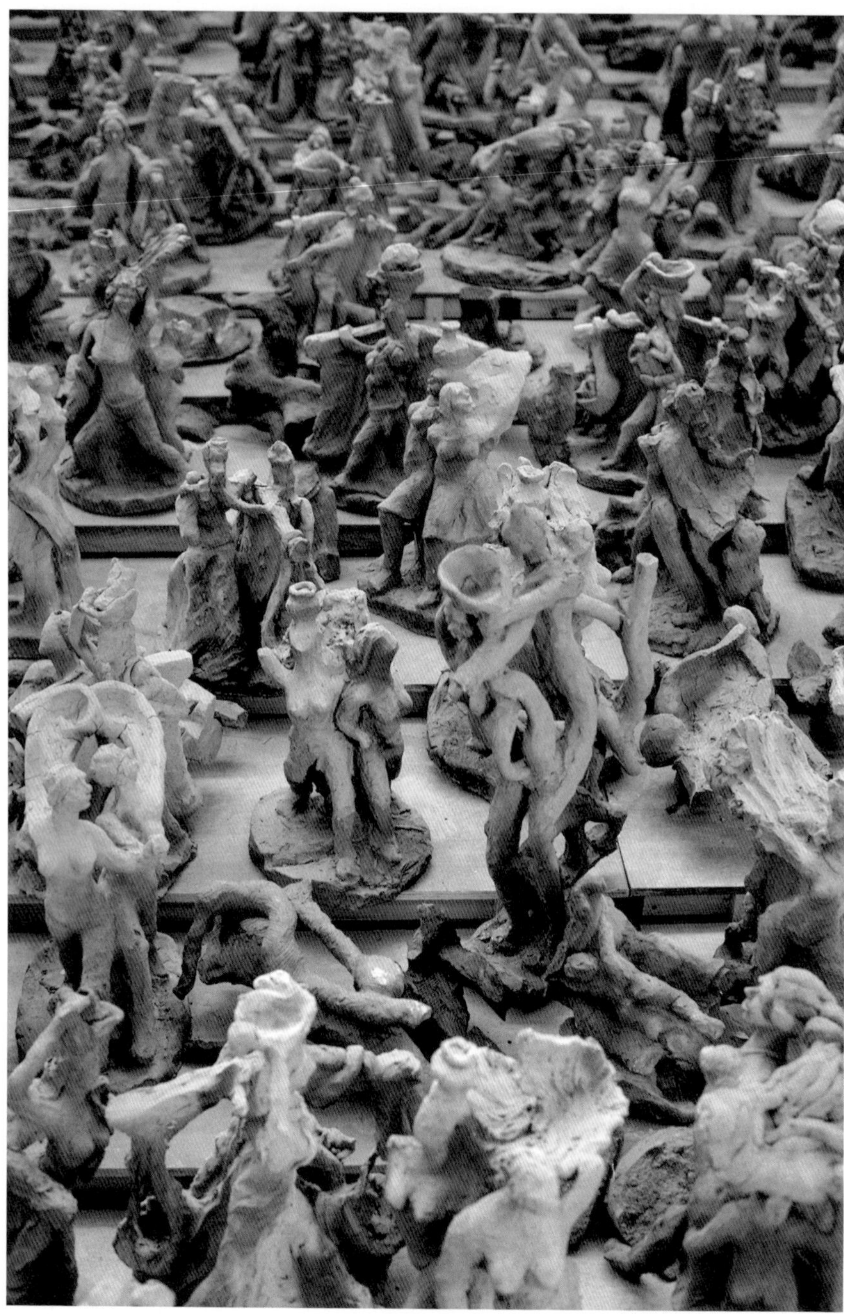

FIGURE EPI.10 Vivan Sundaram, *One and the Many* (detail), 2015, from *409 Ramkinkars*, four hundred terra-cotta figurines. Made in collective workshop by sculptors Krishna Kumar, Saroj Kumar, Sashikanth, Rathan Kumar Verma. Courtesy of the artist.

to replicating its traditional forms. Here, as she has stated, we witness a familiar archival impulse in which the contemporary is staged through "a detour to the past" and reanimated "around a figure that acts as a peg for a range of experiences from the cerebral to the sensual, for the now."[24] In other words, the artist's recall of Baij purposefully evokes Sundaram's earlier "retake" of Amrita, effecting some of the same temporal-historical disjunctures witnessed in that project. In fact, *409 Ramkinkars* gathers together many techniques, gestures, and preoccupations apparent in Sundaram's artistic career as it has been discussed in this book: in it we can see an extension of the historical engagement with the intellectual culture of modern Bengal, along with the multimedia framework and site-specificity, that characterized *History Project*. Similarly, the repurposed materials in these multimedia assemblages—some devised from metal, car parts, and brightly colored fiberglass, others crafted from rubber, wood, and terra-cotta—recall the terra-cotta shards of *Black Gold*, the peculiar figural forms of *Postmortem*, and the recycling operations of *Trash* and *Gagawaka*. Moreover, the turn to performance, spectacular scale, and collaborative spirit of the project all have precedents in the various elements of *Gagawaka* and strike the same dissonant chord of "making strange" via Brecht. Simultaneously pointing backward and forward in time, inward to an individual figure, and outward onto a vast spectrum of repeating issues and themes, *409 Ramkinkars* was both a powerful collaboration and a kind of elliptical, polyphonic, and reverberative occasion, whose structure and meaning will continue to emerge in the afterlife of the performance and in future engagements with its multiple texts.

The reiterative process of ellipsis is also everywhere in Kapur's writing practice, as I suggested in chapter 3; it marks an individuality of voice and relation to discourse that both resemble and depart from the activities of the artist. As noted, the gestures of repetition, renewal, and return that are evident in *Aesthetic Bind* become most potent in Kapur's writings about artists like M. F. Husain, Bhupen Khakhar, and Nasreen Mohamedi, who were friends and interlocutors through their lives but whose deaths entail new kinds of responsibilities and challenges of reinscription for the art historian-critic. Attempting to grasp the anguish, for example, of Mohamedi's debilitating neuromuscular disease, Kapur wrote in 2015, "This suppressed trauma has only now, from close reading of her diaries, come into focus. As a friend-witness, I am cognizant of Nasreen's courage in life and work and would like to place her revealed affliction within a life-enhancing mise-en-scène. So I look for an allegory."[25] In the same way that Nancy saw ellipsis as a means to approach the work of Derrida, his friend—a means by which to mediate the delicate reality of human intimacy with the creativity and pleasures of writing and the text—Kapur has returned on countless occasions to write about these artists in different affective registers and lyrical modes, from passion, fondness, and love to reassessment, mourning, and individual/collective loss. And yet, these essays do not lead to redundancy or to a cumulative, authoritative closing of the circle. They enact instead a more recursive sensibility to reveal precisely the condition of "not being circular," to repeat inscriptions of memory against absence and loss, and to "come endlessly to the limits" of representation itself.[26]

Kapur's investment in the notion of the avant-garde, I will argue in these final pages, stands as another exemplary instance of this elliptical mode. At times misunderstood, the concept is arguably the most significant "keyword" in the critic's vocabulary, consistently informing her theoretical arguments for the past twenty-five years and included in several of the essays in *When Was Modernism* (2000).[27] In the book's final chapter, in particular, titled "Dismantled Norms: Apropos an Indian/Asian Avant-Garde," first published in 1996, Kapur argued that the notion of the avant-garde needed to be "unstrung from the logic of a Euro-American master discourse" and connected to the "hitherto unlogged initiatives" that belonged to specific national or regional histories like those of India and/or Asia.[28] Kapur's response in that essay to the American theorist Hal Foster has been described as "one of the first serious attempts to converse directly" with the long history of intense discussions surrounding the avant-garde in Euro-American theory.[29] In enacting what she called a "deliberate deflection" of Foster's argument, Kapur drew attention to the narrow geopolitical frames and continued indifference to the non-Western world that shaped existing debates on the avant-garde. She thus made visible what Paul Mann has referred to as avant-garde theory's "discursive economy," namely, its own vested interests in institutions of thought.[30] In later essays, she appeared to harness the concept more firmly to the locus of the city, in particular to the disruptive possibilities contained in the volatile urban-scapes of Mumbai in the 1990s and the fraught landscape of New Delhi in the first decade of the twenty-first century.[31]

Lately, in a short polemic titled *Proposition Avant-Garde*, Kapur has argued some two decades later for the need to "continue with the term" by reinforcing "the postcolonial with an avant-garde discourse."[32] Her proposition takes the form of a manifesto, a kind of ironic retake of this modernist genre, outlining thirteen core claims related to the conditions and urgent challenges of the aesthetic field in India. It is pitched from a specific axis, the geopolitical south, and through a decisive set of historical energies—from Bandung to Fanon to *negritude*—that reshape the dominant story of radicalism in twentieth-century art. Here, Kapur has enumerated all manner of temporal, social, and geopolitical contingencies that constitute the "seismic terrain" of our world today, and she has put forth the perennial problem of art's possibilities for existence within it. At the heart of the proposition is Kapur's call to "continue with the term avant-garde," to imbue it with "dense and diverse (cultural) annotation," and to give "valence and purpose to the key avant-garde dialectic," namely, the imbrication between art and life across the widest possible political scale.[33] Her manifesto therefore reactivates her earlier usages and raises several questions at the outset: Why, it seems reasonable to ask, does Kapur remain attached to the notion of the avant-garde in relation to contemporary art in India when that concept has been increasingly disparaged as outdated, exhausted, or overexposed? And how should we understand the centrality and organizing role of the avant-garde in Kapur's theoretical imagination over time?

The idea of the avant-garde is a truly ubiquitous one today, often synonymous with *any* experimental art or a rejection of the status quo in general. Kapur's usage, by contrast, is highly particular and might be seen as an act of vigilance *against* the problem of the concept's increasingly nonspecific character. To begin to understand her relation to this idea is to grasp its intellectual origins in a tradition of Marxist aesthetic theory that evolved from debates surrounding the German literary critic Peter Bürger's influential text *Theory of the Avant-Garde* (1974) and Italian theorist Renato Poggioli's earlier text by the same name (1971). Ever since Bürger's diagnosis that the avant-garde had failed—it failed to resist the forces it opposed, like the market and the institutions of art—the questions of the "death" of the avant-garde has been at the center of these debates. In what Mann has called this "seemingly inexhaustible discourse of exhaustion," there is a dizzying lack of consensus around the questions of where, when, how, and under what conditions an avant-garde project becomes absorbed or obsolete or inevitably co-opted by the systems it opposes. The death of the avant-garde thus represents not its termination, according to Mann, but its "most productive, voluble, self-conscious and lucrative stage."[34]

While some might view the avant-garde as a historical project that has been superseded (with what, however, is not at all clear), Kapur is among those critical theorists who recognize it as a productive discourse of aesthetics driven by its own self-conscious contradictions and the tension of its unrealizability. From this position, the avant-garde is an antiteleological category that, "far from being dead, remains vitally alive" through its internal contradictions and ongoing rearticulation in new and different social and political circumstances.[35] It provides, as Kapur states, a "template for radical disruption," an open-ended placeholder with "deconstructive leverage," rather than a concrete course of action or a doctrine with a fixed design.[36] In other words, it is precisely the lack of an end-game that imbues the avant-garde with its greatest possibilities. This is what John Roberts has called the "suspensive function" of the avant-garde—namely, the indefinite open-endedness of the discourse itself, its constructive paradoxes and contradictions, and the supple way in which this theoretical framework returns us to the most penetrating aesthetic questions in the end: What is an artist? What is an artwork? What constitutes value in art? What are the progressive possibilities and limitations of art's relationship to the world? And so on.[37]

It would be a mistake to view Kapur's commitment to the avant-garde concept as a symptom of what Rosalind Deutsche has called "left melancholy," the attachment on the part of Marxist theorists to past political ideals like unified social movements or a politics defined exclusively by class.[38] For this would imply an adherence to traditionalism, a sense of orthodoxy and inflexibility, and a foundationalist worldview that cannot be accurately attributed to Kapur. On the contrary, her account of a disaggregated society, defined in and through the struggles of India's marginal constituencies along gender, caste, and tribal inequalities, presents a disparate political geography that does not presume such a social totality. Nor does Kapur call for an old-style oppositional avant-garde; she speaks rather of a "conjunctural politics" and modes of resistance that are tethered to situational and locational criteria. For her, the term must be qualified with "dense and diverse (cultural) annotation" in order to give it new purpose and life.[39] Elsewhere in the text, Kapur insists on self-revision: her earlier model of "agonistic reckonings," she states, "seems difficult" within a neoliberal era, and the terms of reference "have to be vastly complicated" yet again.[40] In other words, Kapur's proposition is a revitalizing endeavor, an elliptical project of creative renewal, an ongoing, flexible, and dynamic procedure, rather than a static or nostalgic return to the past. It is a proposition that favors instability and indeterminacy while drawing attention, through its stylistic play, to the forms available for political speech in the present. "Far from hubris," Kapur reminds us, "this is a case to sustain the singularity of the human voice within an amply articulated plurality."[41]

In the end, Kapur's proposition is a philosophical one that rejects the morbid discourses of death that foreclose on a historicized concept of the avant-garde and, indeed, on the role and practice of theory itself. It is an invitation to rethink one of *the* key theoretical terms in the realm of aesthetics in the past half a century, to review and recalibrate its usage and scope, and to dislodge it from its previous scripts. It is a call to rework our existing vocabulary in ever more democratic directions and to understand art's discursive economy in a historically informed way. It argues for an avant-garde consciousness, as well as a consciousness of the avant-garde *debate*. The critic and art historian George Baker, drawing on Said and Adorno, has identified what he calls "late criticism." For Baker, late criticism represents a form of possibility, a "splinter of redemption" in the new era of irrelevance for art criticism.[42] Late criticism is, according to Baker, a criticism of "willfully anachronistic criteria"—not a nostalgic relationship to the past but a means of exacerbation and intervention.[43] The point, Baker argues, "is not to consider criticism as dead, but instead as *confronting* its death, and making of this confrontation a project."[44] Here, then, is a final way to understand Kapur's resurrection of the (exhausted) concept of the avant-garde in the (outmoded) form of the manifesto: not a weary program of Marxist didactics but an assiduously self-conscious undertaking involving ellipsis, reckoning, confrontation, and renewal.

....

Taken together, the liveliness of these current projects and the inventiveness of the artist and the critic seem to intensify and complicate description and vocabulary and to frustrate our efforts to follow in real time: on the one hand, ellipsis, reiteration, recursivity, and return; on the other, dilemma, conundrum, obduracy, and bind. There is no question that these radical acts of imagination are shot through with mortality and the finality of death; and yet, they follow a logic of creation and reproduction that wholly support the intelligence of life. If there is a somewhat morbid fascination with the reconstitutive promise offered by death—found in archives, bodies, narratives, and ideas and encoded in postmortem invitations and reincarnate propositions—this is one effect of a dialectical thought practice that has consistently resisted both origins and ends. As we have seen in these recent projects, our practitioners confront the ambivalence of memorialization by everywhere undermining the normative procedures through which past, present, and future are entangled and produced. Moreover, the scale and force of these efforts appear to escalate in proportion to the urgency and excruciating uncertainty of our times. This uncomfortable sense of intensification and compression, this lack of arrival or satisfactory resolution, this refusal to shy from conflict and contradiction, this way of seizing a certain legacy of culture and turning it critically into one's own, this constant striving toward a better future through creative practice and critical thought, this embedded outlook on the eternal: Is this the fragile inheritance that is bequeathed to us? This book has argued that it surely is, and that a new self-fashioning must necessarily begin out of these inscrutable resources and radical knowledge acts. As to whether all this amounts to the "late style" of my subjects—it is ultimately, of course, too early to tell.

NOTES

Preface

1 Two major exhibitions recently embraced this challenge by presenting a broad retrospective of Sundaram's career over fifty years. They were *Step Inside and You Are No Longer a Stranger*, curated by Roobina Karode, Kiran Nadar Museum of Art, New Delhi, February 9 to June 30, 2018; and *Vivan Sundaram: Disjunctures*, curated by Deepak Ananth, Haus der Kunst, Munich, June 29 to January 1, 2019.

2 Anders Stephanson, "Interview with Craig Owens," in *Beyond Recognition: Representation, Power, and Culture*, ed. Scott Bryson, Barbara Kruger, Lynne Tillman, and Jane Weinstock (Berkeley: University of California Press, 1992), 307.

3 Edward Said, *Beginnings: Intention and Method* (New York: Columbia University Press, 1985), 10.

Introduction

1 Fredric Jameson, "Periodizing the 60s," in *The 60s Without Apology*, ed. Sohnya Sayres, Anders Stephanson, Stanley Aronowitz, and Fredric Jameson (Minneapolis: University of Minnesota Press, 1988), 178–209.

2 See Sabih Ahmed, "Landing Imaginaries: An Interview with Geeta Kapur," in *Sarai Reader 09: Projections* (Delhi: Sarai Programme, CSDS, 2013), 248–56.

3 Vivan Sundaram, interview with Nandita Raman, International Center of Photography, March 17, 2016, http://www.icp.org/interviews/vivan -sundaram.

4 Sundaram, interview with Nandita Raman.

5 Geeta Kapur, "Learning from John Berger," Thewire.in, October 1, 2017, https://thewire.in/98557/learning-john-berger/.

6 Geeta Kapur, "Vagabondage: artandlife in the sixties" (paper presented at Revisiting the Global 1960's: An Interdisciplinary International Conference, School of Arts & Aesthetics, JNU, New Delhi, March 4–5, 2011), 12–13.

7 Geeta Kapur, "Art in These Dark Times," *Economic and Political Weekly* 12, no. 11 (March 12, 1977): 450–51. On the Emergency, see also Emma Tarlo, *Unsettling Memories: Narratives of the Emergency in Delhi* (Berkeley: University of California Press, 2003); Emilia Terracciano, *Art and Emergency: Modernism in Twentieth-Century India* (London: I.B. Tauris, 2017).

8 Arindam Dutta, "SAHMAT, 1989–2004: Liberal Art Practice against the Liberalised Public Sphere," *Cultural Dynamics* 17, no. 2 (July 2005): 193–226; Jessica Moss and Ram Rahman, eds., *The Sahmat Collective: Art and Activism in India since 1989* (Chicago: Smart Museum of Art, University of Chicago, 2013).

9 Belinder Dhanoa, *The Kasauli Art Centre* (New Delhi: SSAF-Tulika Books, forthcoming).

10 David Scott, *Omens of Adversity: Tragedy, Time, Memory, Justice* (Durham, NC: Duke University Press, 2014).

11 Scott, *Omens of Adversity*, 2. Emphasis in original.

12 Edward Said, *The World, the Text, and the Critic* (London: Vintage, 1991), 29.

13 See Martha Buskirk, Amelia Jones, and Caroline Jones, "The Year in 'Re-,'" *ArtForum International* 52, no. 4 (December 2013): 127–30.

14 Jacques Derrida, "The Double Session," in *Dissemination*, trans. Barbara Johnson (Chicago: University of Chicago Press, 1983).

15 Nicolas Bourriaud, *Postproduction* (New York: Lukas and Sternberg, 2002), 44.

16 Hal Foster, *The Return of the Real: The Avant-Garde at the End of the Century* (Cambridge, MA: MIT Press, 1996); see also Peter Bürger, *Theory of the Avant-Garde* (Minneapolis: University of Minnesota Press, 1984).

17 Foster, *The Return of the Real*, x.

18 Frantz Fanon, *The Wretched of the Earth* (New York: Grove, 1963), 40.

19 Vivan Sundaram, "Recycling Photographs," in *Photography Theory*, ed. James Elkins (London: Routledge, 2007), 338. See also Deepak Ananth, "An Unfinished Project," in *Amrita Sher-Gil: An Indian Artist Family of the Twentieth Century* (Munich: Schirmer/Mosel, 2007), exhibition catalogue, 13–31.

20 Sundaram, "Recycling Photographs," 338.

21 Vivan Sundaram, *Re-take of Amrita: Digital Photomontages* (New Delhi: Tulika, 2001), 5.

22 Sher-Gil's unusual biography is worth noting: Amrita was born in Budapest to a Hungarian mother and Sikh father and spent the first eight years of her life in Hungary with her sister, Indira. The family moved to India in 1921 and spent much of the next eight years in Simla before relocating to Paris for her art education. She returned to India in 1934 (at age 21) and lived eventually with her Hungarian husband, Victor Egan, on the family's sugar plantation in the Gorakhpur district of Uttar Pradesh. She moved to Lahore in 1941, where she died suddenly later that year. For further biography of Sher-Gil and the Sher-Gil family, see the Tate Modern exhibition catalogue *Amrita Sher-Gil*; Yasodhara Dalmia, *Amrita Sher-Gil: A Life* (New Delhi: Penguin Viking, 2006); Vivan Sundaram, ed., *Amrita Sher-Gil: A Self-Portrait in Letters and Writings*, 2 vols. (New Delhi: Tulika, 2009); and Vivan Sundaram, *Umrao Singh Sher-Gil: His Misery and His Manuscript* (New Delhi: Photoink, 2008).

23 Sundaram, *Re-take of Amrita*, 5.

24 Geeta Kapur, "The Evolution of Content in Amrita Sher-Gil's Paintings," *Marg* 25, no. 2 (March 1972): 41.

25 See Geeta Kapur, "Re-imagining *Place for People*," in *Horn Please: Narratives in Contemporary Indian Art*, Kuntsmuseum Bern (Berlin: Hatje Cantz, 2007), 27–52.

26 Marsha Meskimmon, *Contemporary Art and the Cosmopolitan Imagination* (New York: Routledge, 2011).

27 Sundaram, *Umrao Singh Sher-Gil and Amrita Sher-Gil*.

28 Geeta Kapur, *When Was Modernism: Essays on Contemporary Cultural Practice in India* (New Delhi: Tulika, 2000), 399.

29 Kapur, *When Was Modernism*, 395.

30 Kapur, *When Was Modernism*, 392.

31 Kapur, *When Was Modernism*, 375.

32 Paul Rabinow, ed., *The Foucault Reader* (New York: Pantheon, 1984), 82.

33 Rabinow, *Foucault Reader*, 97.

34 Rabinow, *Foucault Reader*, 76.

35 Rabinow, *Foucault Reader*, 89–90.

36 Rabinow, *Foucault Reader*, 54.

37 Rabinow, *Foucault Reader*, 45.

38 Étienne Balibar, "The Genealogical Scheme: Race or Culture?" *Trans-Scripts* 1 (2011): 2–9.

39 Sundaram, interview with Nandita Raman.

40 See *Abby Grey and Indian Modernism: Selections from the NYU Art Collection* (New York: Grey Art Gallery, NYU, 2015), exhibition catalogue, 29–30.

41 The thesis was later published as Geeta Kapur, *In Quest of Identity: Art and*

Indigenism in Post-colonial Culture with Special Reference to Contemporary Indian Painting (Baroda: Vrishchik, 1973).

42 Said, *Beginnings*, 5.

43 Gilles Deleuze and Félix Guattari, "Introduction: Rhizome," in *A Thousand Plateaus: Capitalism and Schizophrenia* (Minneapolis: University of Minnesota Press, 1987), 5.

44 Deleuze and Guattari, "Introduction: Rhizome," 9.

45 Deleuze and Guattari, "Introduction: Rhizome."

46 Tania Roy, "Wreck, Restoration, and the Work of Carrying On: History on Vivan Sundaram's Boat-Works," *Cultural Politics* 5, no. 3 (2009): 378.

47 Mariam Ghani, "'What We Left Unfinished': The Artist and the Archive," in *Dissonant Archives: Contemporary Visual Culture and Contested Narratives in the Middle East*, ed. Anthony Downey (London: I.B. Taurus, 2015), 57. See also Nicolas Bourriaud, *The Radicant* (New York: Lukas and Sternberg, 2009).

48 Stuart Hall, "The Neoliberal Revolution," *Soundings* 48 (summer 2011): 9.

49 Geeta Kapur, "A Cultural Conjuncture in India: Art into Documentary," in *Antinomies of Art and Culture: Modernity, Postmodernity, Contemporaneity*, ed. Terry Smith, Okwui Enwezor, and Nancy Condee (Durham, NC: Duke University Press, 2008), 38.

50 Kapur, "Cultural Conjuncture," 30.

51 Kapur, "Cultural Conjuncture," 55.

52 Hall, "Neoliberal Revolution," 26.

53 Sarat Maharaj, ed., *Farewell to Post-Colonialism: Querying the Guangzhou Triennial, 2008* (Dublin: Visual Arts Ireland, 2009), 5. See also Anthony Gardner, "Whither the Postcolonial?," in *Global Studies: Mapping Contemporary Art and Culture*, ed. Hans Belting, Jacob Birken, and Andrea Buddensieg (Berlin: Hatje Cantz, 2011), 142–57; Gayatri Chakravorty Spivak, *A Critique of Postcolonial Reason* (Cambridge, MA: Harvard University Press, 1999).

54 Hal Foster, *Design and Crime (and Other Diatribes)* (New York: Verso, 2002), 129.

55 Ann Laura Stoler, *Duress: Imperial Durabilities in Our Times* (Durham, NC: Duke University Press, 2016).

56 Cited in Stoler, *Duress*, 19.

57 In her book, *Worldly Affiliations: Artistic Practice, National Identity, and Modernism in India, 1930–1990* (Berkeley: University of California Press, 2015), Sonal Khullar also draws on this Said-ian framework to conceptualize the trajectory of modernism in India. Khullar argues that affiliation "denotes a historical process by which a national art world came together and became conjoined with an international art world" (14), but she is less concerned with the question of transmission at the heart of Said's account of the affiliative scheme.

58 Said, *The World*, 17.

59 Said, *The World*, 17.

60 Said, *The World*, 25.

61 Said, *The World*, 20.

62 Said, *The World*, 16.

63 Said, *The World*, 7.

64 Said, *The World*, 20.

65 Karl Mannheim, "The Problem of Generations," in *Essays on the Sociology of Knowledge*, ed. Paul Kecskemeti (London: Routledge and Kegan Paul, 1952; first published 1923), 278.

66 Mannheim, "The Problem of Generations," 291.

67 See Jane Pilcher, "Mannheim's Sociology of Generations: An Undervalued Legacy," *British Journal of Sociology* 45, no. 3 (1994): 481–95.

68 David Scott, "Stuart Hall at Eighty," *Small Axe* 16, no. 2 (July 2012): viii.

69 David Scott, "The Temporality of Generations: Dialogue, Tradition, Criticism," *New Literary History* 45, no. 2 (spring 2014): 157–81.

70 Scott, "Temporality of Generations," 165.

71 Scott, "Temporality of Generations," 166.

72 Rosalind Krauss, *The Originality of the Avant-Garde and Other Modernist Myths* (Cambridge, MA: MIT Press, 1985), 157.

73 Griselda Pollock, "The Politics of Theory: Generations and Geographies in Feminist Theory and the Histories of Art," in *Generations and Geographies in the Visual Arts: Feminist Readings*, ed. G. Pollock (London: Routledge, 1996), 13.

74 Susan Bean, ed., *Midnight to the Boom: Painting in India after Independence* (Salem, MA: Peabody Essex Museum, 2013), 123.

75 Bean, *Midnight to the Boom*, 192 and 195.

76 Chris Dercon and Nada Raza, eds., *Bhupen Khakhar: You Can't Please All* (London: Tate, 2016).

77 See Ranjit Hoskote, "A Crazy Pair of Eyes: Remembering Bhupen Khakhar," in *Touched by Bhupen* (Mumbai: Galerie Mirchandani + Steinruecke, 2013), exhibition catalogue, 34.

78 Gulammohammed Sheikh, "Buddy," in *Touched by Bhupen*, 162.

79 Gulammohammed Sheikh, ed., *Contemporary Art in Baroda* (New Delhi: Tulika, 1997).

80 Geeta Kapur, "The Uncommon Universe of Bhupen Khakhar," in *Pop Art and Vernacular Cultures*, ed. Kobena Mercer (London: Iniva, 2007), 110–35.

81 The show was the first in a series of five exhibitions curated by Kapur under the larger rubric *Aesthetic Bind* at the Gallery Chemould Prescott Road in Mumbai in 2012–13. I discuss the project in more detail in my epilogue.

82 See also the different chapters on Khakhar in two recent monographs: Khullar, *Worldly Affiliations*, and Karin Zitzewitz, *The Art of Secularism: The Cultural Politics of Modernist Art in Contemporary India* (London: Hurst, 2014).

83 Nancy Adajania, "Vivan Sundaram," in *Horn Please*, 108.

84 Adajania, "Vivan Sundaram," 108.

85 Geeta Kapur, "Mortality Morbidity Masquerade," in Dercon and Raza, *Bhupen Khakhar*, 160. The insight recalls the ingenious character of the 2013 exhibition's title, *Touched by Bhupen*.

86 Emilia Terracciano, "A Day in the Life of Khakharpur," *Art India* 17, no. 4 (July 2013): 78.

87 Vandana Kalra, "A Drawing by Dost," *Indian Express*, June 7, 2008.

88 Adajania, "Vivan Sundaram," 108.

89 Kapur, "Uncommon Universe," 112.

90 Kapur, "Uncommon Universe," 114.

91 Terracciano, "Day in the Life of Khakharpur," 79.

92 Marcia Tucker, *Bad Painting* (New York: New Museum, 1978).

93 Susan Sontag, *Against Interpretation and Other Essays* (1966; New York: Picador, 1996), 8.

94 Sontag, *Against Interpretation*, 93.

95 Sontag, *Against Interpretation*, 93–94.

96 Félix Guattari, "Genet Regained," in *The Guattari Reader*, ed. Gary Genosko (London: Wiley-Blackwell, 1996), 218–30.

97 Sontag, *Against Interpretation*, 12.

98 "Independent Critic: Charting a Course—Conversation between Geeta Kapur & Sabih Ahmed," *Take on Art* 2, no. 2 (July–December 2016): 16.

99 Kapur, "Mortality Morbidity Masquerade," 158.

100 Kapur, "Mortality Morbidity Masquerade," 163; emphasis added.

101 Kapur, "Mortality Morbidity Masquerade," 163.

102 Said, *The World*, 24.

103 Said, *The World*, 29.

104 Said, *The World*, 30.

105 Raymond Williams and Terry Eagleton, "The Politics of Hope: An Interview," in *Raymond Williams: A Critical Reader*, ed. Terry Eagleton (Cambridge: Polity, 1991), 176–83.

106 Kapur, "Evolution of Content"; Geeta Kapur, "Body as Gesture: Women Artists at Work," in *When Was Modernism*, 3–60; Geeta Kapur, "Familial Narratives and their Accidental Denouement," in *Where Three Dreams Cross: 150 Years of Photography from India, Pakistan, and Bangladesh* (London: Whitechapel Gallery, 2010), 48.

107 Kapur cites six different essays on Khakhar that she authored between 1969 and 2007 in a footnote. See Dercon and Raza, *Bhupen Khakhar*, 165n1.

108 Homi Bhabha (in conversation with Susan Bean), "India's Dialogical Modernism," in Bean, *Midnight to the Boom*, 24.

109 David Scott, *Conscripts of Modernity: The Tragedy of Colonial Enlightenment* (Durham, NC: Duke University Press, 2004), 4.

110 Scott, *Conscripts of Modernity*, 4.

111 David Scott, *Refashioning Futures: Criticism after Postcoloniality* (Princeton, NJ: Princeton University Press, 1999).

112 Bourriaud, *Postproduction*, 18.

113 Geeta Kapur, "Curating across Agonistic Worlds," in *InFLUX: Contemporary Art in Asia*, ed. Parul Dave Mukherji, Naman P. Ahuja, and Kavita Singh (New Delhi: Sage, 2013), n25.

Chapter 1. Earthly Ecologies

1 On communalism (or sectarian strife) and the visual arts in India, see Jessica Moss and Ram Rahman, eds., *The Sahmat Collective: Art and Activism in India since 1989* (Chicago: Smart Museum/University of Chicago Press, 2013); and Zitzewitz, *Art of Secularism*.

2 *The Times of India*, November 15, 1988.

3 Neville Tuli, *Indian Contemporary Painting* (New York: Harry N. Abrams, 1998), 396.

4 T. J. Clark, *Image of the People: Gustave Courbet and the Second French Republic 1848–1851* (Greenwich, CT: New York Graphic Society, 1973), 17.

5 Clark, *Image of the People*, 17.

6 Rob Nixon, *Slow Violence and the Environmentalism of the Poor* (Cambridge, MA: Harvard University Press, 2011), 35.

7 Nixon, *Slow Violence*, 2.

8 Gastón Gordillo, "Ships Stranded in the Forest: Debris of Progress on a Phantom River," *Cultural Anthropology* 52, no. 2 (April 2011), 141–67; Wu Hung, *A Story of Ruins: Presence and Absence in Chinese Art and Visual Culture* (London: Reaktion, 2011); Ann Laura Stoler, "Imperial Debris: Reflections on Ruins and Ruination," *Cultural Anthropology* 23, no. 2 (2008): 191–219; Julia Hell and Andreas Schönle, eds., *Ruins of Modernity* (Durham, NC: Duke University Press, 2010).

9 Walter Benjamin, "Theses on the Philosophy of History," in *Illuminations*, ed. Hannah Arendt (New York: Schocken, 1968), 257–58.

10 Gordillo, "Ships Stranded in the Forest," 142.

11 Cited in Svetlana Boym, "Ruins of the Avant-Garde: From Tatlin's Tower to Paper Architecture," in Hell and Schönle, *Ruins of Modernity*, 58.

12 Stoler, "Imperial Debris," 198.

13 See Rasna Bhushan, "Tracking," in *Engine Oil and Charcoal: Works on Paper, 1991* (LTG Art Gallery, New Delhi, October 7–26, 1991), exhibition catalogue.

14 On the historical relationships between oil and war, see Iain Boal, T. J. Clark, Joseph Matthews, and Michael Watts, *Afflicted Powers: Capital and Spectacle in a New Age of War* (London: Verso, 2005); and William Engdahl, *A Cen-*

tury of War: Anglo-American Oil Politics and the New World Order (London: Pluto, 2004).

15 Bertolt Brecht, "On Form and Subject Matter," in John Willett, ed., Brecht on Theatre: The Development of an Aesthetic (London: Methuen, 1964), 30.

16 Brecht, "On Form and Subject Matter," 31.

17 Amitav Ghosh, "Petrofiction: The Oil Encounter and the Novel," in The Imam and the Indian (New Delhi: Ravi Dayal and Permanent Black, 2002), 75–89.

18 Ghosh, "Petrofiction," 76.

19 Ghosh, "Petrofiction," 75.

20 Ghosh, "Petrofiction," 79.

21 See Jeff Diamanti and Brent Ryan Bellamy, eds., "Energy Humanities," special issue, Reviews in Cultural Theory 6, no. 3 (2016); Imre Szeman and Dominic Boyer, eds., Energy Humanities: An Anthology (Baltimore: Johns Hopkins University Press, 2017); Patricia Yaeger, ed., special issue, PMLA 126, no. 2 (2011).

22 Allan Stoekl, foreword to Oil Culture, ed. Ross Barrett and Daniel Worden (Minneapolis: University of Minnesota Press, 2014), xii.

23 Imre Szeman, "How to Know about Oil: Energy Epistemologies and Political Futures," Journal of Canadian Studies 47, no. 3 (fall 2013), 145–68.

24 Jennifer Wenzel, "Taking Stock of Energy Humanities," in "Energy Humanities," special issue Reviews in Cultural Theory 6, no. 3 (2016): 31.

25 Andrew Apter, The Pan-African Nation: Oil and the Spectacle of Culture in Nigeria (Chicago: University of Chicago Press, 2005); Barrett and Worden, Oil Culture; Fernando Coronil, The Magical State: Nature, Money, and Modernity in Venezuela (Chicago: University of Chicago Press, 1997); Stephanie LeMenager, Living Oil: Petroleum Culture in the American Century (New York: Oxford University Press, 2014); Timothy Mitchell, Carbon Democracy: Political Power in the Age of Oil (London: Verso, 2011).

26 Mitchell, Carbon Democracy, 5.

27 Allan Sekula, Fish Story (Rotterdam: Richter Verlag, 1995).

28 Sekula, Fish Story, 49.

29 Sekula, Fish Story, 12.

30 Sekula, Fish Story, 32. However, Laleh Khalili, who specializes in Middle East politics and has conducted similar ethnographic work on the shipping infrastructure of the Gulf, claims Sekula as "the most astonishing, affecting, thought-changing" thinker on the subject. Her deep indebtedness to Sekula runs throughout her own extraordinary blog: https://the gamming.org.

31 Benjamin Buchloh, "Allan Sekula: Photography between Discourse and Document," in Sekula, Fish Story, 199.

32 Ian Mayes, "A Nasty Slip on Iraqi Oil," The Guardian, June 7, 2003.

33 For such a history, see David Painter, Oil and the American Century: The Political

Economy of US Foreign Oil Policy, 1941–1954 (Baltimore: Johns Hopkins University Press, 1986); Joe Stork, *Middle East Oil and the Energy Crisis* (New York: Monthly Review Press, 1975).

34 Neil Harris, *Cultural Excursions: Marketing Appetites and Cultural Tastes in Modern America* (Chicago: University of Chicago Press, 1990); Emily Rosenberg, *Spreading the American Dream: American Economic and Cultural Expansion, 1890–1945* (New York: Hill and Wang, 1982).

35 The discrepancies inherent in the history of oil painting are elaborated in my book *India by Design: Colonial History and Cultural Display* (Berkeley: University of California Press, 2007). On Ravi Varma, see Kapur, *When Was Modernism*; Tapati Guha-Thakurta, "The Period of Colonialism and Nationalism, 1757–1947," in *Art of India: Prehistory to the Present*, ed. Fred Asher (Hong Kong: Encyclopaedia Britannica, 2003), 109–28; Partha Mitter, *Art and Nationalism in Colonial India* (Cambridge: Cambridge University Press, 1994); Erwin Neumayer and Christine Schelberger, *Raja Ravi Varma: Portrait of an Artist* (New Delhi: Oxford University Press, 2005); Christopher Pinney, *Photos of the Gods: The Printed Image and Political Struggle in India* (London: Reaktion, 2004); A. Ramachandran, "Raja Ravi Varma: The Marketing Strategies of a Modern Indian Artist," in *Indian Art: An Overview*, ed. Gayatri Sinha (New Delhi: Rupa, 2003).

36 Saloni Mathur, "A Retake of Sher-Gil's 'Self-Portrait as Tahitian,'" *Critical Inquiry* 37, no. 2 (2011): 515–44.

37 Wu Hung, *Vivan Sundaram: Re-take of Amrita* (New York: Sepia International/Alkazi Collection, 2006); Sundaram, *Re-take of Amrita*.

38 The phrase is Jordanna Bailkin's, "India Yellow: Making and Breaking the Imperial Palette," *Journal of Material Culture* 10, no. 2 (2005): 197–214.

39 Frederick Bohrer, *Orientalism and Visual Culture: Imagining Mesopotamia in Nineteenth-Century Europe* (Cambridge: Cambridge University Press, 2003).

40 Scholars have established how American knowledge of the Near East arose in close connection to museums and archaeology, on one hand, and to an explicit Judeo-Christian agenda of pursuing the "truth" of the Old Testament, on the other. The excavation of Nippur in southern Mesopotamia, for example, by the Babylonian Exploration Fund (BEF) between 1888 and 1900, where tens of thousands of cuneiform tablets were unearthed, was one of the largest expeditions undertaken by Americans, and it spawned a rivalry among the University of Pennsylvania, Johns Hopkins, Yale, and the University of Chicago for institutional leadership in the study of the ancient Near East. The history of these archaeological expeditions is thus in part a history of how knowledge was secularized within American higher education —an incomplete process at best, the repercussions of which continue to be felt today. See Magnus Bernhardsson, *Reclaiming a Plundered Past: Archaeology and Nation Building in Modern Iraq* (Austin: University of Texas Press, 2005); Bruce Kuklick, *Puritans in Baby-*

lon: *The Ancient Near East and American Intellectual Life, 1880–1930* (Princeton, NJ: Princeton University Press, 1996); Edward Said, *Orientalism* (New York: Vintage, 1979); Lester Vogel, *To See a Promised Land: Americans and the Holy Land in the Nineteenth Century* (University Park: Pennsylvania State University Press, 1993).

41 Benjamin R. Foster, Karen Polinger Foster, and Patty Gerstenblith, eds., *Iraq beyond the Headlines: History, Archaeology, and War* (London: World Scientific Publishing, 2005), 3.

42 Bell was unquestionably a complicated figure, both a champion of Arabist causes and thoroughly shaped by British imperial ideologies of the era. She also defied standards of female behavior and was once described by a male rival as a "flat-chested, man-woman, globe-trotting, rump-wagging, blathering ass." Her unexplained suicide in Baghdad in 1926 has been related to her increasing redundancy and lack of fit as a subject of empire in an era of decolonization. See Liora Lukitz, *A Quest in the Middle East: Gertrude Bell and the Making of Modern Iraq* (London: I.B. Taurus, 2006), 3. Also, Elizabeth Burgoyne, *Gertrude Bell: From Her Personal Papers, 1889–1914* (London: Ernest Benn, 1958); Janet Wallach, *Desert Queen: The Extraordinary Life of Gertrude Bell* (New York: Doubleday, 1996).

43 Gertrude Bell, *Amurath to Amurath* (London: W. Heinemann, 1911), 115–16, cited in Bernhardsson, *Reclaiming a Plundered Past*, 65.

44 Bernhardsson, *Reclaiming a Plundered Past*, 12.

45 Gertrude Bell, Letter to Mother, March 3, 1926, cited in Bernhardsson, *Reclaiming a Plundered Past*, 153.

46 See "Chapter 4: Mandated Archaeology" in Bernhardsson, *Reclaiming a Plundered Past*, 130–63.

47 Gertrude Bell, Letter to Father, May 4, 1924, cited in Bernhardsson, *Reclaiming a Plundered Past*, 153.

48 Bernhardsson, *Reclaiming a Plundered Past*, 155.

49 Benedict Anderson, "Census, Map, Museum," in *Imagined Communities: Reflections on the Origin and Spread of Nationalism* (New York: Verso, 1991); David Boswell and Jessica Evans, eds., *Representing the Nation: Histories, Heritage and Museums* (London: Routledge, 1999); Ivan Karp, Corrine A. Kratz, Lynn Szwaja, and Tomas Ybarra-Frausto, eds., *Museum Frictions: Public Cultures/Global Transformations* (Durham, NC: Duke University Press, 2006); Barbara Kirshenblatt-Gimblett, *Destination Culture: Tourism, Museums, and Heritage* (Berkeley: University of California Press, 1998).

50 "Free to Do Bad Things," *Guardian Unlimited*, April 12, 2003.

51 Sundaram's peers in Baroda, as well as Navjot Altaf and the PROYOM Study Circle in Bombay, were all reading Neruda in those days, according to Nancy Adajania. See her chapter "Disputations with Marxism" in *Navjot Altaf: The Thirteenth Place* (Mumbai: Guild Art Gallery, 2016).

52 Cited by Ajay Sinha, "Envisioning the Seventies and the Eighties," in *Con-*

temporary Art in Baroda, ed. Gulammohammed Sheikh (New Delhi: Tulika, 1997), 174.

53 Sinha, "Envisioning the Seventies and the Eighties," 174.

54 Juan Pablo Pérez Alfonzo, quoted in LeMenager, *Living Oil*, 92.

55 LeMenager, *Living Oil*, 92.

56 Susan Sontag, *Regarding the Pain of Others* (New York: Picador, 2003), 66.

57 On the role of new visual technologies in contemporary "war-making" practices, see Judith Butler, "Contingent Foundations," in Linda Nicholson, ed., *Feminist Contentions: A Philosophical Exchange* (New York: Routledge, 1995), 35–58; Judith Butler, *Precarious Life: The Powers of Mourning and Violence* (London: Verso, 2004); Caren Kaplan, *Aerial Aftermaths: Wartime from Above* (Durham, NC: Duke University Press, 2018); Stephen Eisenman, *The Abu Ghraib Effect* (London: Reaktion, 2007); Derek Gregory, *The Colonial Present: Afghanistan, Palestine, Iraq* (Oxford: Blackwell, 2004); Nicholas Mirzoeff, *Watching Babylon: The War in Iraq and Global Visual Culture* (New York: Routledge, 2005); Sontag, *Regarding the Pain of Others*; Paul Virilio, *Desert Screen: War at the Speed of Light* (London: Bloomsbury Academic, 2005).

58 W. G. Sebald, *On the Natural History of Destruction*, trans. Anthea Bell (New York: Modern Library Classics, 2004) 19.

59 Sebald, *Natural History of Destruction*, 19.

60 Sebald, *Natural History of Destruction*, 25.

61 Peter Adey, Mark Whitehead, and Alison J. Williams, eds., *From Above: War, Violence and Verticality* (London: Hurst, 2013); Derek Gregory, "Drone Geographies," *Radical Philosophy* 183 (2014): 7–19; Hugh Gusterson, *Drone: Remote Control Warfare* (Cambridge, MA: MIT Press, 2016); Kaplan, *Aerial Aftermaths*; Roger Stahl, "What the Drone Saw: The Cultural Optics of the Unmanned War," *Australian Journal of International Affairs* 67, no. 5 (2013): 659–74.

62 Hito Steyerl, "In Free Fall: A Thought Experiment on Vertical Perspective," in *To See Without Being Seen: Contemporary Art and Drone Warfare*, ed. Svea Braunert and Meredith Malone (St. Louis: Mildred Lane Kemper Art Museum, 2016), 79.

63 Salman Rushdie, *The Moor's Last Sigh* (New York: Vintage, 1995), 4–6.

64 Press statement from the Kochi Biennale Foundation. See http://www.biennialfoundation.org/biennials/kochi-muziris-biennale-india/.

65 See Robert E. D'Souza and Sunil Manghani, eds., *India's Biennale Effect: A Politics of Contemporary Art* (London: Routledge, 2017); Charles Green and Anthony Gardner, *Biennials, Triennials, and Documenta: The Exhibitions That Created Contemporary Art* (London: Wiley-Blackwell, 2016); Elena Filipovic, Marieke van Hal, and Solveig Øvstcbø, eds., *The Biennial Reader* (Berlin: Hatje Cantz, 2010); Rachel Weiss, ed., *Making Art Global (Part 1): The Third Havana Biennale 1989* (London: Afterall, 2012).

66 "Artist Reinvents the Muziris Story," *Hindu*, December 21, 2012.

67 Stoler, "Imperial Debris," 200.

68 W. J. T. Mitchell, ed., *Landscape and Power* (Chicago: University of Chicago Press, 2002).

69 Lukitz, *Quest in the Middle East*, 34. On the visual culture of the Delhi Durbar see Julie Codell, ed., *Power and Dominion: Photography and the Imperial Durbars of British India* (Berlin: Prestel, 2008).

70 Lukitz, *Quest in the Middle East*, 35.

71 Lord Curzon, quoted in Bernhardsson, *Reclaiming a Plundered Past*, 94.

72 Lord Curzon, quoted in Stork, *Middle East Oil*, 11.

73 "Vivan Sundaram and Anil Bhatti: A Conversation," in *Long Night: Drawings in Charcoal* (New Delhi: Lalit Kala Galleries/Chemould Gallery, 1988), exhibition catalogue.

Chapter 2. The Edifice Complex

1 Lord Curzon, quoted in Giles Tillotson, "A Visible Monument: Architectural Policies and the Victoria Memorial Hall," in *The Victoria Memorial Hall, Calcutta: Conceptions, Collections, Conservation*, ed. Philippa Vaughan (Mumbai: Marg, 1997), 8.

2 Umberto Eco, "The Poetics of the Open Work" (1962). Reprinted in *Participation: Documents of Contemporary Art*, ed. Claire Bishop (Cambridge, MA: MIT Press, 2006), 20–40.

3 Alexander Alberro and Blake Stimpson, eds., *Institutional Critique: An Anthology of Artists' Writings* (Cambridge, MA: MIT Press, 2011); John Welchman, ed., *Institutional Critique and After* (Zurich: JRP Ringier, 2006).

4 Vivan Sundaram, *History Project* (New Delhi: Tulika, 2017).

5 Miwon Kwon, *One Place after Another: Site-Specific Art and Locational Identity* (Cambridge, MA: MIT Press, 2002), 26.

6 James Meyer, "The Functional Site: Or, the Transformation of Site-Specificity," in *Space, Site, Intervention: Situating Installation Art*, ed. Erika Suderburg (Minneapolis: University of Minnesota Press, 2000), 25.

7 Arthur Danto, "The Vietnam Veteran's Memorial," *The Nation*, August 31, 1986, 152.

8 Charles Griswold, cited in Marita Sturken, "The Wall, the Screen and the Image: The Vietnam Veterans Memorial," in *The Visual Culture Reader*, ed. Nicholas Mirzoeff (London: Routledge, 1998), 165.

9 For example, Tony Bennett, *The Birth of the Museum: History, Theory, Politics* (London: Routledge, 1995); Carol Duncan, *Civilizing Rituals: Inside Public Art Museums* (London: Routledge, 1995); Andrew McClellan, *Inventing the Louvre: Art, Politics, and the Origins of the Modern Museum in Eighteenth-Century Paris* (Berkeley: University of California Press, 1994); Daniel Sherman and Irit Rogoff, eds., *Museum Cultures: Histories, Discourses, Spectacles* (Min-

neapolis: University of Minnesota Press, 1994); Peter Vergo, ed., *The New Museology* (London: Reaktion, 1989).

10 Tapati Guha-Thakurta, *Monuments, Objects, Histories: Institutions of Art in Colonial and Postcolonial India* (New York: Columbia University Press, 2003); Saloni Mathur and Kavita Singh, eds., *No Touching, No Spitting, No Praying: The Museum in South Asia* (New Delhi: Routledge, 2015).

11 Mulk Raj Anand, "Museum: House of the Muses," *Marg* 19 (December 1965): 3.

12 Anand, "Museum: House of the Muses," 5.

13 Pierre Cabanne, *Dialogues with Marcel Duchamp* (Boston: Da Capo Press, 1987), 38. See also Thierry de Duve, ed., *The Definitively Unfinished Marcel Duchamp* (Cambridge, MA: MIT Press, 1991).

14 Jacques Derrida, *The Truth in Painting*, trans. Geoff Bennington and Ian McLeod (Chicago: University of Chicago Press, 1987), 45.

15 Derrida, *Truth in Painting*, 54.

16 Derrida, *Truth in Painting*, 81.

17 Derrida, *Truth in Painting*, 78–79.

18 Derrida, *Truth in Painting*, 73.

19 Derrida, *Truth in Painting*, 74.

20 James Mill, *The History of British India*, vol. 1 (London: Baldwin, Cradock and Joy, 1826), 2.

21 Andreas Huyssen, *Present Pasts: Urban Palimpsests and the Politics of Memory* (Stanford, CA: Stanford University Press, 2003), 110.

22 Jan Estep, "Reading Hirschhorn: A Problem of (His) Knowledge or Weakness as a Virtue," *Afterall* 9 (2004): 83–89.

23 Ranajit Guha, *Dominance without Hegemony: History and Power in Colonial India* (Cambridge, MA: Harvard University Press, 1998), 191.

24 See Ranajit Guha, introduction to *A Subaltern Studies Reader, 1986–1995* (Minneapolis: University of Minnesota Press, 1997), xxi.

25 Arindam Dutta, *The Bureaucracy of Beauty: Design in the Age of Its Global Reproducibility* (New York: Routledge, 2007), 286. See also his essay, "Staging Absence," in Sundaram, *History Project*, 165–92.

26 Guha, *Dominance without Hegemony*, x.

27 Guha, *Dominance without Hegemony*, 5.

28 Guha, *Dominance without Hegemony*, 5.

29 Guha, *Dominance without Hegemony*, xii.

30 Huyssen, *Present Pasts*, 35.

31 See Hal Foster, *The Art-Architecture Complex* (New York: Verso, 2011), 43.

32 Hans Haacke, "Der Bevölkerung," *Oxford Art Journal* 24, no. 2 (2001): 131.

33 Paul Williams, *Memorial Museums: The Global Rush to Commemorate Atrocities* (New York: Berg, 2007).

34 Huyssen, *Present Pasts*, 3. See also his earlier book, *Twilight Memories: Marking Time in a Culture of Amnesia* (New York: Routledge, 1995).

35 Huyssen, *Present Pasts*, 30.

36 Hal Foster, "An Archival Impulse," in *The Archive*, ed. Charles Merewether (London: Whitechapel Gallery, 2006), 144.

37 Foster, "Archival Impulse."

38 James Young, *At Memory's Edge: After-Images of the Holocaust in Contemporary Art and Architecture* (New Haven, CT: Yale University Press, 2000), 92.

Chapter 3. The World, the Art, and the Critic

1 Said, *The World*, 140.

2 Harold Bloom, *The Anxiety of Influence: A Theory of Poetry* (1973; New York: Oxford University Press, 1997), 5.

3 Nonetheless, substantive engagements with Kapur's work include essays by her co-curator and coauthor, Ashish Rajadhakshya; Ajay Sinha's "Modernism in India: A Short History of a Blush," *Art Bulletin* 90, no. 4 (December 2008): 561–68; and the following interviews: Ahmed, "Landing Imaginaries"; Natasha Ginwala, "Geeta Kapur: On the Curatorial in India (Parts 1 and 2)," *Afterall On-line* (July and October 2011), https://www.after all.org/online/geeta-kapur-part1#.XFJBqyd7nxU, accessed January 30, 2019; Ameet Parameswaran and Rahul Dev, "To Be Partisan, Unsettled, and Alert: Conversation with Geeta Kapur," *Art Margins On-line* (March 11, 2015), http://www.artmargins.com/index.php/interviews-sp-837925570 /756-to-be-partisan-unsettled-and-alert-conversation-with-geeta-kapur-.

4 Rushdie, *Moor's Last Sigh*, 242. For additional comments about Rushdie's novel and the Indian art world, see Khullar, *Worldly Affiliations*, 168–75.

5 Ahmed, "Landing Imaginaries," 250.

6 Geeta Kapur, "Partisan Views about the Human Figure (1981)," in *Horn Please*, 33.

7 Ahmed, "Landing Imaginaries," 252.

8 Geeta Kapur, "Where to Look: When There Is No Modern Museum in Sight," in CIMAM *Annual Conference Proceedings: "Fair Trade, The Institution of Art in the New Economy"* (Mexico City: Museo Tamayo and Museo Universitario de Arte Contemporáneo, 2009), 50.

9 James Ackerman, "Towards a New Social Theory of Art," *New Literary History* 4 (1973): 322.

10 The significance of a parallactic view was elaborated by Hal Foster in his introduction to *The Return of the Real*, xii–xiii.

11 See Maurice Berger, ed., *The Crisis of Criticism* (New York: New Press, 1998); James Elkins and Michael Newman, eds., *The State of Art Criticism* (New York: Routledge, 2008); Hal Foster, *Bad New Days: Art, Criticism, Emergency* (New York: Verso, 2015); Raphael Rubinstein, ed., *Critical Mess: Art Critics on the State of Their Practice* (Lenox, MA: Hard Press Editions, 2006).

12 For the complexities of such a radical model of criticism, see Irit Rogoff, "What Is a Theorist?," in Elkins and Newman, *State of Art Criticism*, 108.

13 Maurice Berger, introduction to Berger, *Crisis of Criticism*, 11.

14 Vidya Shivadas, "Mapping the Field of Indian Art Criticism: Post-Independence," unpublished Asia Art Archive Report (2009), 1, https://aaa.org.hk/en/resources/papers-presentations/mapping-the-field-of-indian-art-criticism-post-independence, accessed January 31, 2019.

15 Edward Said articulated these traditions of the intellectual in his account of Jonathan Swift, in *The World*, 80–81.

16 Tom Overton, ed., *Portraits: John Berger on Artists* (London: Verso, 2015), 394–98.

17 Kapur, "Vagabondage," 12–13.

18 See Khullar, *Worldly Affiliations*, 194–98; Shivadas, "Mapping the Field."

19 Kapur, *When Was Modernism*, xiii.

20 Geeta Kapur, "Signatures of Dissent," Art India 6, no. 2 (2001): 80.

21 Kapur, "Vagabondage," 13.

22 Said, *Beginnings*, 5.

23 Said, *Beginnings*, xiv.

24 Geeta Kapur, "Elegy to an Un-named Beloved," in *When Was Modernism*, 61–86.

25 Kapur, *In Quest of Identity*.

26 Kapur, *In Quest of Identity*.

27 Vidya Shivadas, "Museumizing Modern Art: National Gallery of Modern Art, the Indian Case Study," in Mathur and Singh, *No Touching*, 146–69.

28 Geeta Kapur, "Art Criticism in India," in G. Kapur, ed., *Vrishchik 4: The Social Context of Contemporary Indian Art* (1973).

29 Kapur, *In Quest of Identity*.

30 Geeta Kapur, *Contemporary Indian Artists* (New Delhi: Vikas, 1978), x–xi.

31 Kapur, "Partisan Views about the Human Figure," 36.

32 Kapur, "Partisan Views about the Human Figure" (emphasis in original).

33 Geeta Kapur, *Contemporary Indian Art: An Exhibition of the Festival of India, 1982* (London: Royal Academy of Arts, 1982), 3.

34 Kapur, *Contemporary Indian Art*, 4.

35 Kapur, *When Was Modernism*, xiii.

36 Kapur, "Signatures of Dissent," 80.

37 Geeta Kapur, "Mythic Material in Indian Cinema," *Journal of Arts and Ideas* 14–15 (July–December 1987): 79–108; and "Cultural Creativity in the First Decade: The Example of Satyajit Ray," *Journal of Arts and Ideas* 23–24 (January 1993): 17–49.

38 Kapur, "Cultural Creativity," 23.

39 Moinak Biswas, "Introduction: Critical Returns," in *Apu and After: Revisiting Ray's Cinema* (London: Seagull, 2005), 1–18.

40 Biswas, "Introduction," 11.

41 Biswas, "Introduction," 1.

42 Biswas, "Introduction," 11.

43 Kapur, "Cultural Creativity," 19.

44 Kapur, "Cultural Creativity," 20.

45 Kapur, "Cultural Creativity," 34.

46 Kapur, "Cultural Creativity," 42, 44.

47 Kapur, "Mythic Material," 103.

48 Kapur, "Mythic Material," 102.

49 Kapur, "Mythic Material," 79.

50 Kapur, "Mythic Material," 80. See K.G. Subramanyan, *The Creative Circuit* (Calcutta: Seagull, 1992).

51 See Zitzewitz, *Art of Secularism*, 41.

52 The literature on K.G. Subramanyan includes Khullar, *Worldly Affiliations*; Sheikh, *Contemporary Art in Baroda*; R. Siva Kumar, *K.G. Subramanyan: A Retrospective* (New Delhi: National Gallery of Modern Art, 2003); R. Siva Kumar, *Enchantment and Engagement: Murals of K.G. Subramanyan* (Kolkata: Seagull, 2015); Zitzewitz, *Art of Secularism*.

53 Okwui Enwezor, ed., *The Short Century: Independence and Liberation Movements in Africa, 1945–1994* (Munich: Prestel, 2001).

54 Fanon, *Wretched of the Earth*, 220.

55 Fanon, *Wretched of the Earth*, 223.

56 K.G. Subramanyan, *The Living Tradition: Perspectives on Modern Indian Art* (Calcutta: Seagull, 1987), 7.

57 Ashish Rajadhyaksha, "Living the Tradition," *Journal of Arts and Ideas* 16 (January–March 1988): 74.

58 Rajadhyaksha, "Living the Tradition," 74.

59 Geeta Kapur, "Mid-Century Ironies: K.G. Subramanyan," in *When Was Modernism*, 87–144.

60 Kapur, "Mid-Century Ironies," 110.

61 Kapur, "Mid-Century Ironies," 124.

62 Kapur, *When Was Modernism*, xi.

63 Kapur, *When Was Modernism*, xi.

64 Subramanyan, *Creative Circuit*, 88.

65 Subramanyan, *Creative Circuit*, 147.

66 Rogoff, "What Is a Theorist?," 97.

67 Theodor Adorno, "The Essay as Form," *New German Critique* 32 (spring/summer 1984; originally published 1958): 151–71.

68 Adorno, "Essay as Form," 161.

69 Adorno, "Essay as Form," 159.

70 Adorno, "Essay as Form," 165.

71 Adorno, "Essay as Form," 166.

72 Partha Mitter, *Art and Nationalism in Colonial India 1850–1922: Occidental Ori-

entations (Cambridge: Cambridge University Press, 1994); Partha Mitter, *Indian Art* (Oxford: Oxford University Press, 2002); Partha Mitter, *The Triumph of Modernism: India's Artists and the Avant-Garde 1922–1947* (London: Reaktion, 2007).

73 From Ranajit Guha's endorsement on the jacket of Mitter's *Triumph of Modernism*.

74 Partha Mitter, "Ernst Gombrich and the Western Representations of the Sacred Art of India" (lecture delivered at the Institut für Kunstgeschichte, University of Vienna, May 16, 2012), 1.

75 Mitter, "Ernst Gombrich," 3.

76 Sinha, "Modernism in India," 564.

77 Khullar, *Worldly Affiliations*, 144.

78 Nilima Sheikh, "A Post-Independence Initiative in Art," in G. Sheikh, *Contemporary Art in Baroda*, 64.

79 Iftikhar Dadi, "Calligraphic Abstraction: Anwar Jalal Shemza," in Iftikhar Dadi, ed., *Anwar Jalal Shemza* (London: Ridinghouse, 2015), 9–16.

80 Sunil Khilnani, *The Idea of India* (New York: Farrar, Straus and Giroux, 1997).

81 Kapur, *When Was Modernism*, xiv.

82 Kapur, *When Was Modernism*, xiii.

83 Kapur, *When Was Modernism*, xii.

84 Kapur, *When Was Modernism*, xii.

85 Andreas Huyssen, *After the Great Divide: Modernism, Mass Culture, Postmodernism* (Bloomington: Indiana University Press, 1986), 209.

86 Huyssen, *After the Great Divide*, 209.

87 Huyssen, *After the Great Divide*, 209.

88 Stuart Hall, "The Life of Raymond Williams," *New Statesman*, February 21, 2008.

89 See Christopher Prendergast, ed., *Cultural Materialism: On Raymond Williams* (Minneapolis: University of Minnesota Press, 1995).

90 Gauri Viswanathan, "Raymond Williams and British Colonialism," in Prendergast, *Cultural Materialism*, 165.

91 Viswanathan, "Raymond Williams," 163.

92 Prendergast, *Cultural Materialism*, xxxiii.

93 Kapur, *When Was Modernism*, 297.

94 Raymond Williams, "When Was Modernism?," *New Left Review* 175 (May/June 1989): 49–50.

95 Williams, "When Was Modernism?," 50–51.

96 Williams, "When Was Modernism?," 50.

97 Kapur, *When Was Modernism*, 267.

98 Geeta Kapur, "Modernist Myths and the Exile of Maqbool Fida Husain," in *Barefoot Across the Nation: Maqbool Fida Husain and the Idea of India*, ed. Sumathi Ramaswamy (London: Routledge, 2011), 52.

99 Kapur, *When Was Modernism*, 300.

100 Williams, "When Was Modernism?," 50.

101 Williams, "When Was Modernism?," 51.

102 Williams, "When Was Modernism?," 52.

103 Kapur, *When Was Modernism*, 374.

104 Geeta Kapur, "Secular Artist, Citizen Artist," in *Art and Social Change: A Critical Reader*, ed. Will Bradley and Charles Esche (London: Tate/Afterall, 2007), 422–39.

105 Kapur, "Cultural Conjuncture," 38.

106 Accordingly, the title of her forthcoming book is *Critic's Compass: Navigating Practice*. See "Independent Critic: Charting a Course—Conversation between Geeta Kapur and Sabih Ahmed," *Take on Art* 2, no. 2 (July–December 2016): 17.

107 Kapur, "Cultural Conjuncture," 49.

108 Kapur, "Cultural Conjuncture," 52.

109 Geeta Kapur, "Partisan Modernity," in *Mulk Raj Anand: Shaping the Indian Modern*, ed. Annapurna Garimella (Mumbai: Marg, 2005), 28–41.

110 Kapur, "Partisan Modernity," 40.

111 Kapur, "Modernist Myths and the Exile of Maqbool Fida Husain," 53.

112 Kapur, *Contemporary Indian Artists*, 134.

113 Kapur, *Contemporary Indian Artists*, 30.

114 Kapur, *In Quest of Identity*, n.p.

115 Sumathi Ramaswamy, "Introduction: Barefoot Across India-An Artist and His Country," in *Barefoot Across the Nation*, 4.

116 Kapur, "Modernist Myths and the Exile of Maqbool Fida Husain," 49.

117 Kapur, "Modernist Myths and the Exile of Maqbool Fida Husain," 24.

118 Geeta Kapur, "Again a Difficult Task Begins," in *Waiting Is a Part of Intense Living* (Madrid: Museo Reina Sofia, 2015), 161–206.

119 Kapur, "Again a Difficult Task Begins."

120 Roland Barthes, *The Pleasure of the Text*, trans. Richard Miller (New York: Hill and Wang, 1975), 13–14.

121 Adorno, "Essay as Form," 160.

122 Edward Said, *The World*, 146.

123 This distinction between "fault-finding" and a more profound intellectual practice of critique appears in Raymond Williams, *Keywords* (1976; Oxford: Oxford University Press, 2015), 75–76; and Michel Foucault, "What Is Critique?" in *The Politics of Truth*, ed. Sylvère Lotringer and Lysa Hochroth (New York: Semiotext(e), 1997), 24.

124 Joan Scott, "Against Eclecticism," *Differences: A Journal of Feminist Cultural Studies* 16, no. 3 (2005): 127.

125 Judith Butler, "What Is Critique? An Essay on Foucault's Virtue," in *The Political: Readings in Continental Philosophy*, ed. David Ingram (London: Basil Blackwell, 2002), 213.

126 Michel Foucault, "What Is an Author?," in *The Foucault Reader*, ed. Paul Rabinow (1984; New York: Vintage, 2010).

127 Adorno, "Essay as Form," 152.

128 Ahmed, "Landing Imaginaries," 250.

129 Ahmed, "Landing Imaginaries," 250.

Chapter 4. Urban Economies

1 Octavio Paz, *Marcel Duchamp: Appearance Stripped Bare* (1968; New York: Arcade, 1990), cited in John Scanlan, *On Garbage* (London: Reaktion, 2005), 96.

2 Gay Hawkins and Stephen Muecke, "Introduction: Cultural Economies of Waste," in *Culture and Waste: The Creation and Destruction of Value*, ed. Gay Hawkins and Stephen Muecke (New York: Rowman and Littlefield, 2003), xi.

3 Scanlan, *On Garbage*; Lea Vergine, ed., *Trash: From Junk to Art* (Milan: Electa, 1997); Gillian Whiteley, *Junk: Art and the Politics of Trash* (London: I.B. Tauris, 2011).

4 The work has been exhibited in various formats at the Lalit Kala Academy, Delhi (2005); the Chemould Prescott Road, Mumbai (2008); Project 88, Mumbai (2008); Photoink, New Delhi (2008); Sepia International, New York (2008); and the Walsh Gallery, Chicago (2008–9), and was subsequently included in the artist's retrospective exhibitions at the Kiran Nadar Museum of Art, New Delhi (2018), and Haus der Kunst, Munich (2018).

5 Zygmunt Bauman, *Wasted Lives: Modernity and Its Outcasts* (Cambridge: Polity, 2004).

6 Rahul Mehrotra, "Negotiating the Static and Kinetic Cities: The Emergent Urbanism of Mumbai," in *Other Cities, Other Worlds: Urban Imaginaries in a Globalizing Age*, ed. Andreas Huyssen (Durham, NC: Duke University Press, 2008), 205–18.

7 Bauman, *Wasted Lives*, 22.

8 For example, Xing Danwen and Liu Jianhua, cited in Chaitanya Sambrani, *Tracking Trash: Vivan Sundaram and the Turbulent Core of Modernity* (Mumbai: Chemould Prescott Road, 2008), 16. See also Wu Hung's moving account of the project by Zhao Xiangyuan and Song Dong, titled *Waste Not: Zhao Xiangyuan and Song Dong* (Tokyo: Tokyo Gallery + BTAP, 2009).

9 For example, Yacouba Konaté, "Art, Urban Identity and Citizenship," and Kobena Mercer, "Art and the Experience of African Cities," in *Africas: The Artist and the City* (Barcelona: Centre de Cultura Contemporania de Barcelona, 2001).

10 Shannon Jackson, "High Maintenance: The Sanitation Aesthetics of

Mierle Laderman Ukeles," in *Social Works: Performing Art, Supporting Publics* (New York: Routledge, 2010).

11 See *Sarai Reader 02: The Cities of Everyday Life* (Delhi: Sarai Programme, CSDS, 2002); Indira Chandrasekhar and Peter Seel, eds., *body.city: siting contemporary culture in India* (New Delhi: Tulika, 2003); Mehrotra, "Negotiating the Static and Kinetic Cities"; Gyan Prakash, "Mumbai: The Modern City in Ruins," in Huyssen, *Other Cities, Other Worlds*, 181–203; Gyan Prakash and Kevin Kruse, eds., *The Spaces of the Modern City* (Princeton, NJ: Princeton University Press, 2008).

12 Arjun Appadurai, "Deep Democracy: Urban Governmentality and the Horizon of Politics," *Environment and Urbanization* 13, no. 2 (October 2001): 23–43. See also "Illusion of Permanence: Interview with Arjun Appadurai," *Perspecta* 34 (2003): 44–52.

13 Geeta Kapur, "sub-Terrain: artists dig the contemporary," in Chandrasekhar and Seel, *body.city*, 47–83.

14 Chaitanya Sambrani, "Tracking Trash: Vivan Sundaram and the Turbulent Core of Modernity," in *Trash* (Mumbai: Chemould Prescott Road, 2008), exhibition catalogue, 11.

15 Rana das Gupta, *Capital: The Eruption of Delhi* (New Delhi: Penguin, 2014).

16 Ravi Sundaram, *Pirate Modernity: Delhi's Media Urbanism* (London: Routledge, 2010), 26.

17 Mitchell, *Landscape and Power*.

18 John Friedmann, "Place and Place-Making in Cities: A Global Perspective," *Planning Theory and Practice* 11, no. 2 (June 2010): 149–65.

19 James Scott, *Seeing Like a State: How Certain Schemes to Improve the Human Condition Have Failed* (New Haven, CT: Yale University Press, 1999), 56 and 65.

20 Shoma Chaudhury, "Filth Is Something We All Like to Put Our Hands in: Interview," *Tehelka Magazine*, September 6, 2008, http://www.shomachaudhury.com/filth-is-something-we-all-like-to-put-our-hands-in/.

21 Friedmann, "Place and Place-Making," 158.

22 For an account of how waste has been similarly theorized as an imaginative resource within the social sciences, see Lindsey Dillon, "Race, Waste and Space: Brownfield Redevelopment and Environmental Justice at the Hunters Point Shipyard," *Antipode* 46, no. 5 (2014): 1205–21.

23 Mary Douglas, *Purity and Danger: An Analysis of Concepts of Pollution and Taboo* (1966; London: Routledge, 2002).

24 Sundaram, quoted in Sasha Altaf, "Aesthetics of Urban Waste," *The Hindu*, November 23, 2008, https://www.thehindu.com/todays-paper/tp-features/tp-sundaymagazine/Aesthetics-of-urban-waste/article15402219.ece.

25 Gyan Prakash, "Introduction," in Prakash and Kruse, *Spaces of the Modern City*, 1–18.

26 Tania Roy, "Non-Renewable Resources: The Poetics and Politics of Vivan Sundaram's Trash," *Theory, Culture and Society* 30, nos. 7/8 (2013): 267.

27 Sambrani, *Tracking Trash*, 7.

28 Neil Brenner, "Theses on Urbanization," *Public Culture* 24, no. 3 (2012): 85–114.

29 Brenner, "Theses on Urbanization," 94.

30 See Vinay Gidwani and Rajyashree N. Reddy, "The Afterlives of 'Waste': Notes from India for a Minor History of Capitalist Surplus," *Antipode* 43, no. 5 (2011): 1646.

31 Mike Davis, *Planet of Slums* (New York: Verso, 2007).

32 Dipesh Chakrabarty, "Of Garbage, Modernity and the Citizen's Gaze," *Economic and Political Weekly* 27, nos. 10/11 (1992): 541–47.

33 Cited in R. Sundaram, *Pirate Modernity*, 54.

34 Chakrabarty, "Of Garbage," 541.

35 See Vikramaditya Prakash, *Chandigarh's LeCorbusier* (Seattle: University of Washington Press, 2002), 9.

36 Prakash, *Chandigarh's LeCorbusier*, 43.

37 Le Corbusier, "The Master Plan," *Marg* 15, no. 1 (December 1961): 5–9.

38 Prakash, *Chandigarh's LeCorbusier*, 21. See also Shanay Jhaveri, ed., *Chandigarh Is in India* (Mumbai: The Shoestring Publisher, 2016).

39 Soumyen Bandyopadhyay and Iain Jackson, *The Collection, the Ruin and the Theatre: Architecture, Sculpture and Landscape in Nek Chand's Rock Garden, Chandigarh* (Liverpool: Liverpool University Press, 2008); John Beardsley, *Gardens of Revelation: Environments by Visionary Artists* (London: Abbeville, 2003); Tracy Bonfitto, "The Rock Garden: A Study of Memory, Place-Making, and Community in Chandigarh, India" (PhD Diss., University of California, Los Angeles, 2017), https://escholarship.org/uc/item/8oj5t8x4; Sharon Irish, "Intimacy and Monumentality in Chandigarh, North India: Le Corbusier's Capital Complex and Nek Chand Saini's Rock Garden," *Journal of Aesthetic Education* 38, no. 2 (summer 2004): 105–15; Lucienne Peiry and Philippe Lespinasse, *Nek Chand's Outsider Art: The Rock Garden of Chandigarh* (Paris: Flammarion, 2005).

40 M. N. Sharma, cited in John Maizels, "Nek Chand: Creator of a Magical World," in *Vernacular Visionaries: International Outsider Art*, ed. Annie Carlano (New Haven, CT: Yale University Press, 2003), 71.

41 Scott, *Seeing Like a State*, 62.

42 R. Sundaram, *Pirate Modernity*, 87.

43 Asher Ghertner, *Rule by Aesthetics: World-Class City Making in Delhi* (New York: Oxford University Press, 2015); Ananya Roy, "Postcolonial Urbanism: Speed, Hysteria, Mass Dreams," in *Worlding Cities: Asian Experiments and the Art of Being Global*, ed. Ananya Roy and Aihwa Ong (London: Blackwell, 2011), 307–35.

44 Ghertner, *Rule by Aesthetics*, 22.

45 Chaudhury, "Filth Is Something."

46 Ananya Roy, "Transnational Trespassings: The Geopolitics of Urban In-

formality," in *Urban Informality: Transnational Perspectives from the Middle East, Latin America, and South Asia*, ed. Ananya Roy and Nezar AlSayyad (New York: Lexington, 2004), 289–317.

47 Roy, "Transnational Trespassings," 295.

48 Gidwani and Reddy, "Afterlives of 'Waste,'" 1625–58.

49 Gidwani and Reddy, "Afterlives of 'Waste,'" 1640.

50 Arjun Appadurai, "Spectral Housing and Urban Cleansing: Notes on Millennial Mumbai," *Public Culture* 12, no. 3 (fall 2000): 627–51.

51 See Betti-Sue Hertz, ed., *The Matter Within: New Contemporary Art of India* (San Francisco: Yerba Buena Center for the Arts, 2011).

52 Sambrani, "Tracking Trash," 14.

53 Patricia Yeager, "Trash as Archive, Trash as Enlightenment," in Hawkins and Muecke, *Culture and Waste*, 113.

54 Appadurai, "Spectral Housing and Urban Cleansing," 649.

55 Appadurai, "Spectral Housing and Urban Cleansing," 635.

56 Appadurai, "Spectral Housing and Urban Cleansing," 635.

57 Roy, "Transnational Trespassings," 303.

58 Rosalind Morris, ed., *Can the Subaltern Speak? Reflections on the History of an Idea* (New York: Columbia University Press, 2010).

59 Gayatri Chakravorty Spivak, "Can the Subaltern Speak?," in Morris, *Can the Subaltern Speak?*, 28–30.

60 Spivak, "Can the Subaltern Speak?," 64.

61 Cited in Ritu Birla, "Postcolonial Studies: Now That's History," in Morris, *Can the Subaltern Speak?*, 98.

62 Birla, "Postcolonial Studies," 98.

63 Holland Cotter, "Review of Vivan Sundaram, *Trash*," *New York Times*, October 30, 2008.

64 Spivak, "Can the Subaltern Speak?," 61.

65 Tony Cragg, quoted in Vergine, *Trash*, 247.

66 Sambrani, "Tracking Trash," 9.

67 Sambrani, "Tracking Trash," 9.

68 Sambrani, "Tracking Trash," 9.

69 Vinay Gidwani, "Remaindered Things and Remaindered Lives: Travelling with Delhi's Waste," in *Finding Delhi: Loss and Renewal in the Megacity*, ed. Bharati Chaturvedi (New Delhi: Penguin Viking, 2010), 41.

70 Gidwani, "Remaindered Things," 46.

71 Gidwani, "Remaindered Things," 44.

72 Gidwani, "Remaindered Things," 40.

73 Timothy Luke, "Art and the Environmental Crisis: From Commodity Aesthetics to Ecology Aesthetics," *Art Journal* 51, no. 2 (summer 1992): 72–76.

74 Virginia Dominguez, "Of Other Peoples: Beyond the Salvage Paradigm," in *Discussions in Contemporary Culture*, ed. Hal Foster (Seattle: Bay Press/Dia Art Foundation, 1987), 131.

75 See the dialogue between James Clifford, Virginia Dominguez, and Trinh T. Minh-ha in Foster, *Discussions in Contemporary Culture*, 121–50.

Epilogue

1 See Lisa Corrin and Corinne Granof, eds., *A Feast of Astonishments: Charlotte Moorman and the Avant-Garde, 1960s–1980s* (Evanston, IL: Block Museum of Art/Northwestern University Press, 2016).

2 See *Another Life: The Digitized Personal Archive of Geeta Kapur and Vivan Sundaram*, http://www.aaa.org.hk/Collection/CollectionOnline/SpecialCollecti onRootFolder/2.

3 Karen Painter and Thomas Crow, eds., *Late Thoughts: Reflections on Artists and Composers at Work* (Los Angeles: Getty Research Institute, 2006).

4 Edward Said, *On Late Style: Music and Literature against the Grain* (New York: Vintage, 2006), 23.

5 Said, *On Late Style*, 92.

6 Said, *On Late Style*, 114.

7 Said, *On Late Style*, 92. See also Stathis Gourgouris, "The Late Style of Edward Said," *Alif: Journal of Comparative Poetics* 25 (2005): 37–45.

8 Gordon McMullen and Sam Smiles, "Introduction," in *Late Style and Its Discontents: Essays in Art, Literature, and Music*, ed. Gordon McMullen and Sam Smiles (Oxford, UK: Oxford University Press, 2016), 10.

9 Deepak Ananth, "Seams," in Vivan Sundaram, *Gagawaka: Making Strange* (Mumbai: Chemould Prescott Road, 2012), 16.

10 Saloni Mathur and Miwon Kwon, eds., *Making Strange: Gagawaka + Postmortem by Vivan Sundaram* (Los Angeles: Fowler Museum at UCLA, 2015).

11 Geeta Kapur, *Chemould Prescott Road: 50 Years of Contemporary Art; Five Exhibitions Curated by Geeta Kapur*. Mumbai: Chemould Prescott Road, 2018.

12 Kapur has curated major exhibitions at such venues as the Lalit Kala Academy, Delhi (1977); the Royal Academy of Art, London (1982); the National Gallery of Modern Art, Delhi (1994); the Johannesburg Biennale, South Africa (1995); the Tate Modern, London (2001) with Ashish Rajadhyaksha; the House of World Cultures, Berlin (2003); and the Chemould Prescott Road/National Gallery of Modern Art, Bombay (2003) with Chaitanya Sambrani.

13 Geeta Kapur, "Mortality Morbidity Masquerade," in Dercon and Raza, *Bhupen Khakhar*, 158.

14 Saloni Mathur, "Geeta Kapur's Aesthetic Bind," *Artforum* (summer 2014): 362–63.

15 Jacques Derrida, "Ellipsis," in *Writing and Difference*, trans. Alan Bass (Chicago: University of Chicago Press, 1987), 295–300.

16 Jean-Luc Nancy, "Elliptical Sense," *Research in Phenomenology* 18 (1988): 186.

17 Nancy, "Elliptical Sense," 186.

18 Nancy, "Elliptical Sense," 186.

19 Jacques Derrida, *Rogues: Two Essays on Reason*, trans. Pascale Anne-Brault and Michael Naas (Stanford, CA: Stanford University Press, 2005), 1.

20 The relations between history, memory, the archive, and the event were evoked yet again in a subsequent installation by Sundaram, titled *Meanings of Failed Action: Insurrection 1946*. This site-specific work was mounted at the Chhatrapati Shivaji Maharaj Vastu Sangrahalaya (CSMVS) museum in Mumbai in March 2017. Here, the collaboration with theorist and scholar of Indian cinema Ashish Rajadhyaksha and sound art specialist David Chapman produced a blend of installation and performance with sound and light within the central form of a shipping container/boat. The work was also displayed in the artist's retrospective exhibition at the Kiran Nadar Museum of Art in New Delhi in 2018.

21 They were Santanu Bose, Rimli Bhattacharya, and Aditee Biswas, all part of the core team.

22 Soumitra Das, "A Grand Spectacle," *Telegraph* (Calcutta), April 26, 2015.

23 Meera Menezes, "Interview with Vivan Sundaram on the Making of *409 Ramkinkars*," *CriticalCollective.in*, April 14, 2015.

24 Parul Dave Mukherji, "4092015," *CriticalCollective.in*, April 14, 2015.

25 Kapur, "Again a Difficult Task Begins," 176.

26 Nancy, "Elliptical Sense," 186.

27 Keywords, for Raymond Williams, were not neutral definitions; they constituted instead a capacious vocabulary for culture and society, "a vocabulary to use, to find our own ways in, to change as we find it necessary to change it, as we go on making our own language and history." Williams, *Keywords*, xxxv–xxxvi.

28 Kapur, *When Was Modernism*, 374–76.

29 Elizabeth Harney, "Postcolonial Agitations: Avant-Gardism in Dakar and London," *New Literary History* 41, no. 4 (fall 2010): 740.

30 Paul Mann, *The Theory-Death of the Avant-Garde* (Bloomington: Indiana University Press, 1991), 6–7.

31 Geeta Kapur and Ashish Rajadhyaksha, "Bombay/Mumbai 1992–2001," in *Century City: Art and Culture in the Modern Metropolis*, ed. Iwona Blazwick (London: Tate, 2001), 16–41; Geeta Kapur, "Delhi," in *Art Cities of the Future: 21st Century Avant-Gardes*, ed. Antawan I. Byrd et al. (London: Phaidon, 2013), 89–112.

32 Geeta Kapur, "Proposition Avant-Garde: A View from the South," *Art Journal* 77, no. 1 (spring 2018): 87.

33 Kapur, "Proposition Avant-Garde," 87.

34 Paul Mann, *Theory-Death of the Avant-Garde*, 3.

35 John Roberts, "Revolutionary Pathos, Negation, and the Suspensive Avant-Garde," *New Literary History* 41 (2010): 717.

36 Kapur, "Proposition Avant-Garde," 88.

37 Roberts, "Revolutionary Pathos," 720.

38 Rosalyn Deutsche, *Hiroshima after Iraq: Three Studies in Art and War* (New York: Columbia University Press, 2010), 2.

39 Kapur, "Proposition Avant-Garde," 87.

40 Kapur, "Proposition Avant-Garde," 88.

41 Kapur, "Proposition Avant-Garde," 89.

42 George Baker, "Late Criticism," in *Canvases and Careers Today: Criticism and Its Markets*, ed. Daniel Birnbaum and Isabelle Graw (New York: Sternberg, 2008), 31.

43 Baker, "Late Criticism," 31.

44 Baker, "Late Criticism," 35.

BIBLIOGRAPHY

Adajania, Nancy. *Navjot Altaf: The Thirteenth Place*. Mumbai: Guild Art Gallery, 2016.

Adcy, Peter, Mark Whitehead, and Alison J. Williams, eds. *From Above: War, Violence and Verticality*. London: Hurst, 2013.

Adorno, Theodor. *Essays on Music*. Edited by Richard Leppert. Translated by Susan Gillespie. Berkeley: University of California Press, 2002.

Adorno, Theodor. "The Essay as Form." *New German Critique* 32 (spring/summer 1984; originally published 1958): 151–71.

Ahmed, Sabih. "Landing Imaginaries: An Interview with Geeta Kapur." In *Sarai Reader 09: Projections*, 248–56. Delhi: Sarai Programme, CSDS, 2013.

Alberro, Alexander, and Blake Stimpson, eds. *Institutional Critique: An Anthology of Artists' Writings*. Cambridge, MA: MIT Press, 2011.

Ananth, Deepak. "Precarious Poetics." In *Vivan Sundaram: Disjunctures*, 12–39. Munich: Prestel/Haus der Kunst, 2018. Exhibition catalogue.

Ananth, Deepak. "Seams." In *Gagawaka: Making Strange*, 10–27. Mumbai: Chemould Prescott Road, 2012. Exhibition catalogue.

Ananth, Deepak. "An Unfinished Project." In *Amrita Sher-Gil: An Indian Artist Family of the Twentieth Century*, 13–31. Munich: Schirmer/Mosel, 2007. Exhibition catalogue.

Anderson, Benedict. *Imagined Communities: Reflections on the Origin and Spread of Nationalism*. New York: Verso, 1991.

Appadurai, Arjun. *Fear of Small Numbers: An Essay on the Geography of Anger*. Durham, NC: Duke University Press, 2006.

Appadurai, Arjun. *The Future as Cultural Fact: Essays on the Global Condition*. London: Verso, 2013.

Arendt, Hannah, ed. *Illuminations*. New York: Schocken, 1968.

Bal, Mieke. *In Media Res: Inside Nalini Malani's Shadow Plays*. Ostfilern: Hatje Cantz, 2016.

Bandyopadhyay, Soumyen, and Iain Jackson. *The Collection, the Ruin and the Theatre: Architecture, Sculpture and Landscape in Nek Chand's Rock Garden, Chandigarh*. Liverpool: Liverpool University Press, 2008.

Barrett, Ross, and Daniel Worden, eds. *Oil Culture*. Minneapolis: University of Minnesota Press, 2014.

Barthes, Roland. *Image-Music-Text*. Translated by Stephen Heath. New York: Hill and Wang, 1978.

Barthes, Roland. *The Pleasure of the Text*. Translated by Richard Miller. New York: Hill and Wang, 1975.

Bartholomew, Pablo, Rati Bartholomew, and Carmen Kagal, eds. *Richard Bartholomew, the Art Critic*. Noida, India: BART, 2012.

Bauman, Zygmunt. *Wasted Lives: Modernity and Its Outcasts*. Cambridge: Polity, 2004.

Bean, Susan, ed. *Midnight to the Boom: Painting in India after Independence*. Salem, MA: Peabody Essex Museum, 2013.

Bennett, Tony. *The Birth of the Museum: History, Theory, Politics*. London: Routledge, 1995.

Berger, Maurice, ed. *The Crisis of Criticism*. New York: New Press, 1998.

Bernhardsson, Magnus. *Reclaiming a Plundered Past: Archaeology and Nation Building in Modern Iraq*. Austin: University of Texas Press, 2005.

Bhabha, Homi. *The Location of Culture*. New York: Routledge, 1994.

Biswas, Moinak, ed. *Apu and After: Re-visiting Ray's Cinema*. London: Seagull, 2005.

Boal, Iain, T. J. Clark, Joseph Matthews, and Michael Watts. *Afflicted Powers: Capital and Spectacle in a New Age of War*. London: Verso, 2005.

Bohrer, Frederick. *Orientalism and Visual Culture: Imagining Mesopotamia in Nineteenth-Century Europe*. Cambridge: Cambridge University Press, 2003.

Bourriaud, Nicolas. *Postproduction*. New York: Lukas and Sternberg, 2007.

Bourriaud, Nicolas. *The Radicant*. New York: Lukas and Sternberg, 2009.

Bourriaud, Nicolas. *Relational Aesthetics*. Paris: Les Presses du Réel, 1998.

Braunert, Svea, and Meredith Malone, eds. *To See without Being Seen: Contemporary Art and Drone Warfare*. St. Louis: Mildred Lane Kemper Art Museum, 2016.

Brown, Rebecca. *Art for a Modern India, 1947–1980*. Durham, NC: Duke University Press, 2009.

Brown, Rebecca. *Displaying Time: The Many Temporalities of the Festival of India*. Seattle: University of Washington Press, 2017.

Brown, Wendy. *Undoing the Demos: Neoliberalism's Stealth Revolution*. New York: Zone, 2015.

Bürger, Peter. *Theory of the Avant-Garde*. Minneapolis: University of Minnesota Press, 1984.

Butler, Judith. *Precarious Life: The Powers of Mourning and Violence*. London: Verso, 2004.

Chakrabarty, Dipesh. *Provincializing Europe: Postcolonial Thought and Historical Difference*. Princeton, NJ: Princeton University Press, 2007.

Chandrasekhar, Indira, and Peter Seel, eds. *body.city: siting contemporary culture in India*. New Delhi: Tulika, 2003.

Chatterjee, Partha. *The Nation and Its Fragments: Colonial and Postcolonial Histories*. Princeton, NJ: Princeton University Press, 1993.

Chatterjee, Partha. *Nationalist Thought in the Colonial World: A Derivative Discourse*. Minneapolis: University of Minnesota Press, 1993.

Chaturvedi, Bharati, ed. *Finding Delhi: Loss and Renewal in the Megacity*. New Delhi: Penguin Viking, 2010.

Christov-Bakargiev, Carolyn, Arjun Appadurai, and Andreas Huyssen. *In Search of Varnished Blood: Nalini Malani*. Ostfieldern: Hatje Cantz, 2012.

Clark, T. J. *Farewell to an Idea: Episodes from a History of Modernism*. New Haven, CT: Yale University Press, 1999.

Clark, T. J. *Image of the People: Gustave Courbet and the Second French Republic 1848–1851*. Greenwich, CT: New York Graphic Society, 1973.

Cohn, Bernard. *Colonialism and Its Forms of Knowledge: The British in India*. Princeton, NJ: Princeton University Press, 1996.

Dadi, Iftikhar, ed. *Anwar Jalal Shemza*. London: Ridinghouse, 2015.

Dadi, Iftikhar. *Modernism and the Art of Muslim South Asia*. Chapel Hill: University of North Carolina Press, 2010.

Dadi, Iftikhar, and Hammad Nasar, eds. *Lines of Control: Partition as Productive Space*. London: Green Cardamom, 2012.

Dadi, Iftikhar, and Salah Hassan, eds. *Unpacking Europe: Towards a Critical Reading*. Rotterdam: Museum Boijmans Van Beuningen and NAi Publishers, 2001. Exhibition catalogue.

Dalmia, Yasodhara. *Amrita Sher-Gil: A Life*. New Delhi: Penguin Viking, 2006.

Dalmia, Yasodhara. *The Making of Modern Indian Art: The Progressives*. New Delhi: Oxford University Press, 2001.

Dalmia, Yasodhara, and Salima Hashmi, eds. *Memory, Metaphor, Mutations: Contemporary Art of India and Pakistan*. London: Asia House/Green Cardamom, 2006.

das Gupta, Rana. *Capital: The Eruption of Delhi*. New Delhi: Penguin, 2014.

Davis, Mike. *Planet of Slums*. New York: Verso, 2007.

de Duve, Thierry, ed. *The Definitively Unfinished Marcel Duchamp*. Cambridge, MA: MIT Press, 1991.

Deleuze, Gilles, and Félix Guattari. *A Thousand Plateaus: Capitalism and Schizophrenia*. Minneapolis: University of Minnesota Press, 1987.

Demos, T. J. *The Migrant Image: The Art and Politics of Documentary during Global Crisis.* Durham, NC: Duke University Press, 2013.

Demos, T. J. *The Return to the Postcolony: Spectres of Colonialism in Contemporary Art.* Berlin: Sternberg, 2013.

Dercon, Chris, and Nada Raza, eds. *Bhupen Khakhar: You Can't Please All.* London: Tate, 2016. Exhibition catalogue.

Derrida, Jacques. *Dissemination.* Translated by Barbara Johnson. Chicago: University of Chicago Press, 1983.

Derrida, Jacques. *Rogues: Two Essays on Reason.* Translated by Pascale Anne-Brault and Michael Naas. Stanford, CA: Stanford University Press, 2005.

Derrida, Jacques. *The Truth in Painting.* Translated by Geoff Bennington and Ian McLeod. Chicago: University of Chicago Press, 1987.

Derrida, Jacques. *Writing and Difference.* Translated by Alan Bass. Chicago: University of Chicago Press, 1987.

Deutsche, Rosalyn. *Hiroshima after Iraq: Three Studies in Art and War.* New York: Columbia University Press, 2010.

Douglas, Mary. *Purity and Danger: An Analysis of Concepts of Pollution and Taboo.* London: Routledge, 2002. First published 1966.

Downey, Anthony, ed. *Dissonant Archives: Contemporary Visual Culture and Contested Narratives in the Middle East.* London: I.B. Taurus, 2015.

D'Souza, Robert, and Sunil Manghani, eds. *India's Biennale Effect: A Politics of Contemporary Art.* London: Routledge, 2017.

Duncan, Carol. *Civilizing Rituals: Inside Public Art Museums.* London: Routledge, 1995.

Dutta, Arindam. *The Bureaucracy of Beauty: Design in the Age of Its Global Reproducibility.* New York: Routledge, 2007.

Eagleton, Terry, ed. *Raymond Williams: A Critical Reader.* Cambridge: Polity, 1991.

Eisenman, Stephen. *The Abu Ghraib Effect.* London: Reaktion, 2007.

Elkins, James, and Michael Newman, eds. *The State of Art Criticism.* New York: Routledge, 2008.

Enwezor, Okwui. *Archive Fever: Uses of the Document in Contemporary Art.* New York: Steidl/International Center of Photography, 2008.

Enwezor, Okwui, ed. *The Short Century: Independence and Liberation Movements in Africa, 1945–1994.* Munich: Prestel, 2001.

Enwezor, Okwui, and Chika Okeke-Agulu, eds. *Contemporary African Art since 1980.* Bologna: Damiani, 2009.

Enwezor, Okwui, Katy Siegel, and Ulrich Wilmes, eds. *Postwar: Art Between the Pacific and the Atlantic, 1945–1965.* Munich: Prestel/Haus der Kunst, 2017.

Fanon, Frantz. *The Wretched of the Earth.* New York: Grove, 1963.

Fibicher, Bernard, and Suman Gopinath, eds. *Horn Please: Narratives in Contemporary Indian Art.* Berlin: Hatje Cantz, 2007.

Filipovic, Elena, Marieka van Hal, and Solveig Øvstebø, eds. *The Biennial Reader.* Berlin: Hatje Cantz, 2010.

Foster, Hal. *The Art-Architecture Complex.* New York: Verso, 2011.

Foster, Hal. *Bad New Days: Art, Criticism, Emergency.* New York: Verso, 2015.

Foster, Hal. *Design and Crime (and Other Diatribes).* New York: Verso, 2002.

Foster, Hal. *The Return of the Real: The Avant-Garde at the End of the Century.* Cambridge, MA: MIT Press, 1996.

Foster, Hal, ed. *Discussions in Contemporary Culture.* Seattle: Bay Press/Dia Art Foundation, 1987.

Foucault, Michel. *The Politics of Truth.* Edited by Sylvère Lotringer and Lysa Hochroth. New York: Semiotext(e), 1997.

Garimella, Annapurna, ed. *Mulk Raj Anand: Shaping the Indian Modern.* Mumbai: Marg, 2005.

Ghertner, Asher. *Rule by Aesthetics: World-Class City Making in Delhi.* New York: Oxford University Press, 2015.

Ginwala, Natasha. "Geeta Kapur: On the Curatorial in India (Parts 1 and 2)." *Afterall On-line,* July and October 2011. Accessed January 30, 2019. https://www.afterall.org/online/geeta-kapur-part1#.XFJBqyd7nxU.

Green, Charles, and Anthony Gardner. *Biennials, Triennials, and Documenta: The Exhibitions That Created Contemporary Art.* London: Wiley-Blackwell, 2016.

Gregory, Derek. *The Colonial Present: Afghanistan, Palestine, Iraq.* Oxford: Blackwell, 2004.

Guha, Ranajit. *Dominance without Hegemony: History and Power in Colonial India.* Cambridge, MA: Harvard University Press, 1998.

Guha, Ranajit, ed. *A Subaltern Studies Reader, 1986–1995.* Minneapolis: University of Minnesota Press, 1997.

Guha-Thakurta, Tapati. *The Making of a New Indian Art: Artists, Aesthetics, and Nationalism in Bengal, 1850–1920.* Cambridge: Cambridge University Press, 1992.

Guha-Thakurta, Tapati. *Monuments, Objects, Histories: Institutions of Art in Colonial and Postcolonial India.* New York: Columbia University Press, 2003.

Hall, Stuart. *Cultural Studies, 1983: A Theoretical History.* Edited by Jennifer Daryl Slack and Lawrence Grossberg. Durham, NC: Duke University Press, 2016.

Hall, Stuart. *Familiar Stranger: A Life between Two Islands.* Edited by Bill Schwartz. Durham, NC: Duke University Press, 2017.

Hall, Stuart. *Selected Political Writings: The Great Moving Right Show and Other Essays.* Edited by Sally Davison, David Featherstone, Michael Rustin, and Bill Schwarz. Durham, NC: Duke University Press, 2017.

Hawkins, Gay, and Stephen Muecke, eds. *Culture and Waste: The Creation and Destruction of Value.* New York: Rowman and Littlefield, 2003.

Hell, Julia, and Andreas Schönle, eds. *Ruins of Modernity.* Durham, NC: Duke University Press, 2010.

Hertz, Betti-Sue, ed. *The Matter Within: New Contemporary Art of India.* San Francisco: Yerba Buena Center for the Arts, 2011. Exhibition catalogue.

Higgins, John, ed. *The Raymond Williams Reader*. London: Wiley-Blackwell, 2001.

Hoskote, Ranjit. "Biennials of Resistance: Reflections on the Seventh Gwangju Biennale." In *The Biennial Reader*, edited by Elena Filipovic, Marieka van Hal, and Solveig Øvstebø, 306–21. Berlin: Hatje Cantz, 2010.

Hoskote, Ranjit. "The Disordered Origins of Things: The Art Collection as Pre-canonical Space." In *Abby Grey and Indian Modernism: Selections from the NYU Art Collection*, 41–51. New York: Grey Art Gallery, NYU, 2015. Exhibition catalogue.

Hung, Wu. *A Story of Ruins: Presence and Absence in Chinese Art and Visual Culture*. London: Reaktion, 2011.

Hung, Wu. *Vivan Sundaram: Re-take of Amrita*. New York: Sepia International/ Alkazi Collection, 2006.

Hung, Wu. *Waste Not: Zhao Xiangyuan and Song Dong*. Tokyo: Tokyo Gallery + BTAP, 2009. Exhibition catalogue.

Huyssen, Andreas. *After the Great Divide: Modernism, Mass Culture, Postmodernism*. Bloomington: Indiana University Press, 1986.

Huyssen, Andreas. *Present Pasts: Urban Palimpsests and the Politics of Memory*. Stanford, CA: Stanford University Press, 2003.

Huyssen, Andreas. *Twilight Memories: Marking Time in a Culture of Amnesia*. New York: Routledge, 1995.

Huyssen, Andreas, ed. *Other Cities, Other Worlds: Urban Imaginaries in a Globalizing Age*. Durham, NC: Duke University Press, 2008.

Jackson, Shannon. *Social Works: Performing Art, Supporting Publics*. New York: Routledge, 2010.

Jameson, Frederic. Afterword to *Aesthetics and Politics: Theodor Adorno, Walter Benjamin, Ernst Bloch, Bertolt Brecht, Georg Lukács*. London: Verso, 2007.

Jameson, Frederic. *Brecht and Method*. London: Verso, 2011.

Jameson, Frederic. *Valences of the Dialectic*. London: Verso, 2009.

Jhaveri, Shanay, ed. *Chandigarh Is in India*. Mumbai: Shoestring Publishers, 2016.

Jhaveri, Shanay, ed. *Western Artists and India: Creative Inspirations in Art and Design*. Mumbai: Shoestring Publishers, 2013.

Jumabhoy, Zehra, and Boon Hui Tan, eds. *The Progressive Revolution: Modern Art for a New India*. New York: Prestel, 2018.

Kaplan, Caren. *Aerial Aftermaths: Wartime from Above*. Durham, NC: Duke University Press, 2017.

Kapur, Geeta. "Again a Difficult Task Begins." In *Nasreen Mohamedi: Waiting Is a Part of Intense Living*, 161–206. Madrid: Museo Reina Sofia, 2015. Exhibition catalogue.

Kapur, Geeta. *Chemould Prescott Road: 50 Years of Contemporary Art; Five Exhibitions Curated by Geeta Kapur*. Mumbai: Chemould Prescott Road, 2018. Exhibition catalogue.

Kapur, Geeta. *Contemporary Indian Art: An Exhibition of the Festival of India, 1982*. London: Royal Academy of Arts, 1982.

Kapur, Geeta. *Contemporary Indian Artists*. New Delhi: Vikas, 1978.

Kapur, Geeta. "A Cultural Conjuncture in India: Art into Documentary." In *Antinomies of Art and Culture: Modernity, Postmodernity, Contemporaneity*, edited by Terry Smith, Okwui Enwezor, and Nancy Condee, 30–59. Durham, NC: Duke University Press, 2008.

Kapur, Geeta. "Curating across Agonistic Worlds." In *InFLUX: Contemporary Art in Asia*, edited by Parul Dave Mukherji, Naman P. Ahuja, and Kavita Singh, 159–82. New Delhi: Sage, 2014.

Kapur, Geeta. "Delhi." In *Art Cities of the Future: 21st Century Avant-Gardes*, edited by Antawan I. Byrd et al., 89–112. London: Phaidon, 2013.

Kapur, Geeta. "The Evolution of Content in Amrita Sher-Gil's Paintings." *Marg* 25, no. 2 (March 1972): 39–53.

Kapur, Geeta. "Familial Narratives and Their Accidental Denouement." In *Where Three Dreams Cross: 150 Years of Photography from India, Pakistan, and Bangladesh*, 44–61. London: Whitechapel Gallery, 2010. Exhibition catalogue.

Kapur, Geeta. *In Quest of Identity: Art and Indigenism in Post-colonial Culture with Special Reference to Contemporary Indian Painting*. Baroda: Vrishchik, 1973.

Kapur, Geeta. "Modernist Myths and the Exile of Maqbool Fida Husain." In *Barefoot across the Nation: Maqbool Fida Husain and the Idea of India*, edited by Sumathi Ramaswamy, 21–53. London: Routledge, 2011.

Kapur, Geeta. "Mortality Morbidity Masquerade." In *Bhupen Khakhar: You Can't Please All*, edited by Chris Dercon and Nada Raza, 158–65. London: Tate, 2016. Exhibition catalogue.

Kapur, Geeta. "Partisan Modernity." In *Mulk Raj Anand: Shaping the Indian Modern*, edited by Annapurna Garimella, 28–41. Mumbai: Marg, 2005.

Kapur, Geeta. "Partisan Views about the Human Figure (1981)." In *Horn Please: Narratives in Contemporary Indian Art*, edited by Kuntsmuseum Bern, 33–40. Berlin: Hatje Cantz, 2007.

Kapur, Geeta. "Proposition Avant-Garde: A View from the South." *Art Journal* 77, no. 1 (spring 2018): 87–89.

Kapur, Geeta. "Secular Artist, Citizen Artist." In *Art and Social Change: A Critical Reader*, edited by Will Bradley and Charles Esche, 422–39. London: Tate/Afterall, 2007.

Kapur, Geeta. "sub-Terrain: artists dig the contemporary." In *body.city: siting contemporary culture in India*, edited by Indira Chandrasekhar and Peter Seel, 47–83. New Delhi: Tulika, 2003.

Kapur, Geeta. "The Uncommon Universe of Bhupen Khakhar." In *Pop Art and Vernacular Cultures*, edited by Kobena Mercer, 110–35. London: Iniva, 2007.

Kapur, Geeta. *When Was Modernism: Essays on Contemporary Cultural Practice in India*. New Delhi: Tulika, 2000.

Kapur, Geeta, and Ashish Rajadhyaksha. "Bombay/Mumbai 1992–2001." In *Century City: Art and Culture in the Modern Metropolis*, edited by Iwona Blazwick, 16–41. London: Tate, 2001. Exhibition catalogue.

Kee, Joan. *Contemporary Korean Art: Tansaekhwa and the Urgency of Method*. Minneapolis: University of Minnesota Press, 2013.

Khilnani, Sunil. *The Idea of India*. New York: Farrar, Straus and Giroux, 1997.

Khullar, Sonal. *Worldly Affiliations: Artistic Practice, National Identity, and Modernism in India, 1930–1990*. Berkeley: University of California Press, 2015.

Krauss, Rosalind. *The Originality of the Avant-Garde and Other Modernist Myths*. Cambridge, MA: MIT Press, 1985.

Kumar, R. Siva. *Enchantment and Engagement: Murals of K.G. Subramanyan*. Kolkata: Seagull, 2015.

Kumar, R. Siva. *K. G. Subramanyan: A Retrospective*. National Gallery of Modern Art, New Delhi, 2003. Exhibition catalogue.

Kwon, Miwon. *One Place after Another: Site-Specific Art and Locational Identity*. Cambridge, MA: MIT Press, 2002.

LeMenager, Stephanie. *Living Oil: Petroleum Culture in the American Century*. New York: Oxford University Press, 2014.

Maharaj, Sarat, ed. *Farewell to Post-Colonialism: Querying the Guangzhou Triennial, 2008*. Dublin: Visual Arts Ireland, 2009.

Mann, Paul. *The Theory-Death of the Avant-Garde*. Bloomington: Indiana University Press, 1991.

Mathur, Saloni. *India by Design: Colonial History and Cultural Display*. Berkeley: University of California Press, 2007. (Published in India by Orient Blackswan, 2011.)

Mathur, Saloni. "Partition and the Visual Arts: Reflections on Method." *Third Text*, special issue on Partition, 31, nos. 2–3 (fall 2017): 205–12.

Mathur, Saloni. "A Retake of Sher-Gil's 'Self-Portrait as Tahitian.'" *Critical Inquiry* 37, no. 2 (2011): 515–44.

Mathur, Saloni, ed. *The Migrant's Time: Rethinking Art History and Diaspora*. Williamstown, MA: Clark Art Institute/Yale University Press, 2011.

Mathur, Saloni, and Kavita Singh, eds. *No Touching, No Spitting, No Praying: The Museum in South Asia*. New Delhi: Routledge, 2015.

Mathur, Saloni, and Miwon Kwon, eds. *Making Strange: Gagawaka + Postmortem by Vivan Sundaram*. Los Angeles: Fowler Museum at UCLA, 2015. Exhibition catalogue.

McClellan, Andrew. *Inventing the Louvre: Art, Politics, and the Origins of the Modern Museum in Eighteenth-Century Paris*. Berkeley: University of California Press, 1994.

Mercer, Kobena, ed. *Cosmopolitan Modernisms*. London and Cambridge, MA: inIVA/MIT Press, 2005.

Mercer, Kobena, ed. *Pop Art and Vernacular Cultures*. London and Cambridge, MA: inIVA/MIT Press, 2007.

Meskimmon, Marsha. *Contemporary Art and the Cosmopolitan Imagination*. New York: Routledge, 2011.

Mirzoeff, Nicholas. *Watching Babylon: The War in Iraq and Global Visual Culture*. New York: Routledge, 2005.

Mirzoeff, Nicholas, ed. *The Visual Culture Reader*. London: Routledge, 1998.

Mitchell, Timothy. *Carbon Democracy: Political Power in the Age of Oil*. London: Verso, 2011.

Mitchell, W. J. T. *Cloning Terror: The War of Images, 9/11 to the Present*. Chicago: University of Chicago Press, 2011.

Mitchell, W. J. T., ed. *Landscape and Power*. Chicago: University of Chicago Press, 2002.

Mitter, Partha. *Art and Nationalism in Colonial India 1850–1922: Occidental Orientations*. Cambridge, UK: Cambridge University Press, 1994.

Mitter, Partha. "Decentering Modernism: Art History and Avant-Garde Art from the Periphery." *Art Bulletin* 90, no. 4 (2008): 531–48.

Mitter, Partha. *Indian Art*. Oxford: Oxford University Press, 2002.

Mitter, Partha. *The Triumph of Modernism: India's Artists and the Avant-Garde 1922–1947*. London: Reaktion, 2007.

Morris, Rosalind, ed. *Can the Subaltern Speak? Reflections on the History of an Idea*. New York: Columbia University Press, 2010.

Moss, Jessica, and Ram Rahman, eds. *The Sahmat Collective: Art and Activism in India since 1989*. Chicago: Smart Museum/University of Chicago Press, 2013. Exhibition catalogue.

Nancy, Jean-Luc. "Elliptical Sense." *Research in Phenomenology* 18 (1988): 175–90.

Niranjana, Tejaswini. *Siting Translation: History, Poststructuralism, and the Postcolonial Context*. Berkeley: University of California Press, 1992.

Niranjana, Tejaswini, P. Sudhir, and Vivek Dhareshwar, eds. *Interrogating Modernity: Culture and Colonialism in India*. Calcutta: Seagull Books, 1993.

Nixon, Rob. *Slow Violence and the Environmentalism of the Poor*. Cambridge, MA: Harvard University Press, 2011.

Okeke-Agulu, Chika. *Postcolonial Modernism: Art and Decolonization in Twentieth-Century Nigeria*. Durham, NC: Duke University Press, 2015.

Overton, Tom, ed. *Portraits: John Berger on Artists*. London: Verso, 2015.

Owens, Craig. *Beyond Recognition: Representation, Power, and Culture*. Berkeley: University of California Press, 1992.

Painter, Karen, and Thomas Crow. *Late Thoughts: Reflections on Artists and Composers at Work*. Los Angeles: Getty Research Institute, 2006.

Parameswaran, Ameet, and Rahul Dev. "To Be Partisan, Unsettled, and Alert: Conversation with Geeta Kapur." *Art Margins On-line*, March 11, 2015. http://www.artmargins.com/index.php/interviews-sp-837925570/756 -to-be-partisan-unsettled-and-alert- conversation-with-geeta-kapur-.

Pinney, Christopher. *Camera Indica: The Social Life of Indian Photographs*. Chicago: University of Chicago Press, 1998.

Pinney, Christopher. *The Coming of Photography in India*. London: British Library, 2008.

Pinney, Christopher. *Photos of the Gods: The Printed Image and Political Struggle in India*. London: Reaktion, 2004.

Poddar, Sandhini. *V.S. Gaitonde: Painting as Process, Painting as Life*. New York: Prestel, 2014.

Pollock, Griselda. *Differencing the Canon: Feminist Desire and the Writing of Art's Histories*. London: Routledge, 1999.

Pollock, Griselda, ed. *Generations and Geographies in the Visual Arts: Feminist Readings*. London: Routledge, 1996.

Pollock, Griselda, and Fred Orton. *Avant-Gardes and Partisans Reviewed*. Manchester: Manchester University Press, 1997.

Prakash, Gyan. *Another Reason: Science and the Imagination of Modern India*. Princeton, NJ: Princeton University Press, 1999.

Prakash, Gyan. *Mumbai Fables: A History of an Enchanted City*. Princeton, NJ: Princeton University Press, 2011.

Prakash, Gyan, and Kevin Kruse, eds. *The Spaces of the Modern City*. Princeton, NJ: Princeton University Press, 2008.

Prakash, Vikramaditya. *Chandigarh's LeCorbusier*. Seattle: University of Washington Press, 2002.

Prendergast, Christopher, ed. *Cultural Materialism: On Raymond Williams*. Minneapolis: University of Minnesota Press, 1995.

Rabinow, Paul, ed. *The Foucault Reader*. New York: Vintage Books (1984), 2010.

Rajadhyaksha, Ashish. *Indian Cinema in the Time of Celluloid: From Bollywood to the Emergency*. Bloomington: Indiana University Press, 2009.

Rajadhyaksha, Ashish. "Living the Tradition." *Journal of Arts and Ideas* 16 (January–March 1988): 73–86.

Rajadhyaksha, Ashish. "There Is Violence in the Air." In *Vivan Sundaram: Disjunctures*, 168–179. Munich: Prestel/Haus der Kunst, 2018. Exhibition catalogue.

Rajadhyaksha, Ashish, with Paul Willemen. *Encyclopedia of Indian Cinema*. London: British Film Institute, 1995.

Ramaswamy, Sumathi, ed. *Barefoot Across the Nation: Maqbool Fida Husain and the Idea of India*. London: Routledge, 2011.

Rogoff, Irit. *Terra Infirma: Geography's Visual Culture*. Abingdon, VA: Routledge, 2000.

Rogoff, Irit. "What Is a Theorist?" In *The State of Art Criticism*, edited by James Elkins and Michael Newman, 97–109. New York: Routledge, 2008.

Rosengarten, Ruth. *Vivan Sundaram Is Not a Photographer: The Photographic Works of Vivan Sundaram*. New Delhi: Tulika, 2019.

Roy, Ananya, and Aihwa Ong, eds. *Worlding Cities: Asian Experiments and the Art of Being Global*. London: Blackwell, 2011.

Roy, Ananya, and Nezar AlSayyad, eds. *Urban Informality: Transnational Perspectives from the Middle East, Latin America, and South Asia*. New York: Lexington, 2004.

Roy, Tania. "Non-Renewable Resources: The Poetics and Politics of Vivan Sundaram's Trash." *Theory, Culture and Society* 30, nos. 7/8 (2013): 265–76.

Roy, Tania. "Wreck, Restoration, and the Work of Carrying On: History on Vivan Sundaram's Boat-Works." *Cultural Politics* 5, no. 3 (2009): 359–84.

Rubinstein, Raphael, ed. *Critical Mess: Art Critics on the State of Their Practice*. Lenox, MA: Hard Press Editions, 2006.

Rushdie, Salman. *The Moor's Last Sigh*. New York: Vintage, 1995.

Said, Edward. *Beginnings: Intention and Method*. New York: Columbia University Press, 1985.

Said, Edward. *On Late Style: Music and Literature Against the Grain*. New York: Vintage, 2006.

Said, Edward. *Orientalism*. New York: Vintage, 1979.

Said, Edward. *The World, the Text, and the Critic*. London: Vintage, 1991.

Sambrani, Chaitanya. *Tracking Trash: Vivan Sundaram and the Turbulent Core of Modernity*. Mumbai: Chemould Prescott Road, 2008. Exhibition catalogue.

Sambrani, Chaitanya, ed. *At Home in the World: The Art and Life of Gulammohammed Sheikh*. New Delhi: Tulika Books, 2019.

Sambrani, Chaitanya, ed. *Edge of Desire: Recent Art in India*. London: Phillip Wilson, 2005. Exhibition catalogue.

Sangari, Kumkum, ed. *Trace Retrace: Paintings, Nilima Sheikh*. New Delhi: Tulika Books, 2013.

Scanlan, John. *On Garbage*. London: Reaktion, 2005.

Scott, David. *Conscripts of Modernity: The Tragedy of Colonial Enlightenment*. Durham, NC: Duke University Press, 2004.

Scott, David. *Omens of Adversity: Tragedy, Time, Memory, Justice*. Durham, NC: Duke University Press, 2014.

Scott, David. *Refashioning Futures: Criticism after Postcoloniality*. Princeton, NJ: Princeton University Press, 1999.

Scott, David. "Stuart Hall at Eighty." *Small Axe* 16, no. 2 (July 2012): vii–x.

Scott, David. *Stuart Hall's Voice: Intimations of an Ethics of Receptive Generosity*. Durham, NC: Duke University Press, 2017.

Scott, David. "The Temporality of Generations: Dialogue, Tradition, Criticism." *New Literary History* 45, no. 2 (spring 2014): 157–81.

Scott, James. *Seeing Like a State: How Certain Schemes to Improve the Human Condition Have Failed*. New Haven, CT: Yale University Press, 1999.

Sekula, Allan. *Fish Story*. Rotterdam: Richter Verlag, 1995.

Sheikh, Gulammohammed. "Buddy" (translated from Gujarati). In *Touched by Bhupen*. Mumbai: Galerie Mirchandani + Steinruecke, 2013. Exhibition catalogue.

Sheikh, Gulammohammed, ed. *Contemporary Art in Baroda*. New Delhi: Tulika, 1997.

Sherman, Daniel, and Irit Rogoff, eds. *Museum Cultures: Histories, Discourses, Spectacles*. Minneapolis: University of Minnesota Press, 1994.

Sinha, Ajay. "Contemporary Indian Art: A Question of Method." *Art Journal* 58, no. 3 (1999): 31–39.

Sinha, Ajay. "Modernism in India: A Short History of a Blush." *Art Bulletin* 90, no. 4 (December 2008): 561–68.

Sinha, Gayatri, ed. *Art and Visual Culture in India, 1857–2007*. Mumbai: Marg, 2009.

Sinha, Gayatri, ed. *Expressions and Evocations: Contemporary Women Artists of India*. Mumbai: Marg, 1996.

Sinha, Gayatri, ed. *Indian Art: An Overview*. New Delhi: Rupa, 2003.

Smith, Terry, Okwui Enwezor, and Nancy Condee, eds. *Antinomies of Art and Culture: Modernity, Postmodernity, Contemporaneity*. Durham, NC: Duke University Press, 2008.

Sontag, Susan. *Against Interpretation and Other Essays*. New York: Picador, 1996. First published 1966.

Sontag, Susan. *Regarding the Pain of Others*. New York: Picador, 2003.

Sood, Pooja, ed. *The Khoj Book of Contemporary Indian Art, 1997–2007*. Noida, India: Collins, 2010.

Spivak, Gayatri Chakravorty. *A Critique of Postcolonial Reason*. Cambridge, MA: Harvard University Press, 1999.

Stoler, Ann Laura. *Duress: Imperial Durabilities in Our Times*. Durham, NC: Duke University Press, 2016.

Subramanyan, K.G. *The Creative Circuit*. Calcutta: Seagull, 1992.

Subramanyan, K.G. *The Living Tradition: Perspectives on Modern Indian Art*. Calcutta: Seagull, 1987.

Subramanyan, K.G. *The Magic of Making: Essays on Art and Culture*. Calcutta: Seagull, 2007.

Suderburg, Erika, ed. *Space, Site, Intervention: Situating Installation Art*. Minneapolis: University of Minnesota Press, 2000.

Sundaram, Ravi. *Pirate Modernity: Delhi's Media Urbanism*. London: Routledge, 2010.

Sundaram, Vivan. *Gagawaka: Making Strange*. Mumbai: Chemould Prescott Road, 2012. Exhibition catalogue.

Sundaram, Vivan. *History Project*. New Delhi: Tulika, 2017.

Sundaram, Vivan. "Recycling Photographs." In *Photography Theory*, edited by James Elkins, 333–39. London: Routledge, 2007.

Sundaram, Vivan. *Re-take of Amrita: Digital Photomontages*. New Delhi: Tulika, 2001.

Sundaram, Vivan. *Umrao Singh Sher-Gil: His Misery and His Manuscript*. New Delhi: Photoink, 2008.

Sundaram, Vivan, ed. *Amrita Sher-Gil: A Self-Portrait in Letters and Writings*. 2 vols. New Delhi: Tulika, 2009.

Szeman, Imre, and Dominic Boyer, eds. *Energy Humanities: An Anthology*. Baltimore: Johns Hopkins University Press, 2017.

Tarlo, Emma. *Unsettling Memories: Narratives of the Emergency in Delhi*. Berkeley: University of California, 2003.

Terracciano, Emilia. *Art and Emergency: Modernism in Twentieth-Century India*. London: I.B. Taurus, 2017.

Tiampo, Ming. *Gutai: Decentering Modernism*. Chicago: University of Chicago Press, 2011.

Tuli, Neville. *Indian Contemporary Painting*. New York: Harry N. Abrams, 1998.

Vaughan, Philippa, ed. *The Victoria Memorial Hall, Calcutta: Conceptions, Collections, Conservation*. Mumbai: Marg, 1997.

Vergine, Lea, ed. *Trash: From Junk to Art*. Milan: Electa, 1997.

Vergo, Peter, ed. *The New Museology*. London: Reaktion, 1989.

Virilio, Paul. *Desert Screen: War at the Speed of Light*. London: Bloomsbury Academic, 2005.

Wagner, Anne. *A House Divided: American Art since 1955*. Berkeley: University of California Press, 2012.

Weiss, Rachel. "Some Thoughts after Kapur and Mathur." *Art Journal* 77, no. 1 (spring 2018): 95–101.

Weiss, Rachel, ed. *Making Art Global (Part 1): The Third Havana Biennale 1989*. London: Afterall, 2012.

Welchman, John, ed. *Institutional Critique and After*. Zurich: JRP Ringier, 2006.

Whiles, Virginia. *Art and Polemic in Pakistan: Cultural Politics and Tradition in Contemporary Miniature Painting*. London: I.B. Taurus, 2010.

Whiteley, Gillian. *Junk: Art and the Politics of Trash*. London: I.B. Tauris, 2011.

Willett, John, ed. *Brecht on Theatre: The Development of an Aesthetic*. London: Methuen, 1964.

Williams, Paul. *Memorial Museums: The Global Rush to Commemorate Atrocities*. New York: Berg, 2007.

Williams, Raymond. *Keywords*. Oxford: Oxford University Press, 2015. First published 1976.

Williams, Raymond. *The Politics of Modernism: Against the New Conformists*. London: Verso, 1990.

Williams, Raymond. *Problems in Materialism and Culture*. London: Verso, 1980.

Young, James. *At Memory's Edge: After-Images of the Holocaust in Contemporary Art and Architecture*. New Haven, CT: Yale University Press, 2000.

Zitzewitz, Karin. *The Art of Secularism: The Cultural Politics of Modernist Art in Contemporary India*. London: Hurst, 2014.

INDEX